The Fighting Irish

Ireland's Role In World Boxing History

by

Patrick Myler

To Frances, my wife, for staying the distance.

First published 1987
Brandon Book Publishers Ltd
Dingle, Co Kerry, Ireland
and 51 Washington Street
Dover, New Hampshire 03820, USA

Myler, Patrick
The Fighting Irish.
1. Boxing – Ireland – History
I. Title
796.8'309415   GV1127.I.73

ISBN 0-86322-088 6

Cover design: Paula Nolan
Typesetting: Southern Computer Services, Cork
Printed in Ireland

Contents

Mike McTigue, Rinty Monaghan, Jack Doyle and Barry McGuigan

Introduction by Eamonn Andrews

This is an astonishing piece of work over which I am honoured to accept Patrick Myler's invitation and sound the opening bell. Truth to tell, I started to skim the proof pages, stopped, and started all over again. It is a work of true scholarship and diligent research. It puts prize fighting into perspective; and, if it takes you from Mendoza to McGuigan and all the non-boxing ruffians in between, it does so (for the true boxing afficionado) without a moment of dullness and with an affection for the fighter shining all through. As a boy, I read every book about boxing in Kevin Street Public Library before I ever stepped into an amateur boxing ring. If this had been written then, I would have devoured it. It adds new sights to old stories and, at times, sets my heart thumping all over again. It brings back, for instance, my first professional boxing radio commentary on Martin Thornton's debacle against Bruce Woodcock at the Theatre Royal in Dublin, when, *before* the fight, I asked Martin if he had any message for the folks back in the Gaeltacht. 'Tell them,' said he 'that I did me best!'

And what a vindication of the noble art to discover on page two that the Rector of Templecarne Parish near Lough Derg about 1730 hired boxer Jonas Good to protect him from 'so rough, disorderly, drunken and quarrelsome pilgrims'.

Read on. This sport for ruffians is really a refuge for gentlemen.

In boxing my interest is purely scientific. I have no sympathy with either party. I hate the sight of blood.

George Bernard Shaw

I fought for twenty years and anyone who goes into boxing for fun has got to be out of his entire cotton pickin' mind, because it's a rough, rough business.

Jimmy McLarnin

Preface

The term 'the fighting Irish' can be a source of great shame or pride to an Irishman, depending on the context in which it is applied. The traditional image of the drunken, brawling 'Paddy' has been perpetuated by stand-up comics and caricaturists down through the years. Like the tight-fisted Scot, the passionate Frenchman and the stern, work-obsessed German, the popular concept of the devil-may-care Irishman who is ready to fight at the drop of a shillelagh may be a slanderous generalisation but, as with the others, there is at least some basis for the charge.

'Other men go into fights finely, sternly or indifferently but the only man who really loves it, after all, is the green immortal Irishman,' wrote army surgeon Thomas Ellis about the Irish Brigade (the famous Fighting 69th) in the American Civil War. It may be a gross exaggeration to suggest that anyone actually enjoys going to war, but the spirit and bravery shown by the Irish on numerous battlefields has been well chronicled. It is this same inbuilt refusal to back down when the gauntlet is dropped that has characterised the Irish in the sporting arena. Boxing came naturally to them. In the early days of prize-fighting in England, names like Corcoran, Ryan and O'Donnell figured among those who opposed the favourites of 'the Fancy'. Perhaps it was their way of articulating their sense of grievance at the centuries of oppression by the English in Ireland. More likely it was getting well paid for something they liked doing that attracted them to the sport.

When bare-fist boxing began to be promoted in America, it was again the Irish who took most readily to it. The late Nat Fleischer, founder and editor of *The Ring* magazine, remarked that the history of the American ring from the middle of the nineteenth century through the early part of the twentieth was primarily a story of Irish supremacy. The Irish influence has continued through the years. Great champions like John L. Sullivan, James J. Corbett, Gene Tunney, Mickey Walker and Billy Conn, to name but a few, were all born in the United States but came from solid Irish stock. Even though black boxers increasingly dominate the American scene, they are regularly challenged by fighting Irishmen. Gerry Cooney, Sean O'Grady, Jerry Quarry and Shawn O'Sullivan are just some of the Irish descendants who have kept the green flag flying in US rings during recent times.

For all their enormous contribution to the history of the game, it is surprising that so little has been done to record the stories of the outstanding Irish boxers. It was only after I undertook a lingering ambition to fill that gap that I realized why no one had beaten me to the punch. It is only by ploughing laboriously through old newspapers and magazines that one gets a clear picture of the objective. The difficulty of tracing adequate records of Irish boxers is compounded by the fact that virtually all of their activity took place abroad. With a few exceptions, whatever fame or championship success has been achieved occurred in American or British rings. The few books that have been written on Irish boxing have dealt almost exclusively with the amateur side of the game. Indeed, had it not been for the many references to Irish ringmen made in books by British and American authors, the difficulties of researching this book would have proved insurmountable.

Having gathered as much data as I could from whatever source, I faced a dilemma that is not unfamiliar to authors: what do I include and what do I leave out? To those who will feel that I have been unfair in omitting recognition of their particular favourite, or favourites, I apologise. It would have been impossible to provide career details of every Irish boxer who achieved a modicum of fame. As a criterion I have selected those ringmen who have won major championship honours or who have made some impact on the world scene. While following this guideline I have managed to include some mention of most of the well-known characters who have graced (or in a few cases disgraced) Irish boxing.

It has been a fascinating and highly rewarding task and it is my way of saying 'thank you' to the men who have provided me with ineradicable memories of meeting them, reading about them or watching them in action.

I wish to thank most sincerely all those who helped and encouraged me in writing this book. I am especially indebted to Gilbert Odd, Britain's top boxing historian and author, who traced sources of information which had hitherto eluded me. Harry Mullen, current editor of *Boxing News*, was unfailing in offering assistance and I do not know how I would have managed without recourse to the weekly trade paper, for which I thank Harry and his conscientious predecessors. Vic Hardwicke, a diligent collector of boxers' records, tried gallantly, if in vain, to help me gather a complete record of Irish title fights. Denis Morrison, honorary secretary of the Irish ex-Boxers Association, was always ready to help in any way he could, as were photographers Joe Fay and Charlie Collins. So too were Jimmy Ingle, Paddy Hodgins and Billy Roche, who provided valuable information on his grandfather, Jem Roche. Dave Roake and John O'Donnell were especially generous with the loan of rare photographs from their private collections. I thank, too, the directors and staffs of the National Library, Dublin, the Linen Hall Library, Belfast and the library staff of Independent Newspapers for their unfailing assistance. Finally, I am most grateful to Eamonn Andrews for finding time in his extremely busy schedule to write the introduction.

One

The Bare-Fist Pioneers

LONG BEFORE THEY fought for fame and prize-money in the ring the Irish enjoyed a reputation of being ready to fight whenever pride or honour was at stake, to settle an argument, or just for the hell of it. The traditional image of 'the fighting Irish' has its roots well established in ancient history and in legend. Early Irish literature portrayed the natives as a physically strong people with a deep love of sport and outdoor activities. The mythical warrior Cuchulainn was supposedly so agile and powerful that he was designated 'the best all-round athlete in the Gaelic world'. From 632 BC to 1169 AD a spectacular Gaelic sporting festival was held periodically about ten miles from Tara on the site of the tomb of Tailte, an Irish Queen. Known as the Tailteann Games, huge crowds flocked to enjoy the feats of strength, skill and endurance in sports such as running, jumping, wrestling and boxing, as well as horse and chariot racing.

Fist-fighting as a sport largely died out, until its revival in England in the early 18th century. There it grew out of its association with sword and cudgel fighting to become recognised as a sport in its own right. Exhibitions of skill combining the blade, the stick and the fists gave way to the slightly less physically damaging art of bare-knuckle boxing. In Ireland, there is evidence that pugilism had its roots in the peculiarly national phenomenon of 'faction fighting'. This popular pastime was chiefly practised in rural areas around market days, fairs or other organised events. Faction fighting was not a sport but a regular way of sorting out family rows, disputes over land or whatever grievances lingered between groups. Hundreds, sometimes thousands, of agitated people would wage battle, initially with sticks but frequently progressing to stones, swords and even guns. Death and maiming were very often the grim outcome of vicious faction fights. Yet, whatever its toll on life and limb, there are ample grounds for assuming that the participants enjoyed the thrill of it all.

A well-known Cork landlord, Rev Horatio Townsend, wrote to the authorities at Dublin Castle in 1817 urging a stronger police and military presence in the west Cork area, especially around Drimoleague where the clans were notorious for their strength and ferocity. 'In other places people fight for some object of real or imaginary advantage,' observed Townsend, 'but in Ireland they fight for nothing but fighting's sake.'

When they did not get completely out of hand, faction fights were normally contested with heavy blackthorn sticks or with 'the loaded butt', a whip handle loaded with lead at the thick end. There were schools of instruction in the art of stick fighting and champions of battle achieved a high degree of skill and cunning. One noted faction fighter of the early 19th century, James O'Donnell of Ballinascally, County Clare, was recognised as 'a subtle fighter, noted for his ability to goad an opponent into a blind fury and resultant carelessness and loss of concentration. He was also an expert at dealing numbing strokes on elbow and shoulder and at knee-tapping where reflex action caused an enemy to bend double and thus leave himself vulnerable to a smart clout on the head.'

Another dab hand at swinging the shillelagh was the celebrated philanthropist Philip Skelton. In 1725, when Skelton was a sizar at Trinity College, Dublin, he took a trip to the notorious Donnybrook Fair and heard an announcement that a hat was set up as a prize for the best cudgel player. Skelton took up one of the sticks and issued a challenge to anyone in the crowd to oppose him. A young fellow stepped up to accept the invitation. 'Immediately a ring was formed and the two heroes began,' wrote Burdy, Skelton's biographer. 'They fought for a while on equal terms, warding off blows by their science of defence. But at last his opponent was off his guard and Skelton, taking the advantage, hit him some smart strokes about the head and made him throw down his cudgel and admit that he was overpowered. He thus gained the victory and won the hat. Skelton then took the hat in his hand, showed it to the crowd, made a bow to the ladies and told them he fought not for the hat, but just to please them. He refused to take away the prize, but returned it to the donor and then bowed and retired. A hero in romance could not have been more gallant to the fair sex.' Some years later, when he was rector of Templecarne, the wild moorland parish around Lough Derg, Skelton hired the boxer Jonas Good to protect him from 'so rough, disorderly, drunken and quarrelsome pilgrims'.

But, contrary to what some may believe, boxing was not the 'invention' of the Irish. It is to their nearest neighbours, the English, that the credit must go for resurrecting the sport that originated in the Olympic Games of ancient Greece and was adapted by the Romans. Pugilism (from the latin *pugilatis*, the art of fighting with the fist) was a particularly brutal affair under the Romans. Participants wore a form of glove known as the *caestus*, made of leather or iron and covered with spikes or thongs. Moderated forms of the sport spread from Athens and

Rome to other parts of Europe and, eventually, to Britain and Ireland. It was not until the early 18th century, however, that boxing resembling its present form achieved a degree of popularity.

The first known accounts of modern boxing come from England. The *Protestant Mercury* of January 1681 carried the earliest known fight report, on a match between the Duke of Albermarle's footman and a butcher. The sport acquired a somewhat more respectable image with the opening of a boxing academy in Tottenham Court Road, London, by James Figg. At his school, founded in 1719, Figg taught the arts of attack and defence and gave exhibitions of broadsword skill, cudgelling and boxing. Among the nobles who patronised Figg's establishment was Jonathan Swift, Dean of St Patrick's Cathedral in Dublin. But there is no record of the celebrated author of *Gulliver's Travels* testing his sporting prowess against the master.

Figg, acknowledged as the first English boxing champion, further popularised the sport by touring the English countryside, setting up booths at local fairs to stage contests and exhibitions. He retained his profitable standing as English champion by fighting off several challengers. The most persistent of these was Ned Sutton, who made three vain attempts to dislodge him. In their first meeting they started off by opposing each other with cudgels and finished fighting it out with their fists. Figg's championship reign lasted until 1730 when he retired undefeated and handed over the championship of England to his pupil George Taylor. But it is to the third English champion, Jack Broughton, that boxing owes its greatest debt. Stricken with remorse when one of his opponents died after a fierce struggle, Broughton drew up the first set of rules of the ring in 1743. Crude and inadequate they may seem today, but Broughton's Rules 'to be observed in all battles on the stage' eliminated many of the free-for-all tactics that had hitherto been commonplace. The rules, seven in all, remained in force for nearly 100 years and formed the framework of the laws that now govern the game.

To Broughton, too, goes the credit for introducing the first boxing gloves. Unlike the modern, well-padded gloves, 'Broughton's mufflers' contained only a small amount of padding across the knuckles. They were used only in exhibition matches and were mainly to protect the delicate features of the noblemen who sparred at his club. Bare knuckles remained the norm for actual prize-fights for a century after Broughton's death. It was not until 1892 that a couple of hardy sons of Irish emigrants to the United States, John L. Sullivan and James J. Corbett, donned padded gloves for the first world heavyweight championship contest under Marquis of Queensberry rules.

As the popularity of boxing spread throughout England in the 18th century, the prize-money increased together with the size of the crowds of spectators. Whereas initially the pugilists had to rely on what cash might be thrown into the ring (decided by the value of their performance), the better battlers began to arrange specific 'purses', usually with the winner

THE RING

RULES

TO BE OBSERVED IN ALL BATTLES ON THE STAGE

I. THAT a fquare of a Yard be chalked in the middle of the Stage; and on every frefh fet-to after a fall, or being parted from the rails, each Second is to bring his Man to the fide of the fquare, and place him oppofite to the other, and till they are fairly fet-to at the Lines, it fhall not be lawful for one to ftrike at the other.

II. That, in order to prevent any Difputes, the time a Man lies after a fall, if the Second does not bring his Man to the fide of the fquare, within the fpace of half a minute, he fhall be deemed a beaten Man.

III. That in every main Battle, no perfon whatever fhall be upon the Stage, except the Principals and their Seconds; the fame rule to be obferved in bye-battles, except that in the latter, Mr. Broughton is allowed to be upon the Stage to keep decorum, and to affift Gentlemen in getting to their places, provided always he does not interfere in the Battle; and whoever pretends to infringe thefe Rules to be turned immediately out of the houfe. Every body is to quit the Stage as foon as the Champions are ftripped, before the fet-to.

IV. That no Champion be deemed beaten, unlefs he fails coming up to the line in the limited time, or that his own Second declares him beaten. No Second is to be allowed to afk his man's Adverfary any queftions, or advife him to give out.

V. That in bye-battles, the winning man to have two-thirds of the Money given, which fhall be publicly divided upon the Stage, notwithftanding any private agreements to the contrary.

VI. That to prevent Difputes, in every main Battle the Principals fhall, on coming on the Stage, choofe from among the gentlemen prefent two Umpires, who fhall abfolutely decide all Difputes that may arife about the Battle; and if the two Umpires cannot agree, the faid Umpires to choofe a third, who is to determine it.

VII. That no perfon is to hit his Adverfary when he is down, or feize him by the ham, the breeches, or any part below the waift: a man on his knees to be reckoned down.

As agreed by feveral Gentlemen at Broughton's Amphitheatre,
Tottenham Court Road, Auguft 16, 1743.

getting the bigger share unless they agreed to 'winner take all'. They also acquired patrons, who would look after them in their preparations for the fight and back their man with substantial amounts. A winning boxer would earn a fair share of his backer's prize. An example of the system of financial backing for boxing of the period is contained in an advertisement that appeared in a 1742 newspaper:

Thomas Hodgkins, from Shropshire, and Jeremiah MacCarthy, from Ireland, who fought on Wednesday last a severe and bloody battle...at the request of the honourable Gentlemen then present...are to have a second combat for a great sum of money.

To the Irish, prize-fighting provided a ready outlet for those with the strength and courage to channel their natural instincts into a lucrative pastime. Any Irishman who considered himself handy with his fists was encouraged to try his luck in the English ring. Not that the chance of boxing fame alone lured many young Irishmen from their native homes. Poverty was the prime motivator. Although they, alone among migrants to Britain, could avail of Poor Law benefits, the Irish found jobs hard to come by and even then the pay was meagre. Migration from Ireland to Britain had gone on from the early 1600s and there were large colonies of Irish all over the country. The young Irishmen worked mainly as builders' labourers, sedan carriers, porters, coal heavers, milk sellers, street hawkers and farm labourers. Boxing offered those with the talent a way of escape from drudgery and obscurity, just as it does today for the many American blacks and Latin-Americans who find life a perennial obstacle course. It also meant the Irish could indulge their traditional passion for fighting for its own sake. A visitor to England noted that Irish labourers in London 'gave each other pitched battles every Saturday night, when heroes and heroines show their prowess at fisticuffs and roll together in the kennel'.

Despite this common predilection for fisticuffs, no Irishman rose to fame during those very early days of English dominance in the ring. The most one comes across in newspapers and periodicals are occasional mentions of obscure Irish boxers, more often than not omitting their names. A poster that appeared at Broughton's amphitheatre in London in 1742, proclaimed that one John Francis, otherwise known as 'the Jumping Soldier', wished to avenge a defeat in 12 minutes by 'an Irish braggadocio' who had questioned his manhood. 'I now invite him to fight me for two guineas at Broughton's amphitheatre where, I doubt not, I shall give him the truth of a good beating,' declared the affronted John Francis. The Irishman willingly accepted the challenge, reported Pierce Egan in *Boxiana*, and 'he so bothered the gig of the Jumping Soldier that he was not able to move, much more to jump, for some time. Paddy gave him a Tipperary fling, which so completely shook all his recollection out of him that he never troubled the town afterwards with any more of his epistolary challenges'.

However, the respectability pugilism had begun to enjoy took a severe, almost fatal blow in 1750 when Jack Broughton, though almost blinded while losing his English championship to Jack Slack, was accused by his backer, the Duke of Cumberland, of selling him out. The Duke had put £50,000 on his man to win and he angrily denounced the deposed champion. He withdrew all further financial support for Broughton. The sport fell into disrepute as many contests were 'arranged' to ensure betting profits. An unruly element took control. Riots were commonplace when gamblers refused to pay out on obviously 'fixed' matches. Fears of greater public disorder led to an Act of Parliament banning prize-fighting. Fights were still staged away from the eyes of the authorities, but venues had constantly to be switched, often at the last minute, when word got around that the law was about to swoop. Very often a bout would commence, only for the police to step in and arrest the boxers and all concerned with the promotion.

All this uncertainty about dates and locations, together with the recurring allegations of the results being decided in advance, caused a rapid decline in boxing's support. The nobility switched their patronage to the fast-growing sport of horse-racing. Sadly, it was during this 'dark age' of prize-fighting that Ireland produced its first ringmen of note. But they, too, were to be enveloped in the pervading cloud of corruption that hung over the game.

Champions without honour

Only two Irishmen are entered on the roll of the bare-knuckle heavyweight champions of England. At any other period in the sport's history, Peter Corcoran and Duggan (Jack) Fearns would have been feted as heroes. But their brief reigns occurred at a time when boxing was at its lowest ebb. Each of their championship contests carried the taint of being 'fixed', the only real winners being those who were 'in the know' and placed their bets accordingly. The link man between the two Irish 'champions' was Englishman Harry Sellers, who took the title from Corcoran and lost it to Fearns, each time to cries of 'shame' from the outraged spectators. The pity of it all was that Corcoran was quite a talented fighter who might have earned true acclaim had he come along at any other time. He fully deserved to be called the champion of England for he was the best man around, albeit at a time when genuine talent was in short supply. Fearns, on the other hand, had no real claim to greatness. His sole 'achievement' was his dubious title win and he quickly faded into obscurity without defending the championship.

Peter Corcoran from Athy, County Kildare, had fled Ireland after killing a man in a fight over a girl. But, he had only arrived in England when his hot temper got him into a row with a Birmingham butcher over the price of a leg of mutton. The butcher was a noted pugilist and he challenged the young Irishman to fight him with the chunk of meat as the prize if he won. A hungry fighter makes the best fighter, it is often said, and Corcoran proved it by trouncing his rival. He later worked as a coal heaver in London before going to sea. With a reputation as a capable man with his fists, he once disposed of a whole press gang in a brawl at Portsmouth, so it was claimed. Out of uniform, he became a publican, running the Black Horse Inn at St Giles, in London's East End.

By 1770, Corcoran was an established pugilist and several impressive wins took him into the leading contender's spot for Bill Darts' English championship. He was backed by Colonel O'Kelly, a shady character who had risen from poverty and illiteracy in Ireland to become a successful gambler, racehorse owner and associate of the nobility. O'Kelly used his considerable influence to press his man's claim to be the rightful champion. A match to decide the issue was organised for Derby Day in 1771 at Epsom Race-course in Surrey. The championship fight followed the last race of the day.

The dual attraction of the big race and the title bout ensured a huge attendance. Whatever value they might have got from the racing, those who stayed on for the boxing lived to regret it. The contest was over almost as soon as it began. After a minute or two of harmless sparring Corcoran landed a heavy blow to the champion's face. Darts promptly surrendered. Loud cries of 'fix' and 'shame' rang around the race-course. It was alleged that O'Kelly had paid Darts £100 to lose, thus not only ensuring his man's ascension to the championship throne but picking up a small fortune in bets. Pierce Egan, writing some years later in *Boxiana*, did not agree with the general assumption that the affair was a frame-up. 'Surely,' he suggested, 'no thoroughbred sportsman could commit such bare-faced robbery. And, upon the best information, we are assured that Darts in his prime was never half man enough for Corcoran!'

Guilty or not, the mud stuck to both victor and vanquished. Darts, who ran a tavern in Holborn, London, found himself suddenly short of customers and he died in poverty ten years later. Corcoran, too, failed to prosper from the affair. He defended his title against Sam Peters and won in ten minutes. Again there was much disquiet expressed about the manner of his success. He accepted the challenge of a west of England man, Harry Sellers, to meet for the championship in a ring pitched in front of the Crown Inn at Staines, Middlesex. This time it was Corcoran's turn to relinquish his hold on the title without putting up much of an effort, although his lack of training might have been a contributory factor in his defeat. The only known account of the contest, in October 1776, described it thus:

> At the first onset, Corcoran gave his antagonist a violent blow which threw him to the farthest end of the stage, and the odds increased from three to four to one in Peter's favour. Sellers now fought very shy for about 18 minutes in order to wind his antagonist, which having accomplished, he advanced boldly and beat him by

straightforward hitting in ten minutes.

Charges that Corcoran had made considerable monetary gain from the loss of his title were strengthened when, within days of the fight, he had his public house premises (the Blakeney Arms in St Martin's Lane, London) stacked out with every brand of liquor and he had the whole premises painted and decorated, inside and out. Yet only a week earlier he had been threatened with eviction for inability to pay the rent. His trade slumped and he fell heavily into debt. He ended up begging on the streets of London and when he died a public subscription was raised to meet the cost of his burial. It was a sad postscript to the story of the first Irish-born champion of England.

Sellers, Corcoran's conqueror, held the title for four years before yielding it to Duggan Fearns, an Irish boatswain. The championship bout was staged at Slough in Buckinghamshire on 25 September 1779 for a purse of £50. The farcical affair was all over in 90 seconds. Sellers went down from the first punch landed and declined to continue. No one took Fearns' claim to the championship seriously and there is no further record of his ring career, if there was one, or of his subsequent life. Interest in boxing had plunged to such a low that it was virtually ignored by the newspapers.

Perhaps Fred Henning, in *Fights for the Championship*, summed up boxing's 'dark age' best of all:

> Under the nominal leadership of Mr Fearns, prize-fighting sank to the very lowest ebb, but he formed the climax and capped the careers of what we have rightly named a 'batch of blackguard bruisers'.

Cheated of the championship

In Michael Ryan the Irish found their first genuine hero of the ring. A brave battler and, more important, an honest one, Ryan failed to emulate his fellow countrymen, Corcoran and Fearns, in assuming the role of English heavyweight champion. But in his two attempts to unseat the redoubtable Tom Johnson, Ryan lifted Irish spirits and swept away the taint of villainy left by the infamous pair. Thanks to the unstinted efforts of men like Ryan and Johnson, boxing was restored to a degree of respectability. The crowds began to flock back when they could be assured of value for their money and the patrons reappeared to lend their valued support. Yet, as the first encounter between Ryan and Johnson proved, the sport had not managed to rid itself completely of those who would resort to skullduggery to make sure their man won the battle.

Perhaps today it would be considered gamesmanship, but Tom Johnson's cornermen saw the opportunity to exploit his opponent's weakness. Michael Ryan might have been 'manly and athletic and one of the hardest hitters in the kingdom,' but his Achilles' heel was his hot temper. It cost him dearly in both his assaults on the English championship.

Both men carried unbeaten records into the ring when they squared off for a purse of 300 guineas in Buckinghamshire in December 1787. Ryan, who had done all his fighting in Ireland, was the betting favourite at six to four. Left-handed, or what is now termed a southpaw, his favourite punch was a downward chopping action, which had finished off most of his rivals to date. Ryan appeared to justify the odds by getting the better of the early stages. In one determined attack he caught the English champion with a tremendous blow to the temple which sent him reeling against the ropes, arms dangling by his sides, an open target. As the Irishman attempted to follow up, Richard Humphries, one of Johnson's seconds, ran forward and grabbed Ryan in his arms. It was a blatant abuse of the rules and Ryan's cornermen were justified in demanding Johnson's disqualification. The English corner alleged that their man had been hit while his hands touched the ground and that the fight should only continue after a half-minute's rest. When one of Ryan's men conceded the point, Ryan was furious. He turned on the appeasing cornerman and had to be restrained from attacking him.

After lengthy argument Ryan agreed to go on with the contest. That first round had lasted 20 minutes. Rounds under the rules that governed bare-knuckle boxing were of indeterminate length, ending only when a man was knocked to the ground. A round, therefore, could last merely a few seconds or half an hour or more, depending on how long the pugilists remained on their feet. Quite often a boxer under pressure would deliberately touch down to end the round and avail of the allotted 30 seconds rest period. If he did not answer the call of 'Time' for the next round, he was deemed to have lost the fight. All bouts were fought to the finish, when one man was unable to continue or when both parties agreed to call it a draw. A drawn contest did not mean the two contestants were evenly matched, as it does nowadays, but that the fight ended inconclusively. Matches were of no fixed duration and could drag on for several hours until someone collapsed from exhaustion. There was no points scoring in those days.

Ryan was still fuming when he toed the line for the second round. The lengthy interruption while both sides argued was to the English champion's advantage, for he had clearly regained his composure. The crowd applauded Ryan's sportsmanship in agreeing to continue, but he seemed to have lost his zest for the encounter. Johnson used his superior skill to dominate the remainder of the fight and Ryan gave up the uneven struggle after 30 minutes.

The Irishman's supporters were not satisfied that their man had been beaten fairly and demanded a return. It was over a year before Johnson agreed to give Ryan a second chance at the title. Once again, the stakes were set at 300 guineas, a considerable sum for the time. The ring was erected on a stage on private grounds near Rickmansworth in Hertfordshire. Both boxers began cautiously, their skill at parrying and feinting being likened to that of fencing masters. It was several minutes before the first blow was struck, a heavy thump to the chest dropping the Englishman to the floor. Johnson set out to avenge his hurt and the second round was fiercely contested. Now it was Ryan's turn to go down after a solid blow to the head.

With neither boxer showing any marked superiority in the exchanges, Richard Humphries, whose timely intervention in the first encounter had swayed things in Johnson's favour, again brought his brand of gamesmanship into play. Exploiting Ryan's renowned short temper, Humphries began to shout anti-Irish jibes at the challenger. His tactics brought the desired result. Ryan, clearly agitated at the repeated insults, threw caution to the wind. His wild swings were easily avoided by the cool champion, whose carefully placed counter-punches wrought havoc on the Irishman's features. After 33 minutes Ryan looked such a sorry sight that his cornermen accepted the inevitable and conceded defeat on his behalf.

That was the end of Ryan's title aspirations, but there were hopes that his son, Bill, might earn greater glory for Ireland when he beat Tom Belcher, brother of English champion, Jem, in a major upset. Bill weighed around 11 stone (154 pounds) and would be classed as a light-middleweight today. In the bare-knuckle era, weight differences meant little. If a small man was willing to concede several stone and take on a bigger opponent, no one would try to stop him. Whatever hopes the Irish might have cherished of Bill Ryan's success were dashed when he was beaten in a return match with Belcher and later lost an even tougher battle with an alcohol problem. He was the despair of his backers. If they took their eyes off him for an hour, bewailed a contemporary, he would get 'completely besotted'.

Pierce Egan, the supreme boxing reporter of the period, evaluated Bill Ryan as 'a much superior fighter than his veteran sire', but conceded that he was 'so rivetted by the charms of the bottle that his constitution was soon undermined and, at a very premature age, he paid the debt of nature'. Another early scribe, Henry Downs Miles, dismissed Egan's view as unworthy. In his book *Pugilistica, the History of British Boxing*, Miles stated that Michael Ryan's renown 'consisted of being beaten twice by Tom Johnson, which was no disgrace, and then by Mike Brady, an Irish rough, which was'. Furthermore, he dismissed the younger Ryan as 'a drunken Irish braggadocio'.

But then Miles was unfairly dismissive in his treatment of Pierce Egan and was especially critical of his alleged partiality towards Irish boxers. Egan was not beyond putting an 'O' in front of a boxer's name if he thought it would make him sound more Irish, charged Miles. Others recognised Egan, the son of an Irish paviour who settled in London, for his true worth. A largely self-educated man, Egan's undisciplined writing style bears out his lack of formal learning, but no one can match him as a chronicler of pugilism. His vivid descriptions of the bare-knuckle encounters and the atmosphere surrounding them are true masterpieces of journalism. His five volumes of *Boxiana: Sketches of Ancient and Modern Pugilism*, published in London between 1812 and 1829, are classics of boxing literature. 'The man who has not read *Boxiana* is ignorant of the power of the English language', observed *Blackwood's Magazine* in 1820. Many years later, the American writer A.J. Liebling, whose *The Sweet Science* is a modern gem, said of Egan: 'He was the greatest writer about the ring who ever lived'.

Mendoza shows the Irish how

Up to the latter part of the 18th century, boxing in Ireland was on a small scale, poorly organised and rarely reported in the newspapers. Any pugilist worth his salt had to go to England if he hoped to make a name for himself. Daniel Mendoza changed all that. The London Jew, who revolutionised boxing with his scientific approach, is credited with popularising boxing in Ireland through his visit in 1791. After touring the country giving sparring exhibitions the English champion set up a school in Dublin where he taught the rudiments of the game to 'sons of the gentry'. His gymnasium became the nucleus of the amateur sporting clubs which soon began to spring up all over the land. Mendoza was the first to recognise the true commercial potential of prize-fighting. He helped promote his own contests, issued tickets and took money at the 'gate', a practice unknown up to then. He developed boxing as a science, introducing the value of footwork, which had hitherto been considered unmanly. He also demonstrated the usefulness of a left-hand jab. Frequently and accurately used, the straight jab could steadily weaken and discourage an opponent, while preserving the boxer's own hands from the hazards of striking bony heads with roundarm swings. As he stood only 5' 7" and weighed 11st 6lbs (160 lbs), it is obvious that Mendoza adopted his scientific tactics to overcome bigger, stronger men. He showed how a small, skilful boxer could conquer a comparative giant through guile and patience. Champion of England from 1791 to 1795, Mendoza had his last fight at the ripe old age of 57.

In 1791 Philip Astley, the noted equestrian and showman, built a theatre in Dublin at the corner of Bride Street and Peter Street. He wanted something special as an attraction on opening night and he chose wisely in booking the newly crowned champion of England. As well as sparring several rounds with his brother, Mendoza gave details of his life and career to an enraptured audience. And what stories he had to tell, like that of the gang of pirates who boarded his ship on the way to Ireland. He knocked two of the intruders overboard, causing one to drown, and forced the rest to flee in their small boats. A fanciful tale, no doubt, but it served to endear him to his growing 'fan club'.

Astley's Theatre was filled to capacity while Mendoza was engaged, many theatregoers preferring his brand of entertainment to the rival attraction of singer Elizabeth Billington at the Smock Alley Theatre. One night Astley cancelled the boxing show to stage a benefit variety concert for his son, only to find that those who had turned up demanded to see Mendoza in action. Fears of a riot were only quelled on the intervention of the Duke of Leinster who was among the audience. He convinced Astley that he had better summon the boxing champion if he didn't want the place pulled down around his ears. The theatre owner had to agree to the change of programme.

Despite his general popularity Mendoza did suffer a certain amount of prejudice during his stay in Dublin. As well as receiving hate letters and abuse from some sections of the theatre audience, he was attacked by a gang of ruffians while on his way to Astley's and he had to resort to a disguise for several days afterwards. One Squire Fitzgerald, a noted sportsman, accosted Mendoza at a city club and insulted him and his race. He branded the boxer 'an imposter' who would stand little chance against a worthwhile opponent such as the squire himself. He demanded that Mendoza fight him there and then. Dan tried to reason with him, to no avail. He then offered to spar with him, wearing gloves. 'Gloves be damned,' retorted Fitzgerald, 'I've come to show you what an Irishman can do to a Jew with his bare fists.' The Duke of Leinster said he would give Mendoza 50 guineas if he would accept the challenge. Dan saw there was no way out.

The room was cleared of all but the backers of each man. The doors were locked and the rivals stripped to the waist. Fitzgerald went on the attack right away, while the English champion contented himself with smart defensive action while sizing up his antagonist's strength. This didn't please the squire, who called him a coward. 'But I'm only playing with you,' replied Mendoza. His constant grin enraged the Irishman even more. 'Fight and don't try your accursed tricks with me,' snorted the squire. 'Well, if you'll have it, you'll have it,' said Mendoza, his smile vanishing. He lashed Fitzgerald's face with both fists, causing the blood to flow and closing one of the squire's eyes. For half an hour the foolhardy Irishman took a beating until at last his backers convinced him his task was hopeless.

Squire Fitzgerald now showed himself to be a true sportsman. Taking Mendoza's hand and holding it aloft, he said, 'You beat me fairly and I may tell you that you are the only man to have done so, or who ever floored me. In the heat of the battle I used offensive expressions and I ask you to forgive me. You are a great fighter, a true son of the Fancy, a credit to the sport and your race. I'm proud to shake the hand of the bravest and most skilful man I've ever met.' When word of the scrap got out, Mendoza was idolised by the Irish with the intensity of a modern pop star. The enthusiasm he generated stirred the ambitions of promising pugilists and spawned renowned

Daniel Mendoza and his brother in Dublin

Dan Donnelly

Irish champions like Dan Donnelly, Jack Langan and Simon Byrne. And it opened the way to the New World, where Irish prize-fighters were to the forefront in creating the climate that was to make America the foremost boxing nation in the world.

In his memoirs, published in 1816, Mendoza expressed his high regard for the Irish people, although still suffering hurt at the treatment he received from some elements:

> No people are more hospitable and generous than the respectable part of the Irish nation. Their liberality and kind attention to strangers are well known and universally acknowledged. I should feel the greatest regret if, in mentioning the instances of ill conduct of some of the vilest part of the community, I should be supposed to be casting illiberal reflections on the Irish in general. On the contrary, I am happy to avail myself of this opportunity of declaring that, during my residence with them, the generous reception I experienced from numerous persons of all ranks demands my most grateful acknowledgements and will never be forgotten by me.

Victims of their brutal business

Pugilism might have provided a passport to a comfortable lifetime for the fortunate few, but it frequently took a heavy toll of permanent injury and death. Broken noses and jaws were commonplace. Slashing blows often caused frightening eye injuries, sometimes blindness. Ribs and internal organs took a severe degree of abuse. More often than not, the winner of a long drawn-out tussle suffered nearly as much punishment as the defeated man. Broken hands were the price regularly paid for participation in the art of bare-knuckle boxing. Men who ended fights badly bruised would be surgically 'bled' before being put to bed for as long as it took them to recover. Some never did.

One particularly brutal battle fought on the Curragh of Kildare, some 30 miles from Dublin, in 1813 left the contestants so physically damaged that it ended both their fighting careers. Irish lightweight Dan Dougherty, according to Pierce Egan 'as game a pugilist as ever stripped a shirt over his head', was knocked out in 26 rounds by England's Tom Belcher and had his features 'materially altered'. One of his eyes was completely closed. His lip was split almost up to his nose. Three of his teeth were dislodged and his overall appearance was 'truly piteous'. And the victor's right hand was so disfigured, with one of his fingers permanently bent, that he could never again take part in a prize-fight. He did have the consolation of having the spot where the fight took place named after him. It was known as Belcher's Hollow until the Irish found a hero of their own a year later by the name of Dan Donnelly.

In the year 1800 Jem Belcher, Tom's brother, became the 20th man to claim the heavyweight championship of England. Three days before

Christmas, in a ring pitched on Wimbledon Common, he put his title at stake against his Irish challenger, Andrew Gamble. Many of the Irishman's supporters made the arduous sea journey especially to see Gamble make his bid but they were sorely let down. He fought gamely enough but apart from the third round, when he threw the champion to the ground and fell upon him to increase the effect, he was never really in it. A tremendous dig to the stomach in the fifth round deprived Gamble of his breath and a follow-up smash to the kidneys dropped him in agony. He had not recovered by the call of 'Time' for the next round. His disappointed fans made their way solemnly across the Common where the decaying corpse of highwayman Jerry Abbershaw swung from the gibbet.

Perhaps they were just making excuses for his poor showing, but it was the firm belief of many that Gamble had lost his true appetite for boxing following the fatal outcome of an earlier contest. Andrew, from the Liberties district of Dublin, had arrived in England with an impressive record of 18 straight successes and he was strongly tipped to dethrone the English champion. Though awkwardly built and knock-kneed he stood six feet and was very strong. Somewhat slow moving in the ring, he packed a heavy punch and had a sound defence. After winning his English debut, Gamble was matched with Trooper Noah James at Wimbledon Common. The Irishman was the betting underdog at six to four, as the Horse Guardsman had proven his ability and courage in 17 previous fights. Honours were fairly even until the 12th round, when Gamble landed a fierce right that split the Englishman's nose and sent blood flying in all directions. Worse was to follow. In the 20th round James suffered a broken collarbone when he was thrown heavily and, a round later, his jaw was shattered. He struggled on gallantly for another four rounds, until he collapsed and lay motionless. He died within hours. Distraught, Gamble donated part of his purse to his victim's young widow.

Twenty-one years later, it was an Irishman's turn to succumb to a fatal knockout. Daniel O'Leary, dropped by a tremendous right that caught him on the temple, died from a ruptured vessel in his brain. The fight, staged at Epsom Downs in Surrey for 25 guineas a side, had lasted just over an hour. The winner, Jack Cooper, known as 'the Tremendous Little Gypsy', was sent for trial to Croydon Assizes, charged with 'feloniously killing and slaying Daniel O'Leary'. He was found guilty of manslaughter and was sentenced to six months' imprisonment. Passing judgement, Justice Burrough stated that he did not think it was a fair fight and that Cooper was guilty of improper conduct in striking a man on a part of the head which any man knew was dangerous.

It was the fate of another Irish boxer of the period not to die from ring injuries, but to endure a kind of living death: sentenced to spend his remaining days in a distant penal colony. His crime: stealing £60 from a public house in London. It was not the sort of adventure Jack O'Donnell had envisaged when he set off from Ireland as a youth. He showed such natural fighting ability in impromptu street scraps in London that a prominent boxing instructor took him under his wing. By the time he was 18 Jack was ready for his ring debut. He beat Pardo Wilson in ten rounds. His next opponent was a fellow named Smith who revelled in the occupation of a 'boot closer'. There is a popular boxing expression 'he wasn't fit to tie his opponent's boots'. It might have originated in this 1802 contest. Smith was no match for the Irish prospect, who was borne off on the shoulders of his growing band of followers.

O'Donnell had his first brush with the law when he stepped into the ring to face one Henigan. Prize-fighting was still illegal and both boxers were arrested and bound over to keep the peace. The Irishman showed his contempt for the law by promptly accepting a match with Caleb Baldwin. Somewhat overawed by his opponent's reputation as a talented ringman, O'Donnell suffered his first setback. At one point it seemed as if he might pull off an upset when he cut Baldwin's eyebrow with a sharp blow. He followed up to throw the Englishman to the ground. But a clever stroke of gamesmanship saved the day for Baldwin. He manoeuvred so that his back was to the setting sun and, at the same time, ensuring that it shone in O'Donnell's eyes. Baldwin took control of the action and finished it in the eighth round with a mighty 'cross buttock'. This particular tactic was a legitimate and highly effective way of downing an opponent in the bare-knuckle era. *Fistiana*, published in 1868, described it as 'the most fatal of falls' and instructed students in the way it might be operated: 'Get your arm firmly over your adversary's neck, grasping his loose arm with the other hand, get his crutch upon your hip or buttock, give him a cant over your shoulder, he goes over with tremendous violence, and you fall upon his abdomen.' By modern standards it hardly seems justified to be ever considered as a boxing tactic, but, until the Marquis of Queensberry decreed it illegal in 1867, it was a common method of bringing a contest to a summary conclusion.

O'Donnell's defeat by Baldwin seemed to knock much of the heart for further combat out of him. He was beaten in 15 rounds by Tom Belcher and was trounced by a man named Emery. However, he regained his former taste for victory by gaining revenge over Emery and dismissed the cocky challenge of a novice by the name of Wasdale in three rounds. His star seemed to be in the ascendant again, but he fell in with a gang of robbers and paid the dreadful penalty of being transported for life. He was never to see England, or his native Irish shores, for the rest of his days.

Dan Donnelly: the man and the myth

Without doubt, the outstanding Irish pugilist of the entire period of bare-knuckle combat was Dan Donnelly. He may, or may not, have been the most fistically gifted of them all, but no one matched his popularity in his homeland. Quite astonishing scenes of rejoicing followed his famous victory over the Englishman George Cooper on the Curragh of Kildare and the footprints left by the brawny Dublin carpenter as he strode up the hill after his triumph are preserved to this day, over 160 years later. Over the years, visitors to the historic spot have trod the same path and thus enabled the Irish champion's exit from the ring to be perpetually marked out in the turf. At the base of Donnelly's Hollow, named in his honour, stands a five feet high monument bearing a plaque with a brief description of Donnelly's career. It is thought to be the only place in the world where a monument has been erected to commemorate a boxing contest. Some two miles from there in the town of Kilcullen is an even more remarkable reminder of the hero of Kildare. In a glass case at The Hideout tavern is displayed what is reputed to be Dan Donnelly's right arm, surely the world's oddest boxing 'souvenir'. The story goes that the arm was severed by grave robbers who raided the Bully's Acre graveyard at Kilmainham, Dublin, and was used initially by anatomy students at Edinburgh University, then as a peepshow exhibit in a travelling circus. In 1904 it was purchased by the well-known Belfast bookmaker and sports enthusiast Hugh 'Texas' McAlevey for display in his public house, the Duncairn Arms. Fifty years later it passed to the late Jim Byrne, owner of The Hideout, and there it remains, a ready topic of query and discussion among locals and amazed visitors.

The years have lent enchantment to another story, almost certainly a myth, that Donnelly is the only boxer ever to have received a knighthood from a member of the British royal family. Legend has it that, on meeting the prize-fighter, the Prince Regent (later King George IV) remarked, 'I am glad to meet the best fighting man in Ireland', to which the bold Donnelly replied, 'I am not just that, your royal highness, but I am the best in England'. The Prince was supposedly so impressed with the boxer's brash charm that he thereupon bestowed on him the right to be known as 'Sir Daniel'. Certainly Donnelly himself did little to dispel the popular belief that he had earned his knighthood. A huge copper spirit jug, used by Donnelly at one of the four public houses he ran in Dublin and now in the possession of a retired solicitor, has a small plaque attached bearing the words, 'Sir Dan Donnelly, Irish Champion, Pill Lane, 1820'.

Much of the lasting hero-worship of Donnelly can be attributed to the numerous poems and ballads that were penned in the wake of his sudden death at the age of 32. The most enduring ballad, *Donnelly and Cooper,* was still a popular choice among the street singers who, up to the 1930s, trotted out the seemingly never-ending verses for a few pennies. The song relates Dan's great battle to overcome his English rival and how Miss Kelly, sister of his patron Captain William Kelly, bet her coach and horses and all her estate on his winning. The last verse of the ballad goes:

You sons of proud Britannia,
 your boasting now recall,
Since Cooper by Dan Donnelly
 has met his sad downfall;
In eleven rounds he got nine knock downs,
 likewise a broke jaw-bone,
'Shake hands,' said she, 'brave Donnelly,
 the battle is all our own.'

So much for the legends. How well does the real Dan Donnelly match up? Certainly the massive turnout for his funeral, with men tussling for the honour of drawing his hearse, from which the horse was un-yoked, show that he had acquired the status of a demigod among the poor. *The Sporting Magazine* reported that 'at least 80,000 men, women and children attended the funeral, the roads and streets leading to the burial ground being covered with a moving mass of rags and wretchedness.' The privileged classes had their heroic statesmen and generals. To those in the lower strata of society, Donnelly represented their struggle for survival and ultimate triumph against the odds. His act of bloodying an English nose also struck a blow for their desire to win freedom from their country's English rulers. In 1800, when Donnelly was a teenager apprenticed to a Dublin timber merchant, Ireland lost whatever limited independence it had enjoyed when the Act of Union of Great Britain and Ireland gave full control of the country's affairs to the government at Westminster.

On strict appraisal of Donnelly's boxing record there is little to support his ranking as a ring great. True, he never lost a fight, but the records show that he only had three major contests, none of them against men of championship status. It would be interesting to see how he would have fared against the two English title-holders who were around when he was at his peak, but efforts to match him with Tom Cribb and Tom Spring failed to materialise. The closest he came to proving his true worth was in a sparring match with Spring in which gloves were worn. Donnelly gave a praiseworthy account of himself against one of the most gifted ringmen of the day, but exhibition bouts are far from the real thing. Had the Irishman been more painstaking in his pursuit of the English champions and had he applied himself more diligently to the rigours of training, he might well have proven his boast to the Prince Regent. However, like far too many of his fellow Irishmen down the years, dedication to the task was not his most notable attribute.

Born in Townsend Street, Dublin, the ninth of 17 children, Dan was drawn into boxing as a career after he was seen chastising a bully who had insulted his ailing father in a pub. He came under the patronage of Captain William Kelly, a noted horse-owner and eccentric, whose other interests included playing the uileann pipes and joining in the popular family diversion of 'dancing in their pelts'. When Donnelly had absorbed his patron's teaching of the rudiments of boxing he was matched with

Tom Hall from the Isle of Wight. Hall was touring Ireland giving exhibitions and agreed to meet Donnelly at the Curragh on 14 September 1814. It seemed that every available horse-drawn vehicle in Dublin was used that day to ferry eager fans to the scene of the fight. Those without transport happily walked the 30 miles. Donnelly proved too big and strong for the visitor, who was three inches shorter and two stone lighter. Several times Hall dropped to his knees to avoid further punishment and avail of the 30 seconds rest between rounds. Finally, an exasperated Donnelly struck Hall on the side of the head as Hall's knee touched down. The incident ended the 15th round and Hall failed to answer 'Time' for the next round. His cornermen claimed he should be awarded the fight because of Donnelly's foul blow. The Irishman's supporters had no doubt that their man had proved his superiority and carried him triumphantly from the ring. On his way back to his living quarters at nearby Calverstown Donnelly's coach was halted several times and the hero of the hour was invited to join the victory celebrations in the local taverns. It was the same when he got back to Dublin. The wild drinking spree and merrymaking lasted a full week, with the Irish champion in the midst of it all, caring nothing that every penny he earned in the fight was spent.

The scenes were repeated after Donnelly's legendary victory over George Cooper 15 months later. As for the match with Hall, every inch of grass in the natural amphitheatre of the Hollow was occupied by some 20,000 fans. Cooper, a bargeman from Stone in Staffordshire, was a skilful and courageous boxer, but he was at a disadvantage in height and weight to the six feet, 14st (196lbs) Irish champion. At one stage it looked as if the Englishman's greater experience would tell but Donnelly came storming back to turn the tide and finish it off with a tremendous right that smashed his rival's jaw. The ecstatic cheering that greeted the climax could be heard in villages several miles away and bonfires were lit in celebration.

Donnelly's great weakness ruined his chances of making a success as a publican, for he was his own best customer at his premises in Capel Street, Dublin. Subsequent efforts to do better as the landlord of taverns in The Coombe, Poolbeg Street and at the corner of Greek Street and Pill Lane (now Chancery Street) proved equally unprofitable. He was too generous in lavishing drink on his worshippers, true and less genuine, and loved to join in the constant revelry. He quickly fell into debt and overcame his initial reluctance to travel to England to pick up some ready cash from boxing exhibitions. Before long the calls grew for the Irish champion to prove his claim to be the best fighting man in England. Though he had not gone there to engage in an actual prize-fight, principally because he was far from fit, he accepted a challenge from Tom Oliver, from Bledlow in Buckinghamshire, who had beaten George Cooper in 17 minutes and was known as 'the Bravest of the Brave'. It would obviously be a severe test of Donnelly's true worth but he refused to take it seriously. He rarely went to bed without a bottle of whiskey for company, unless it was with a fair wench procured on regular diversions from his training camp in Surrey. So careless was the man that, as Pierce Egan so quaintly put it, 'he picked up a disease in the promiscuousness of his amours'.

The fight with Oliver was staged at Crawley Downs in Sussex on 21 July 1819. Encouraging shouts of 'Bravo, Dan' and 'Ireland for ever' greeted Donnelly as he entered the ring, evidence of the many supporters who had travelled from Ireland to will him to victory. For once the Irish champion was meeting a man as big and as strong as himself. Oliver gave him a desperately hard time for the one hour and ten minutes it lasted. Dan's great determination saw him through some rough passages, although his lack of conditioning almost brought about his downfall. He made heavy weather of a fight he needed to win impressively if his threat to the English champion was to be taken seriously. A solid right to the head, followed by a mighty cross buttock, finished off Oliver in the 34th round, but Donnelly was disappointed with his performance and admitted he 'fought like a wooden man'.

The fruits of his labours were quickly swallowed up in the more notorious drinking and gambling dens of London's West End and he had just two pounds in his pocket when his wife arrived to take him home to Dublin. It was the end of Dan Donnelly the prize-fighter and aspirant to the championship of England. He never fought again. A billed exhibition stint at Donnybrook Fair in 1819 flopped when he failed to turn up. He preferred the company of his drinking pals to the role of chief attraction at the fair. And it was while engaged in that same pastime that he took ill at his Pill Lane pub and he died on the morning of 18 February 1820. Death was attributed to his drinking a large dose of water after playing a strenuous game of fives, but there were many rumours of what might have been responsible, the wildest being his poisoning by a jealous Englishman. Pierce Egan gave his appraisal of the archetypal Irishman in *Boxiana*:

> Donnelly was a creature of the moment. He was excellent company, creating mirth and laughter all around him. His sayings were droll in the extreme and his behaviour was always decorous. He was generous, good natured and grateful. Tomorrow might, or might not, be provided for and it never created any uneasiness in his mind. He would say, 'Devil may care'. He was an Irishman, every inch of him.

Pugilism: the case for the defence

Boxing has always had its critics. It is not surprising that a sport which has as its main objective the rendering of one man unconscious by another should draw its fair share of detractors. Even today, with its tighter controls and inbuilt safeguards, serious injuries and death are far too frequent. It is difficult to defend boxing against the constant demands for its abolition. Can it really have a place in a society that pretends to uphold the dignity of the person? Yet the anti-boxing brigade tend to spoil their case by over-playing their hand, such as when they use renowned figures like Muhammad Ali and Joe Louis as examples of the physical and mental damage participation in the sport can cause. Conveniently ignored is the fact that the disease which affects Ali, Parkinson's Syndrome, is suffered by many people in all walks of life, and that Louis' father, who never boxed, ended his life in a mental institution.

Boxing is a brutal sport. That cannot be denied. But it is also one of the most skilful of games. To the connoisseur, the pleasure of watching a craftsman making an oppponent miss by a slight movement of his head, his feinting to create an opening for a points-scoring jab, or his use of sheer skill to overcome a more powerful rival, is more rewarding than seeing a man knock another senseless. Good boxers know the risks and come prepared. They are among the most physically fit and mentally alert of sportsmen, and the financial rewards are greater than in any other sport.

One of pugilism's earliest defenders against the abolitionists was an Irish ringman with a literary leaning, Tom Reynolds from Middletown, County Armagh. 'Show me the man who is completely opposed to pugilism and you will find his character to be a bad neighbour and a tyrant under his own roof.' He vehemently rejected charges that boxing matches debased, demoralised or brutalised Britain as a nation. On the contrary, he insisted, boxing introduced chivalrous notions of honour, courage, fortitude and love of manly fair play, features that were strongly indented in the British character.

> Compare the population of Ireland, where the stick has been thrown aside and the fist used, to the other parts. The difference in the number of deaths by violence will strike conviction in the dullest. In fact, though chivalry did much to smooth down the roughness of the darker ages, 'tis only the boxing glove can give the true polish of civilisation to the world.

Reynolds was obviously a cut above the average boxer of the time in that he was well educated and prided himself on his ability to 'write a good letter'. Yet his entry into the fight trade came about through less than respectable circumstances. He was in prison at the time. Failure to pay his bills while operating as a potato dealer in London caused him to be thrown into the notorious Fleet Prison. Sparring matches were a popular way for convicts to put in their recreation periods and Tom found it to his liking. He was so encouraged with his showings that, on his release, he secured a match with Abraham Belasco. Reynolds, nicknamed 'the Murphy Dealer' because of his previous occupation, won a fiercely-fought tussle in 66 rounds. He was preparing to advance his boxing career when misfortune struck again.

Installed as the landlord of a public house in Drury Lane, London, he fell through a trap-door into a cellar, badly injuring himself. It looked like he could forget about the ring. However, he made such a fine recovery that he agreed to undertake a tour of Ireland to box exhibitions. In July 1820 he met John Dunn at Donnelly's Hollow for a purse of £50. He gave Dunn such a hiding that, after 54 minutes, he stopped fighting and refused to strike his helpless victim. Captain Kelly, Dan Donnelly's former patron, who was in Dunn's corner, accepted Reynolds' merciful gesture and signalled his man's retirement.

Reynolds' compassionate side was again in evidence when, on his return to England, he hit a fellow named Sammonds so hard that the recipient turned a complete somersault and lay motionless for ten minutes. Seeing his opponent's distress on awakening, Tom counted out five of the £40 he had earned for his win and handed them over to Sammonds. Pierce Egan noted that Reynolds was a much improved fighter from his travels in Ireland, although he thought that Tom, a mild, inoffensive man outside the ring, had 'rather too much of the bulldog in his mode of fighting'. There is no further record of his pugilistic achievements, except that he challenged any man in England to fight him for 200 guineas a side. He did appear again as a trainer to promising young Irish boxers Jack Langan and Simon Byrne. By this time he was running a successful bar in Abbey Street, Dublin, 'which he conducted with great regularity until his sand ran out,' recorded Egan. He died, aged 40, on 15 May 1832.

Jack Langan: 'never a braver man'

Boxing fans, along with those who supported such grotesque sports as dog fighting, bull baiting and cock fighting in the Regency period, came under the collective term of the Fancy. It applied to all those associated with such 'amusements', irrespective of class. For the big fight at Worcester Race-course on 7 January 1824 between Tom Spring, the champion of England, and his Irish challenger Jack Langan, the Fancy was out in force. In his inimitable way, Pierce Egan described the huge gathering as

> a union of all ranks, from the brilliant of the highest class in the circle of Corinthians, down to the Dusty Bob graduation in society, and even a shade or two below that. Lots of the Upper House and the Flash House, proprietors of splendid parks and demenses, inmates from proud and lofty mansions, thousands from the peaceable cot and myriads of coves from no houses at all - in a word, it was a conglomoration of the Fancy.

The West Midlands town of Worcester, though used to crowds on race days, had never known anything like the 30,000 congregation for the English title fight. From early morning the streets were filled with coaches and four-horse chaises, mails and vehicles of every description arriving to the blowing of horns and the ringing of bells. For the first time at a boxing contest a grandstand was erected, with an admission fee of ten shillings. Some of the more daring spectators who paid nothing perched precariously on the masts of ships in the adjacent River Severn. Inside the ground scaffolding was erected to accommodate some of the overflow crowd. There was minor panic when part of the scaffolding collapsed. Many people were injured, though no one was killed.

Tom Spring was the first of the contestants to arrive in the ring, to tumultuous cheers. Nattily dressed, the English champion was driven up to the scene in a post-chaise. He had to wait half and hour before his Irish challenger put in an appearance. Further delay occurred when Tom Reynolds, one of Langan's seconds, objected to a belt made of whalebone worn by Spring. After some discussion the Englishman agreed to remove the belt and the contest was free to begin. It was noticeable that Spring had all the physical advantages. At six feet, he was three inches taller and, at 13st 6lbs (188lbs), the heavier by 20 pounds. Spring, whose real name was Winter, was not reckoned to be a very damaging puncher, but he was a gifted ringman with style and grace. Langan's build drew admiration, his arms and upper body being described as 'fine and athletic', although his legs were thin. Some expressed the opinion that he had trained too hard and had lost too much weight.

Langan felt quietly confident as he awaited the call of 'Time' for this, the most important occasion of his life to date. Many an adventure he had packed into those 26 years. Like the time he almost starved to death, along with the rest of the crew of the Charlotte Gambier, on a nightmare journey to South America to fight for the cause of independence. Though suffering the ravages of pain and sickness, he was able to treat the people of St Marguerite Island to their first glimpse of boxing when he beat Jack Power, an admiral's boatswain. Or the time he spent in Dublin's Marshalsea Prison for failure to pay the terms of a paternity suit. Jack, then a publican in King Street, Dublin, had fallen for the charms of a pretty young dairymaid. When Cathy Flynn presented him with a child, Langan's normally jovial disposition undertook a change. He refused to marry her, alleging that he was the one who had been seduced, not the other way round as she claimed. The court ruled in Cathy's favour. He was ordered to pay £100 for damage to her character. Feeling he had been unjustly treated he fled to England, where he worked as a sawyer. But his conscience got the better of him and he returned home to face the music. Though jailed for absconding he was discharged when he appeared before the insolvents' court. Cathy Flynn spoke up in his favour, stating that she had no desire to see him locked up.

Langan, born in Clondalkin, now a densely populated Dublin suburb but then a quiet village, had moved as a child with his family to Ballybough Lane where his father opened a provisions business 'for man and horse'. A lively youth, Jack enjoyed nothing better than a good scrap and he was only 13 when he downed a much bigger and older opponent in a contest staged on the banks of the Grand Canal. He was apprenticed to a sawmill owner while pursuing his boxing ambitions by running up a string of wins over local opposition. One of those successes was over Jimmy Lyons in a fight that began with snowballs and ended with fists. Tutored by Dan Donnelly, Langan beat the highly regarded Pat Slantea in 13 rounds and then, after a split with Donnelly, he got great satisfaction out of trouncing Pat Halton, a protégé of Donnelly's.

But now it was the big one, the challenge for the heavyweight championship of England. Not only was the greatest prize in boxing within his grasp, but the £600 which Tom Spring had put up to match his own sidestake. Langan opened the contest confidently and he scored 'first blood' with a sharp blow to the Englishman's lip. This was an important point in a bare-knuckle bout, with bets hanging on which boxer was first to draw blood. It was Langan's turn to shed blood in the second round. Spring's greater mobility made him an elusive target and his stinging punches closed the challenger's left eye by the sixth round. Langan was most effective when he got to close quarters, where he showed great strength in throwing the bigger man to the ground. In a spectacular show of force he tossed Spring clean out of the ring to end the 29th round, to cries of 'Bravo, Langan' from his supporters. At this stage the crowd began to converge on the ring, making it difficult for the boxers to use the extremities of the space. Stewards used long poles and then whips in a futile effort to clear the area around the ring.

As the fight progressed it was Spring's superior skill which kept him on top, but Langan's great heart kept him in with a fighting chance. The Irishman drove a vicious blow to Spring's head to floor him in the 65th round. Langan threw himself on top of the limp figure. Spring, spitting blood, was hauled to his corner by Tom Cribb, the former English champion. Pale and looking distressed, Spring recovered sufficiently to drop his spirited challenger. Near chaos prevailed as the unruly crowd almost smothered the contestants. They had only about five feet of the centre of the ring in which to manoeuvre. Those at the back of the attendance couldn't see what was happening. For the Langan fans among them, perhaps it was just as well. The Irishman was in a sorry state as he dropped, exhausted, to end the 77th round. Asked if he wanted to retire he retorted, 'No, I am not beaten - I can fight for hours if I must'. The battle had already gone on for two and a half hours.

When 'Time' was called Langan tried but failed to rise from his sitting position on his second's knee. It was the end of one of the bravest challenges for the championship of England. Tom Cribb shook the Irishman's hand and remarked, 'You are a brave man indeed, Jack'. Ned Painter, the champion's other cornerman, added, 'I never saw a better'. There was much critical comment afterwards about the way the crowd had converged upon the ring during the contest and, in a letter to one of the newspapers which carried much correspondence on the controversy, Langan claimed he had been unfairly treated by Spring's supporters. He challenged the champion to a return match and was willing to back himself for a sum from £300 to £1,000. It was an offer Spring could not refuse.

The second encounter, at Birdham Bridge near Chichester in Essex on 8 June 1824, was even more savagely fought than the first. In fact, so severe was the punishment suffered by both men that neither fought ever again. One of the conditions laid down by the Irishman was that Spring's seconds wear kneepads. He complained that Ned Painter had used his knee on him when the crowd closed in on the ring in the first meeting. Langan again drew first blood with a stiff blow to the English champion's mouth and he threw Spring heavily to end the second round. But generally he found it difficult to land decisive punches on his constantly shifting target. Spring had suffered throughout his career from brittle hands and the pain showed on his features as his left fist swelled up. His right hand, too, was clearly giving him trouble by the 17th round, when Langan tossed him to the ground with a powerful cross buttock. The Irishman was not escaping unscathed, however, his face showing signs of the punishment he was taking in the grim struggle.

So battered were Langan's features by the 39th round that one of his seconds, Tom Belcher, implored him to quit. Jack would not hear of it. He gambled on Spring's hands giving out completely, and then the fight - and the English championship - would be his. But Spring was not prepared to release his hold on the title just yet. Though suffering agony every time he connected to Langan's head, he still managed to dole out dreadful punishment. After a lengthy exchange in the 56th round, Pierce Egan reported, Langan 'went down like a log of wood from a terrific facer'. Both men's faces were so bloody and swollen that they were scarcely recognisable. Even though Spring's hands were so puffed up that he could hardly close them, he still slammed home punch after punch on an incredibly brave challenger. Langan, dropped time and again, resisted calls for his retirement. 'I can still win it,' he insisted. Even Ned Painter, Spring's cornerman, took pity on the Irishman. 'A better man was never seen in the ring, Langan, but you can't win,' said Painter. 'It's no use fighting on. It could be dangerous for you.' Langan mumbled in answer, 'I will fight on. No one shall take me away.'

When 'Time' was called for the 75th round, Langan almost had to be carried to the line. His knees buckling beneath him, he struck out pathetically at the shadowy figure before him and was severely chastised for his efforts. The sickening spectacle finally ended in the 76th round. Langan was barely able to strike a fighting pose as Spring, ignoring the pain from his throbbing hand, measured his range for a mighty right-hander that put the Irishman down and out. The savage contest had lasted an hour and 49 minutes, almost an hour shorter than their first encounter. The victor immediately went to Langan's corner and offered his outstretched hand.   Jack, his battered head lying limply on his chest, looked up and muttered, 'Is the battle over?' Spring nodded and tried to console the beaten man, saying, 'Jack, you and I must be friends for the rest of our lives and anything that is in my power I will do to serve you.'

Pierce Egan, who counted Langan among his closest friends, said it was one of the fairest fights he had witnessed but that the Irishman's bravery had not been enough to counter Spring's superior skill and cool confidence. Spring, realising that his hands would not stand up to further abuse, quit the ring to become a publican. Langan followed the same route, taking the licence of a premises in Liverpool where his lively personality ensured a regularly full house. After a few years he had made enough money to retire to a house he bought in Cheshire. It was there that he died, aged 47, on St Patrick's Day 1846.

Death stalked Simon Byrne

Irishman Simon Byrne earned himself a niche in boxing history in 1833 when his unsuccessful bid to wrest the English heavyweight championship from James 'Deaf' Burke lasted for three hours and 16 minutes.   The 99-rounds contest is the longest championship fight in history, either with bare knuckles or gloves. Sadly, the effort cost Byrne his life.   It was a fateful end to the Irishman's career, for three years earlier he had dealt out such a beating to Sandy McKay that the latter failed to recover consciousness. He was put on trial for manslaughter but was acquitted. Byrne seemed unable to avoid prolonged encounters in the ring.   His first notable win, over Mike Larkins at Blessington Race-course in County Wicklow, went 138 rounds. Yet he never trained for lengthy fights. Most of his 'preparation' for a bout seemed to consist of discussing it with his friends in various taverns throughout Ireland and England.   Though he stood an inch over six feet, his 13st 8lbs (190lbs) was mostly positioned around his waistline and he was notably round-shouldered.   He hardly cut an impresssive figure for a would-be champion of England.

When Byrne got his first crack at the title, in 1831, the contrast in appearance between the champion, Jem Ward, and himself was the subject of much comment. Ward's deep chest, broad shoulders, well-shaped body and bright, glistening features stood out starkly against the ungainly figure of the Irishman. 'There was a heavy, sluggish look about Byrne,' noted an observer, 'and the meat hung in collops over his drawers, while he had a corporation that would have done credit to a city alderman.' Yet there was enough support for Byrne's assault on the title to draw a crowd of 15,000 to the Warwickshire venue.   Among the ringsiders were the Duke of Beaufort, the Marquis of Worcester and the Marquis of Queensberry. Byrne's fighting stance made him look even more clumsy, his left hand extended and his right arm held low to protect his ample midsection. Ward, the English-born son of an Irish butcher, was neatly balanced and held his arms high, ready for attack or defence. Byrne's supporters accepted that he was a long way behind the champion on skill, but they felt that, because of his reputation as a long stayer, he would outlast Ward.

For 25 rounds Byrne could make no impression on the Englishman and the odds were 20-to-1 against him. But just when he seemed close to collapse he rallied and in a determined attack caught Ward with a hard blow to the throat. The champion staggered back against the ropes, gasping for breath. Byrne tried to follow up his advantage but he was over-anxious and his wild swings were way off target. Now recovered, Ward picked off Byrne with stinging punches. By the 33rd round it was clear that Simon Byrne, bleeding badly from the nose and unable to breathe properly, had no chance of winning and his seconds retired him. While the winner jumped over the ropes and back again to show how fresh he was, Byrne sat slumped in his corner. Ward took him by the hand and remarked, 'You're a brave man, Simon, and I had a rare job to beat you'.

When Ward later announced his retirement from boxing the English championship was claimed by James Burke, another son of Irish settlers. Immediately Burke was challenged by Simon Byrne. When the championship bout was scheduled for Ascot Race-course, Byrne asked Ned Neale, a former prominent pugilist, to help him get into trim. 'A mountain of fat' when he arrived in Liverpool to commence training, he lost almost two stone (28lbs) by the time of the fight but still looked poorly conditioned in comparison to the heavily muscled champion. The Irishman's main plan of campaign seemed to be to rush Burke to the ropes and hold him by the neck with his left hand while belting him with his right. This tactic proved moderately successful until the 19th round, when he damaged his right hand. His chief weapon was now gone. Yet he managed to deal out sufficient punishment to keep the champion worried about the outcome. Both men were weary from their efforts and the pounding their bodies were taking. In the 93rd round Byrne was knocked over by the sheer weight of the champion's charge and Burke then fell on top of him. Simon was barely able to stand during the following rounds, yet he held his ground while trying to keep off the Englishman with his one good hand. Finally, even his great spirit reached its limit and he collapsed in a heap at Burke's feet. The champion, sagging noticeably at the knees, gave a huge grin of relief that it was over.

After being carried unconscious from the ring, Byrne was put to bed in his quarters and surgically bled. He remained in a state of stupor. The left side of his head was badly bruised, his left eye was completely closed and his mouth and face much swollen. His body, too, bore many bruises. The following day his condition worsened; his head was shaved and leeches were applied to the bruised parts. He recovered sufficiently to thank those who were attending him but he then relapsed and died.

At the inquest into his death some witnesses deplored the fact that boxers were often carried to the 'scratch' when they could not make it alone. This subsequently led to a change in the rules, requiring that 'a man must walk to the scratch in eight seconds after Time is called'. The surgeon who attended Byrne attributed his death to 'the congested state of the brain, combined with violent and prolonged exertions, and the mental suffering under defeat'. He emphasised the point that the anguish felt by Byrne over his loss was largely to blame for his death. Had he won, suggested the doctor, there was a good chance he would have recovered, as the blows alone were not enough to cause his death. The coroner returned a verdict of manslaughter against Burke. He stood trial at Hereford Assizes and was found not guilty. Byrne, only 32 when he died, was buried at St Albans in Hertfordshire; a public appeal raised £262 for his widow.

The Irish, shocked at the loss of their championship hope, vented their anger on Burke, whom they accused of deliberately causing Byrne's death. They vowed to avenge it by finding an Irishman who would relieve him of the English title. They soon found the man they sought in Samuel O'Rourke. As Samuel had run up quite a reputation on his home territory, his backers sent over a challenge to Burke to meet O'Rourke in Ireland. In view of the animosity shown towards him in the wake of the Simon Byrne tragedy, it was not surprising that he turned down the invitation. Besides, the boxing spotlight was now beaming towards a new and exciting base across the Atlantic. America had become aware of the attractions of prize-fighting and beckoned the cream of England's and Ireland's talent. The response was overwhelming. Almost overnight, England was forced to yield its hold on the sport and concede it to the New World. And the United States has enjoyed world supremacy over ring affairs ever since. It was on American soil that James 'Deaf' Burke, from England, and Samuel O'Rourke, from Ireland, were to settle the bitter differences that had followed them across the ocean.

Two

The American Invasion

AROUND THE YEAR 1830 bare-knuckle boxing began to establish its roots on American soil. The New World offered plenty of opportunities to hardy young men with surplus energy to burn and a yearning for fame and fortune. The ring could provide a short-cut to the goal that motivated many an Irishman fleeing from the famine and deprivation of his homeland. To those with talent in their fists England was no longer the place to look to. After Simon Byrne's tragic end no Irish challenger emerged for the English championship. Instead, the best of them set sail for the American continent. The early progress of American pugilism was nursed along by men with names like Murphy, Duffy, Kelly, Sullivan, O'Brien and Morrissey.

Not all of them fulfilled the dream they were prepared to shed their blood for, but enough came through to form the nucleus of the great American boxing tradition. The late Nat Fleischer, founder and editor of *The Ring* magazine, said in his book *The Heavyweight Championship:*

American ring history from the middle of the 19th century through the early part of the 20th is primarily the history of Irish supremacy. In every division the headliners were, with few exceptions, either emigrants from the land of Erin or native sons of Hibernian parents who had come to these shores to seek their fortune.

Before the Irish invasion, boxing in the United States had been largely confined to matches between black slaves, forced to fight each other for the entertainment of their white masters who had been introduced to pugilism in England. The greatest of these black battlers was Tom Molineaux, who had won his freedom and travelled to England to challenge Tom Cribb for the English championship. Twice he tried and twice he failed. In the first match Molineaux was cheated of certain victory by one of Cribb's cornermen, who accused the American of concealing bullets in his fists just when the English title-holder was set for defeat. Molineaux, who enjoyed the good life at the expense of his health, went rapidly downhill and was in Ireland when he died, aged 34. He was buried in a pauper's grave in County Galway.

The first generally recognised American champions were a New Yorker of Dutch extraction, Jacob Hyer, and his son Tom. But as Daniel Mendoza had taught boxing to the Irish, it was another Englishman, William Fuller, who spread the fistic gospel in the United States. Fuller, who had once been beaten by Molineaux in Scotland, spent six years in America. He opened a gymnasium and training school in Charleston, West Virginia, where he taught eager young men the rudiments of the Noble Art of Self Defence. In the meantime, word had spread across the Atlantic of the potential gold mine that was the American ring. First of the English champions to arrive in the US was James 'Deaf' Burke, in 1836. It was not long before Burke heard the unwelcome news that he had been followed by Samuel O'Rourke, the man set up by the Irish as the avenger. O'Rourke played his allotted role to perfection. He took every opportunity of accosting Burke and calling him a murderer, regardless of the fact that the Englishman had been exonerated of blame for Simon Byrne's death. Burke eventually conceded to the pressure and agreed to fight O'Rourke just outside the Irishman's adopted 'home town' of New Orleans.

The unsavoury element that attached itself to the early days of prize-fighting in the United States was borne out in a report in the *New Orleans Item*:

> From an early hour swarms of men - fashionable Creoles, French gamblers, half-breeds, Yankee sharps, Irish toughs and smugglers and picaroons from the Barataria swamps and lakes - began to leave New Orleans for the field of battle. A regulation 20-foot ring, with outer ropes after the English fashion, was erected. The heterogeneous mob closed thick around the enclosure, reflecting the belligerent mood which was natural in the gathering of so many and varied nationalities. Hardly a man was there who had not ruffian stamped on his face, save the few Englishmen and Creole aristocrats, and there was a free and ostentatious display of pistols, bowie knives, bludgeons and sling shots. The rough element - in a heavy majority - was the O'Rourke contingent, and Caldwell whispered to his English friend, Brandham the cotton buyer, that Burke wouldn't have a chance with that gang.

How right that observer was proved. From the outset of the fight the English champion was subjected to a barrage of insults from O'Rourke's supporters, who called upon their man to destroy Byrne's 'assassin'. The fight was only a few minutes old when one of O'Rourke's seconds, Mickey Carson, 'accidentally' fell against Burke, knocking him off balance. O'Rourke had been well rehearsed for this ploy and he rushed in to throw his opponent heavily to the ground. A furious Burke scrambled to his feet and warned Carson not to try anything like that again. Carson responded by drawing a knife from under his shirt and waving it under the startled boxer's nose. When Burke had O'Rourke in trouble after landing a solid thump to the face, Carson again intervened. Burke turned on him and sent his tormentor sprawling with a hefty blow. This was the signal for the Irishman's followers to invade the ring. All thoughts of the boxing match were abandoned as the mob sought to wreak vengeance for Simon Byrne. Burke courageously, if foolishly, stood his ground and attempted to fight off the howling rabble. But Jim Phelan, one of his seconds, urged him, 'Run for your life!'

The Englishman's friends had been prepared for such an eventuality and when Burke reached a nearby wood, with the mob in hot pursuit, he found a horse ready for him. He was handed a bowie knife and advised to seek refuge in the St Charles Theatre. The frightened boxer, clad only in his ring pants and shoes, burst in on Julius Brutus Booth in rehearsal for *Macbeth*. The tragedian, whose son John Wilkes Booth was to earn infamy as the man who assassinated President Abraham Lincoln, agreed to keep Burke in the safety of his dressing room until the police came to ensure his safe passage out of New Orleans. While the English champion lost little time in returning to the safety of his homeland, O'Rourke drifted around the United States before ending up as a lumberjack in Canada. He lost what money he earned in gambling and, desperate, he turned to smuggling. His dangerous lifestyle ended when he was murdered in a row with a timber worker.

Many of the Irish immigrants who took to the early American prize-ring reflected little credit on their homeland or the country of their adoption. If they were not cavorting with gamblers, gunmen or shady ladies, they were using whatever power their boxing success brought to make their way in business or in crooked politics. Some met violent deaths.

Such a fate befell Yankee Sullivan, born James Ambrose in Bandon, County Cork, who found his way to America after somehow gaining his freedom from the dreaded Botany Bay penal colony. He had been sentenced to deportation there after being convicted of robbery in England. Sullivan had done some boxing before his sentence and he was able to pick up the threads of his career on reaching New York. After several impressive wins, he opened a saloon with his earnings and threw out a challenge to Tom Hyer for the championship of America. Hyer showed no urgency in picking up the gauntlet and the rowdy Irishman lashed him about his 'cowardice' whenever they met. There were a couple of bar-room brawls between the pair before Hyer at last agreed to meet Sullivan in the ring. The date chosen for the contest was 7 February 1849 and the venue was the island of Rock Point in Maryland. The reason for the remote location was for fear of intervention by the police, as prize-fighting was illegal. A magnificent solid silver belt was put up for the winner by Colonel Hiram Johnson, proprietor of the well-known sporting journal *The Whip* and founder of the American Pugilistic Club. The American champion, a handsome, well-built six-footer, was a good four inches taller than Sullivan and outweighed him by 30 pounds. The Irishman tried to offset his height and reach disadvantages by rushing in close, but his wild attempts were easily rebuffed by the cool Hyer. In the 16th round Sullivan, greatly distressed, was lying helpless against the ropes when his second signalled his retirement. The bout had lasted 17 minutes, during which time the challenger had suffered much punishment. While Sullivan was taken to hospital with a hairline fracture of the skull, the American champion was arrested and charged with inciting a riot. Political influence secured his release.

When Hyer retired from the ring, the vacant title was immediately claimed by Yankee Sullivan. His first challenger was a fellow Irishman, John Morrissey. Their clash at Boston Corners, New York, in 1853, ended in uproar and so angered Sullivan that he never entered a ring again. Though now a veteran of 40, Sullivan had the better of the contest up to the 37th round, when Morrissey claimed he had been struck below the belt. As both boxers and their respective cornermen debated the issue, knives and revolvers appeared amid the unruly throng and threats were made on Sullivan's life. He climbed out of the ring and refused to go back, thus passing the American heavyweight championship to Morrissey by default. Both boxers were involved with the corrupt political Tammany Hall organisation and Sullivan blamed Morrissey's greater standing within the party for influencing the outcome of the fight. Sullivan saw no profitable future for himself in New York and he headed west, ostensibly to join the California gold rush. It was not long before he made progress in San Francisco politics, which were just as tarnished as those in New York. Corruption and gangsterism were rife and, in 1856, a group of the city's more respectable citizens formed a vigilante committee with the avowed intention of rooting out the crooked politicians. Among those rounded up and sentenced to stiff jail terms was Yankee Sullivan. When a jailer opened Sullivan's cell door one morning, he found the Irishman's body lying on the stone floor. Whether he had committed suicide rather than face his long sentence or had been murdered by a paid assassin has never been established.

John Morrissey: from pugilism to political power

One of the most remarkable success stories of any Irish emigrant to the United States was that of John Morrissey. Unable to read or write until he was 18, he won the American heavyweight championship, owned a string of lucrative gambling houses and several successful racehorses and, turning to politics, first on the shady side and then as a reform campaigner, became a Congressman and Senator. But his hectic lifestyle proved too strenuous and he dropped dead at the age of 47.

Born in the County Tipperary town of Templemore in 1831,

Morrissey was taken to America by his family when he was three years old. It was while working as a bartender at Troy, in New York, that John showed a liking for boxing. His boss staged regular shows at the back of the tavern and Morrissey emerged the winner of most of his rough-and-tumble scraps. He caught the eye of Kate Ridgeley, proprietor of a dubious dockside boarding house, who invited the young Irishman to join her staff. Morrissey's job was to meet arrivals off the ships and try to entice them to spend their money at Kate's establishment. He also fell for his employer's charms, which did little to endear him to a local pugilist named Tom McCann who considered himself Kate's lover. In a row in the bar of a Broadway hotel, McCann forced Morrissey onto a coal-burning stove in the middle of the room. The stove was knocked over, spilling its contents onto the floor. Morrissey was thrown onto the red-hot coals and held there for several minutes, until he managed to wriggle free and knock his attacker unconscious. His clothes still smouldering, he was promptly given the nickname 'Old Smokey'. It stuck with him throughout his ring career.

Morrissey followed the fashion by joining the gold trail to California. His shrewd business sense told him he could make more money running a gambling joint than digging for the elusive ore. Financed by a syndicate he soon became a wealthy man. His new-found comfort did not deter him from issuing a challenge to George Thompson, a former sparring partner of Tom Hyer, to a fight for a £2,000 sidestake. Thompson's greater experience made him look the likely winner until he got word in his corner that such an eventuality would not be in his immediate interests. The threat prompted him to land a foul blow and earn his disqualification. Morrissey, this prestigious 'scalp' tucked into his belt, returned to New York to take the American championship from Yankee Sullivan, as already described.

A vicious, no-holds-barred battle with one Bill Poole in a saloon ended with Morrissey having to spend several weeks in bed recovering from his lumps and bruises. Poole came off far worse, however. He was bitten right through his cheek by Morrissey and he had only just recovered from this appalling injury when he was shot dead by one of Morrissey's cronies. Morrissey was one of those arrested in connection with the murder, but political muscle was used to get him off the hook. It was with this sordid background that Morrissey squared off with John C. Heenan in 1858 for the heavyweight championship of America. Heenan, the New York-born son of an emigrant from Clareen, near Birr, County Offaly, had been a pal of Bill Poole and welcomed the chance of avenging his death. The ring was pitched at Long Point in Canada, just across the lake from Erie, Pennsylvania. A steamship stood by at the Long Point lighthouse in case the participants and fans needed to switch the venue quickly should the law swoop. The gathering was a typical example of the kind of mob which attached itself to the early American ring. 'A worse set of scapegallowses could scarcely be collected,' noted a contemporary bulletin. 'Low, filthy, brutal, bludgeon-bearing scoundrels - the very class of men who have built up the Tammany Hall party in New York and to whose well-paid labours the party owes almost its existence.'

Heenan, who later married the beautiful actress Adah Isaacs Menken, was a handsome man of 6' 2" and weighed 13st 8lbs (190lbs). Morrissey was three inches shorter and 20 pounds lighter. An old leg injury, suffered by Heenan when he struck himself with a pick-axe while gold prospecting in California, reared up again and prevented him from achieving peak fitness. Indeed, he was described as 'hog fat' by one reporter. The dour Morrissey was as hard as nails, with not an ounce of surplus flesh on his frame. The *New York Times* reckoned that Heenan was 'the more scientific of the combatants, Morrissey being an extremely uncultivated fighter'. But 'Old Smokey' packed enormous strength into his compact body and his ability to soak up punishment was legendary. Noting the challenger's pot belly, Morrissey made that area his target. But Heenan showed his finer skill by neatly evading most of Morrissey's attempts and countering with sharp punches to the face. Morrissey's eye was cut and he looked to be in some distress when fate came to his aid.

Heenan, trying a big right, missed Morrissey's head and struck a wooden corner-post with sickening force. He cried out in pain and could hardly use that hand for the rest of the fight. Morrissey, encouraged by his rival's discomfort and urged on by his supporters, scored well to the body. Heenan, badly out of breath and nursing his damaged hand, had only his gameness to keep him going. 'Both contestants came up tired for the eleventh,' reported the *New York Times*, 'but Heenan the more so. The striking was in favour of Morrissey. On Heenan aiming and missing, Morrissey put in a huge blow on the jugular. Heenan fell flat on his face. The champion stepped away from him. Heenan could not make time.' Much public sympathy was extended to the loser. Many felt it would have been a different story had he been fully fit and had he not injured his hand. Certainly, Morrissey's face was the more disfigured and it was said that the bushy beard he grew was to hide the scars. The bitterness between the boxers extended to Heenan's memorable drawn battle with Tom Sayers for the 'world championship' in 1860, when Morrissey backed the Englishman. Though a return match between Morrissey and Heenan was mooted, Morrissey turned his back on the ring to pursue his financial and political ambitions.

Using his friendship with Cornelius Vanderbilt, the railroad pioneer, to gain access to valuable information on the stock markets, he made a considerable 'killing', enabling him to open a luxurious gambling house in Saratoga, New York. He also purchased several winning thoroughbreds and was prominent in the setting up of the famous Saratoga racing establishment. His progress to politics was a logical next step and, in 1870, he received a nomination from the Fifth New York District to run for the United States Congress. He secured a landslide victory, polling 2,659 more votes than his nearest opponent. Morrissey was re-elected for a second term and became a State Senator for the Seventh District of New York in 1877. He had jumped on the bandwagon for the campaign to reform the notorious Tammany Hall organisation and was hugely successful. Morrissey held onto his seat for another term, but the rigours of his fight for re-election led to a breakdown of his health. Even the sunshine of Florida, where he went to recuperate, failed to revive him and it was there that he died on 1 May 1878.

If you're Irish, you're champion of America!

The immigrant Irish created a monopoly in their hold on the American heavyweight championship. Not that all who claimed the honour were taken too seriously. It seemed that if one was Irish, could fight a bit and shout a lot, his demand to be recognised as American champion was sure of some support. Of course, it was the absence of a ruling body that led to such a proliferation of title claims. The result was confusion in the minds of boxing's followers as to who were the legitimate title-holders. Ring historians differ widely in their assessments of who should be accredited as champions and who should not.

On the retirement of John C. Heenan the American title was disputed by two Irish-born pugilists, Joe Coburn and Mike McCoole. The decider took place at Charlesworth, Maryland, in May 1863 and Coburn won in 67 rounds. Coburn, a childhood emigrant from Middletown, County Armagh, twice met the English champion Jem Mace in contests for the 'world' title, but each bout ended inconclusively. Joe travelled to England to challenge Mace on his own territory, but someone came up with the bright idea of staging the fight in Dublin. Initially, the English champion went along with the idea, until he was persuaded that he was unlikely to get a fair deal meeting Coburn in Ireland. Mace threw in a suggestion: he would choose the referee. Coburn would have none of that, and the match fell through.

His plans frustrated, Coburn returned to the United States. He was followed shortly afterwards by Mace. The English fight scene had gone sour in the aftermath of the unsatisfactory outcome of the Heenan *v* Sayers battle and public interest had waned. Also, the law was coming down heavily on all associated with boxing promotions in Britain and the press denounced it as 'a sport for ruffians'. Similar vigilance by the Canadian police prevented a decision as to who was the rightful 'world champion' when Coburn and Mace finally squared off at Port Ryeson in 1871. The law's intervention came after one hour and 17 minutes, so no verdict could be rendered. A contemporary account states that not one single blow was struck by either contestant during that time, which seems scarcely credible. The return match six months later was staged at St Louis, Missouri, and the spectators got better value for their money. Coburn was the stronger, more forceful participant but he found it very difficult to pierce the Englishman's sound defence. After three hours and 48 minutes, with both men close to collapse and the biting wind freezing the onlookers, it was decided to call a halt and the boxers agreed to a draw. Only 12 rounds had been fought in that time, underlining how long some rounds lasted in the bare-fist era.

If Joe Coburn's claim to the American title had a sound basis, it was sheer effrontery that made Mike McCoole dispute the honour. Known as 'the Deckhand Champion' from his days spent working on the river steamers around Cincinnati, Ohio, McCoole based his right to the championship on weird logic. Having been defeated once by Coburn, he stripped off in readiness for the return match at Cold Spring Station, Indiana, in May 1868. Coburn was about to disrobe when the police stepped in and arrested the boxers. While serving his 40 days' detention McCoole had plenty of time to weigh up the situation. He reasoned that as he had entered the ring prepared for action and Coburn was not yet ready, he had the right to consider himself the true champion. Coburn's reaction to his rival's statement is not recorded. The American public, still feeling the numbing effects of the Civil War (1861-65), cared less.

As if two heavyweight title-holders were not enough, Englishman Tom Allen weighed in with his own claim, having beaten yet another pretender, Bill Davis. McCoole and Allen were matched in a bid to settle the issue at Foster Island, near St Louis, but the Irishman's unruly followers ensured that he escaped certain defeat. McCoole was on the brink of being knocked out when his gang stormed the ring, demanding that Allen be ruled out for an alleged low punch. With revolvers brandished under his nose, the Englishman had no option but to concede the point. Allen had his revenge four years later when he gave McCoole a savage beating and forced him to quit in seven rounds.

High hopes of genuine championship honours were vested by the American Irish on the lofty figure of Ned O'Baldwin, 'the Irish Giant'. A towering 6' 5" O'Baldwin had left his native Lismore, County Waterford, to try his luck in English rings. With some useful 'wins' under his belt he issued a challenge to English champion Jem Mace. When Mace opted to earn his living across the Atlantic, O'Baldwin followed suit. It was in a sparring match with John Morrissey that the big Irishman impressed observers. Though wearing gloves, he managed to floor Morrissey with a solid blow to the jaw. Among those who witnessed this occurance was a promoter with a flair for publicity. He lost no time in matching O'Baldwin with Londoner Joe Wormwald and billing it for 'the heavyweight championship of the world'. A handsome purse of $2,500 was at stake. But the spoilsport local police were not caught up in the general enthusiasm. They made their appearance when the fight was less than ten minutes old and the boxers ended up serving 18 months apiece. O'Baldwin had enough of pugilism's uncertainties and went into business as a liquor store proprietor. A row with his partner led to his being shot dead in a New York saloon at the age of 35.

A similar fate befell another of the Irish pretenders to the American fistic throne, Jim Elliott. But there were few tears shed at the 1883 funeral of Elliott, gunned down in a gambling row at a Chicago tavern. He was a notorious character who would employ any ruse or mean trick to win a contest if he thought he would get away with it. But his crude methods backfired on him when he met fellow Irishman Jim Dunne in New Jersey on 13 May 1863. Both men claimed the American title and so desperate was Elliott to cement his demand that he struck out wildly and repeatedly fouled his opponent, earning his disqualification in the 12th round. And he had no sooner stepped out of the ring when a policeman's hand clamped on his shoulder. He served two years in prison for his part in the affair, as did his opponent.

It was five years before Elliott, born in Athlone, County Westmeath, made his return to boxing. In one of his better efforts he easily beat a rival claimant to the American title, Bill Davis, in nine rounds. The strongest contender for the title at the time was Joe Coburn, but Elliott reasoned that Coburn had forfeited his right by refusing to meet him. In a defence of his 'championship' against Canadian Charlie Gallagher, Elliott reverted to form. The challenger was subjected to such abuse and constant foul blows that his backer refused to allow him to leave his corner for the 24th round.

Having got away with that little bit of skullduggery, Elliott, by way of diversion, turned highwayman. He was captured, convicted of assault and battery with intent to kill, and was committed to the Eastern State Penitentiary in Philadelphia for a term of 16 years and ten months. The boxing world heaved a collective sigh of relief. But it had not seen the last of Jim Elliott. Good behaviour earned him a pardon after eight years and he announced his intention of regaining 'his' American title. The latest claimant was New Yorker Johnny Dwyer, who accepted Elliott's challenge. The Irishman, his reflexes dulled by his long absence from ring action and in far from top condition, was no match for the sharp-hitting Dwyer. He took an unmerciful hammering. Realising he stood no chance of turning the tide, Elliott resorted to his most despicable trick yet. He dipped his fists into a bucket of turpentine which had been concealed in his corner. Dwyer, after taking several blows around the eyes, staggered back, screaming 'Help, I'm blind!' Dropping to his knees, he was lifted up by his seconds and carried to his corner. His seconds worked feverishly to wash out his eyes before the 30-second interval was up. The tears streamed down the Brooklyn boxer's face as he snarled across the ring at his grinning tormentor. He exacted sweet revenge on the shadowy figure in front of him, battering him from one corner to the other. Elliott was helpless before this raging aggressor. By the 12th round Elliott's face was a bloody mess and he was gasping with pain as punches smashed in his ribs. He called it quits. Dwyer, sickened by the indignities to which he had been subjected by a fellow professional, never fought again. He became chief clerk in the Brooklyn County Court.

Elliott tried once more. And he picked a tough one for his farewell appearance. In the opposite corner at Washington Park, Brooklyn, on Independence Day 1882 was the new and undisputed American heavyweight champion, John L. Sullivan. 'The Boston Strong Boy' was 24 years of age and at the peak of his considerable powers. He was undefeated in four years' fighting. Elliott was 44 and out of condition. He had no right to be sharing a ring with the man destined to be the greatest of all the bare-knuckle battlers. Sullivan, in his autobiography published in 1892, told of how he had offered half the gate receipts to any man he could not stop in four rounds, under Marquis of Queensberry rules:

> The challenge was accepted by Jimmy Elliott, a boxer of high pretensions and good ring record. Both hard and soft gloves were offered to him and he chose the former..... Elliott was taller and fully as heavy as I was. As soon as time was called, I let go my left and landed on Elliott's body; the latter countered and hard fighting followed. I then knocked him all over the ring, and sent him flying off his feet amid the yells of the crowd. The second round was far more desperate. I punished him terribly, landing with left and right on Elliott's nose and neck until [Bill] Madden [Sullivan's second] begged me not to hit him again. In the third round Madden told me to finish him, but be careful and not knock him out forever. He was knocked down in this round by just such a blow as I gave Paddy Ryan at Mississippi City the previous February. I then made Elliott a present of $50. Over 5,000 persons were present and they appeared to have been well satisfied with the manner in which things were conducted....

Last of the bare-knuckle breed

Fashions changed in boxing as in other walks of life. In the latter part of the 19th century the trend was turning away from bare-fist battling in favour of gloved combat. Under the new rules drawn up by Arthur Chambers, a former English lightweight champion, and to which the Marquis of Queensberry gave his name, gloves were used for the first time in actual prize-fights. The Queensberry Rules also stipulated that rounds should be confined to three minutes, with one minute's rest in between, and that a man knocked down had ten seconds to regain his feet or else he would be counted out. Not all ringmen were in favour of the new code. The old sport of pugilism under London Prize-Ring Rules, in which rounds were of unlimited duration and where wrestling and other unrefined tactics were allowed, obviously suited the fighters who relied on endurance and raw strength to bring them success. Such a conservative was Paddy Ryan, 'the Trojan Giant' from Thurles, County Tipperary.

Most of Ryan's apprentice days in the American ring are unrecorded, although it is known that by the time he was 19 he was acknowledged as the finest fighter in the Troy district of New York, famed breeding ground of tough warriors. He made sufficient progress within a few years for his backers to throw out a confident challenge to Johnny Dwyer, one of the main claimants to the American heavyweight championship. Dwyer quit the ring before the match could be made. Ryan then invited all-comers for a match at $1,000 a side. It was the veteran Englishman Joe Goss who picked up the gauntlet and the bout was scheduled for Long Point, Canada, on 30 May 1880. For some obscure reason, Goss then insisted on the venue being switched to Collier's Station, on the Pennsylvania-West Virginia border, scene of many famous bare-fist encounters.

Fifteen years younger than the 42-year-old Englishman, Ryan also had all the other physical advantages. He was four inches taller, with a correspondingly longer reach, and he was almost 50 pounds the heavier man. On Goss's side were his greater experience and skills, which he used to outbox the crude Irishman in the early rounds. Goss cleverly drew his opponent into range and then picked him off with precise blows. He easily avoided the wild swipes that came his way. But it was at close quarters that Ryan was most effective. His greater strength enabled him to throw Goss to the ground time and again and the longer the contest went the greater the odds grew in the younger man's favour. Ryan finished it in the 87th round. Goss was carried to his corner and never looked likely to make the 'scratch'.

Ryan was now the undisputed champion of America, but a challenging figure loomed on the horizon. The columns of the *Cincinnati Enquirer* on 9 December 1880 first carried the challenge from a young Bostonian of Irish descent, John L. Sullivan, for a title match for a sidestake of anything from $1,000 to $10,000. Ryan laughed off the invitation. 'Go out and get yourself a reputation', he advised the 22-year-old challenger. Sullivan did just that. He ran up a string of exciting wins, including an eight rounds knockout of Irish-born John Flood, known as 'the Bull's Head Terror', and a second round eclipse of another Irishman, Steve Taylor. In a sparring match with Joe Goss, Sullivan floored the veteran and had to be told to ease up.

The public demanded a showdown between Ryan and Sullivan. Ryan could avoid the issue no longer. He agreed to meet his brash young challenger at Mississippi City on 7 February 1882. The title fight aroused unprecedented interest throughout the United States. Thousands of fans converged on the site, where the ring was pitched in front of the Barnes Hotel, and everywhere the talk was of who would win the battle of the giants. The main newspapers recognised the public excitement and many hired famous novelists and dramatists to provide colourful 'copy' for their readers to savour. Among those assigned to cover the event for a leading English paper was Oscar Wilde. The Irish playwright was on a lecture tour of America when he was asked to stop off at Mississippi for the big fight. An ironic sidelight to Wilde's brief encounter with boxing came 13 years later, when he was imprisoned for his relationship with Lord Alfred Douglas, son of the eighth Marquis of Queensberry, who introduced the rules of modern boxing.

Ladies carrying delicate parasols mingled happily with the 15,000 spectators who occupied the lawn in front of the Barnes Hotel. The fight itself, for all the ballyhoo, proved a major disappointment. Sullivan was so vastly superior to Ryan in boxing ability and punching power that he dismissed the champion in just over ten minutes. The challenger had offered to fight with gloves under Queensberry Rules but Ryan insisted on bare fists. The first round ended inside two minutes with Paddy flat on his back after taking a terrific right. Ryan managed to throw the challenger to end the second round, but he was again stretched by a big right in the next. They traded heavy blows in the fourth, but Ryan was bleeding badly from the mouth and puffing heavily as Sullivan closed and tossed him to the ground with a mighty cross buttock. To add to his discomfort, the champion's truss, which he wore to support a rupture, slipped and could not be adjusted properly. Despite his obvious distress, Paddy battled on gamely.

Another powerful right dropped him like a log in the eighth and his seconds had to carry him back to his corner. They worked feverishly to get him ready for the call of 'Time' but they should not have bothered. Ryan stumbled forward to face a relentless foe. A vicious right caught him behind the ear and sent him crashing to the ground unconscious. There was never a hope of his recovering in the 30 seconds interval. While the beaten champion was still struggling to regain his senses, the jubilant Sullivan leaped over the ropes and dashed the 100 yards to his hotel room. It was said that up to $200,000 changed hands in bets on the fight.

Ryan had staked $1,000 on himself and he had a further shock when he discovered that $300 had been swiped from his trousers pocket during the contest. When the contestants met afterwards for a drink, Ryan candidly admitted that he 'wasn't in it' after the first blow. On being asked for his assessment of Sullivan, he said, 'I have never faced a man who hits so hard and I don't believe there is another man like him in the country. Any man Sullivan can hit he can whip. Before he is downed he must either meet a man who is as hard at hitting as he is or by some wonderfully clever boxer. Such a man as [Jem] Mace, if younger, might defeat Sullivan, but no slouch can do it.'

It might be thought that Ryan had sampled too many Sullivan punches to relish a repeat dose, but they met again three years later in New York. This time they wore gloves. It was all over in 50 seconds. A police captain ordered the slaughter be stopped as Ryan was simply overwhelmed by Sullivan's power. 'I did it to save Sullivan from answering a murder rap,' the policeman explained. Still not content, Paddy had a third go with John L. nearly two years later in San

Francisco. He managed to stick it out for nearly three rounds until he finally got the message. Wisely, he quit the ring for good. He died at Green Island, near Troy, in 1901, aged 48.

Ryan's title defeat by Sullivan marked the end of the era of bare-knuckle boxing, at least in terms of the supreme prize, the heavyweight championship. John L. Sullivan proved such an outstanding performer that he fully deserves ranking as the first heavyweight champion of the world. He was only once beaten in a career total of 48 fights. That was when he defended his title in the first world heavyweight championship contest under Marquis of Queensberry Rules. Though a four to one favourite, Sullivan, his once superb body wracked by years of heavy drinking and idleness, was outclassed by James J. Corbett in the historic duel at the Olympic Club in New Orleans on 7 September 1892. Corbett, one of the most scientific boxers of his time, won by a knockout in the 21st round. Sullivan hid his disappointment by remarking that if he had to lose his title he was glad it was to a fellow American. He might just as well have said a fellow Irishman for, like himself, Corbett was the son of Irish emigrants to the United States. Corbett's parents came from Shrule, near Tuam in County Galway, while Sullivan's father was from Tralee, County Kerry, and his mother was born in Athlone, County Westmeath. To the Boston Irish, Corbett was a 'foreigner' from America's West Coast (he was born in San Francisco) and they deeply resented his demolition of their idol.

Three

Conquerors of the World

BOXING HISTORY HAS produced two Jack Dempseys, each of them an outstanding world champion. Yet in neither case was Jack Dempsey his real name. Mention of the name to most fight fans immediately means the great American heavyweight who was champion of the world from 1919 to 1926. One of the most destructive punchers of all time, William Harrison Dempsey adopted the name Jack in honour of the Irishman who was the first holder of the world middleweight title. To distinguish between the two, the original Jack Dempsey is always given the prefix 'Nonpareil', the unrivalled or incomparable. But Nonpareil Jack Dempsey was not a Dempsey at all. He was born John Kelly near Clane, in County Kildare, on 15 December 1862 and was taken to America as a child. The family settled in the Brooklyn district of New York. When he started boxing, young Kelly took the name Jack Dempsey to spare his parents' feelings as they had no great love of the sport.

Dempsey fought in the era that bridged both bare-knuckle and gloved combat. He excelled in both codes. Indeed, he must be considered one of the most outstanding of the fighting Irish. He was especially noted for the accuracy and timing of his punching, his excellent footwork and his skill at feinting to create openings. He was only beaten three times in 68 contests. Twelve were draws. If this seems extraordinarily high, it must be noted that during the period any fight that ended inconclusively was recorded as a draw. Unless there was a knockout or a retirement, there was no way of deciding a winner. Usually in a long drawn-out contest, participants and spectators would be equally bored with the affair and there would be general agreement to call a halt. Thus a draw would be declared. The system of awarding points and of limiting the length of contests did not come along until much later.

The first Jack Dempsey actually started out as a wrestler and was 23 when he turned to boxing. His first contest took place in near-zero temperatures in a tiny delapidated hall on Staten Island, New York. His opponent, Irishman Ed McDonald, was disqualified for a low blow in the 26th round. Not the most auspicious start to Dempsey's boxing career, perhaps, but he quickly ran up a reputation with a succession of good wins. He laid claim to the world lightweight championship, but decided to leave that to his pal Jack McAuliffe, another Irish immigrant, while he concentrated on the new middleweight division. A Canadian, George Fulljames, also claimed the middleweight title and the two met to decide the issue at Staten Island in July 1884. Dempsey won in 22 rounds. The cunningness that went into promoting illegal prize-fighting is typified in the staging of Dempsey's title defence against Jack Fogarty two years later. The boxers, along with some 300 fans, met at a Manhattan rendezvous. They hired cabs to take them to a ferry bound for New Jersey, across the Hudson river. The New York police, seeing the ferry depart with the crowd aboard, were happy that they had driven the fight off their territory and went back to their stations. This was what the fight crowd had been waiting for. The ferry took them back again to New York, where the contest was staged at the Clarendon Hall on 13th Street with not a lawman in sight. Dempsey gave Fogarty a savage hiding and won in the 27th round. He picked up $1,500 in prize money and a world championship belt donated, ironically, by the *Police Gazette*.

Even more extraordinary circumstances marked the Irishman's bout with New Yorker Johnny Regan. Twice postponed because of police interference, the title fight eventually took place in two stages in rings 25 miles apart. It started on a remote beach at Huntingdon, on Long Island. By the eighth round the tide had come in and a contemporary sketch shows the boxers milling away with the water swirling around their ankles. A tugboat was engaged to transport the contestants and the small band of spectators to a field on higher ground. The resumed bout was then threatened by a blinding snowstorm but Dempsey brought the affair to a timely conclusion with a powerful right to his challenger's jaw in the 45th round.

Dempsey's first defeat was the subject of great controversy and led to the banning of the so-called 'pivot' punch. Its practitioner, George LaBlanche, had already been beaten by Dempsey and did not really fancy his chances in the return. Together with his trainer, Jimmy Carroll, LaBlanche worked out the new punch. He had to wait for 32 rounds, by which time he had absorbed a sound beating, before he got a chance to bring his secret weapon into play. After deliberately missing with a right swing which left him with his back to his opponent, LaBlanche pivoted around on his heel, bringing his stiffened right arm in a sweeping arc to land a terrific back-handed blow on Dempsey's jaw. The effect was dramatic. Dempsey fell as if he were shot. Dan Costigan, the Irishman's manager, protested violently but the referee refused to declare it a foul punch and named LaBlanche as the winner. Although the resultant outcry caused the 'pivot' punch to be outlawed, the verdict stood. Dempsey had lost his unbeaten record. But he retained recognition as world middleweight champion.

Failing health threatened to curtail the Irishman's career, but he was tempted by a $12,000 purse to defend his title against Bob Fitzsimmons in 1891. The winner would receive $11,000 with just $1,000 for the loser. Dempsey figured he would have little trouble accounting for the ungainly-looking challenger. Fitzsimmons, born in England, raised in New Zealand and Australia and now an American citizen, was an odd sight with his balding, freckle-covered head, his powerful upper torso and spindly legs, but he was a skilled boxer and carried a devastating punch in both hands. Dempsey had never seen him fight and cared nothing for his reputation. At the weigh-in for the fight at the New Orleans Olympic Club Fitzsimmons extended his hand to the champion and said, 'May the best man win, Jack,' to which Dempsey retorted, 'He will'. The captain of the local police force, which had sanctioned the bout, examined the five-ounce gloves and proclaimed his satisfaction, although he wondered how they could hurt each other with 'these pillows'.

The fight was surprisingly one-sided. Dempsey, the betting favourite, was totally unable to fathom his opponent's style. Fitzsimmons picked him off with his long leads and defended well against the champion's attacks. Dempsey was floored at the start of the second round when he ran into a smart counter-punch. He had to defend desperately to last out the round. He recovered sufficiently to make the Englishman wince from a solid dig to the heart. Dempsey gave a reasonable account of himself for the next few rounds but was brought to his knees in the seventh as the result of a neat left-right combination. Jack struggled aloft and cleverly lured the anxious challenger onto a good right to the neck. Fitzsimmons merely grinned and, pushing up the champion's left arm, sunk a right into his ribs. Dempsey slumped against the ropes and slid slowly to the floor. The bell saved him from being counted out. 'Saved' is hardly an appropriate word, for it only meant he had to suffer further abuse to his pain-wracked body. Three times in the tenth round he was knocked down and was again 'rescued' by the bell. A pitiful sight with blood flowing freely from both eyebrows, nose and mouth, only his great courage kept him going. Even Fitzsimmons showed compassion, imploring him to quit. Jack would not hear of it. Floored six times in the 11th and 12th rounds, he refused his cornermen's pleas to throw in the towel. He was down again within 30 seconds of the 13th round starting. He somehow managed to scramble to his feet, only to reel into his tormentor's arms. Fitzsimmons told him in the clinch, 'You've had enough, I don't want to hurt you any more'. The Irishman's defiance showed through the blood and the bruises as he snarled, 'I'm good enough to beat you yet'. Fitzsimmons shrugged his shoulders, then measured his distance with his extended left arm before crashing a thunderous right to the jaw. This time there was no getting up. Back in his dressing room, the dethroned champion wept bitterly. 'It wouldn't hurt so much if I lost my title to an Irishman or an American,' he sobbed, 'but to an Englishman; that's what kills me.'

While Fitzsimmons went on to secure his place in history by becoming the first boxer to win world titles at three different weights (middleweight, light-heavyweight and heavyweight), it was near to the end of the road for Nonpareil Jack Dempsey. He did not fight again for over a year, returning to beat Mike Keogh in four rounds; he took another 18 months' rest before boxing a 28-round draw with Australian Billy McCarthy. He called it quits after losing in three rounds to Tommy Ryan, the world welterweight champion, in 1895. His last ring appearance was in an exhibition bout with John L. Sullivan. It was a benefit show for Dempsey, short of cash and in poor health. Within five months he was dead, a victim of what was then a deadly disease, tuberculosis. He was only 33 years of age when he was buried at Portland, in Oregon.

Champion who never met his master

Only three world boxing champions have managed to remain unbeaten throughout their careers. Heavyweight Rocky Marciano is the only one with a 100% record, winner of all his 49 contests. Bantamweight Jimmy Barry, an American of Irish descent, was never beaten in 70 bouts, although he was held to a draw on nine occasions and fought two 'no decision' contests. The remaining member of the unique trio is Irish-born Jack McAuliffe. He fought 53 times, winning 41, drawing nine and had three 'no decision' bouts.

While the record books appear to uphold his status among the premier ringmen of his time, closer scrutiny of McAuliffe's career serves to take at least some of the glitter off his proud record. What the bare statistics do not show is that he was on the lucky end of some highly dubious decisions during his 13-year spell in the ring. And there is strong justification for the assertion by some historians that he should not be recognised as a world champion, but merely as American title-holder. The experts are divided on the merits of McAuliffe's claim to world champion status. In his favour is the fact that he did defeat three English challengers, Harry Gilmore, Sam Collier and Jack Hyams. Gilmore, who gave the Irishman a great tussle before succumbing in the 28th round, was in his eighties when he gave this assessment of his victor:

> To a greater degree than any other lightweight champion I have known, Jack McAuliffe outclassed the best men of his day. That was because he was a natural-born fighter... He took to the gloves like a duck takes to water and time and practice made him a number one

...npareil Jack Dempsey

Jack McAuliffe

Peter Maher knocked out by Bob Fitzsimmons at the Olympic Club, New Orleans

boxer. On top of that he was a lightning fast thinker and as fine a general as ever performed between the ropes. That's a combination that's hard to beat and I never saw it equalled in my experience.

McAuliffe was born at Meelin, midway between Newmarket and Rockchapel in County Cork on 24 March 1866. His father, who emigrated to America before Jack was born, survived several skirmishes with raiding Indians while serving with the US Army and saved enough money to bring over his family. They settled at Bangor, Maine. After some years the McAuliffes moved to Williamsburg in Brooklyn where they set up home in the predominently Irish 14th Ward. It was a tough district and young Jack learned the value of a good pair of fists. He worked in the same Brooklyn cooperage as Nonpareil Jack Dempsey and the pair became firm friends.

Harry Smith's saloon on the Bowery was the scene of McAuliffe's first ring appearance. He beat a local favourite, Bob Mace, in three rounds. After winning a tournament advertised as 'the amateur featherweight championship of America', Jack collected a couple of other prestigious prizes before turning professional under the guidance of Billy Madden, former mentor of John L. Sullivan. He toured the States taking on all-comers in contests limited to four rounds, picking up valuable experience as well as handy cash. He did suffer one 'knockout', but it was after a contest and the blow was from a chair flung into the ring by the enraged father of a boxer Jack had just beaten.

McAuliffe issued a challenge to Billy Frazier who, as well as holding the position of boxing instructor at Harvard University, claimed the American lightweight title. The match was staged in Boston in October 1886 for a purse of $100, as well as a belt emblematic of the American championship. The bout was under Marquis of Queensberry Rules and skin-tight gloves were worn. While Frazier made the 133-pounds weight limit with three pounds to spare, McAuliffe was five and a half pounds overweight. The trouble with Jack was that he enjoyed his food and beer and wasn't particular about training. Nevertheless, he knocked out Frazier in the 21st round, only to find the loser refusing to concede the American title as McAuliffe had not made the required poundage. An irate McAuliffe demanded another match, but Frazier withdrew on the night of the proposed return, complaining of stomach cramp. His forfeiture of the title left McAuliffe undisputed American champion. In fact, he extended his claim to the world crown. One man prepared to dispute that assertion was the English champion Jem Carney.

Excitement was at fever pitch at 1 AM on 16 November 1887 when the showdown battle began. Only 50 invited spectators were present in the huge barn at Revere, in Massachusetts, when the antagonists squared off. The big wooden doors were bolted from the inside and the fight took place in the eerie glow of several oil lamps. Each of the boxers had put up a sidestake of $2,500. McAuliffe, the betting favourite, was the more skilful. Carney, who had won the English title under London Prize-Ring Rules, was more accustomed to the rough and tumble of bare-knuckle fighting, but he was the stronger hitter. For the first ten rounds the Irishman had the better of the exchanges, but he then complained of feeling unwell, a recurrence of a stomach complaint that had caused a six weeks' postponement of the fight. He looked to be in trouble as Carney stepped up his attacks. In the 36th round Carney rushed in, head down, and butted McAuliffe in the stomach, completely winding him. Jack's seconds demanded the Englishman's disqualification, but this plea died quickly when Billy Tracey, one of Carney's seconds and a notorious gun-fighter, stepped up to the ring and fingered his revolver. Carney's continuous rough tactics drew howls of protest from the Irishman's corner. Carney was warned by the referee for kicking his opponent, gouging him in the eyes with his thumbs and for biting him on the shoulder!

By the 60th round McAuliffe was looking dejected, but he summoned new energies to drop the Englishman two rounds later for a count of nine. It was his last big effort. Carney appeared set for victory as he sent his rival sprawling in the 70th round but the Irishman's cohorts stormed the ring, pulling down the ropes and posts, and shouting that the police were about to invade the barn. The ruse didn't work and some semblance of order was restored. The tussle dragged on into the 74th round when the McAuliffe mob again invaded the ring after their man was floored. Bottles and sticks were brandished by the opposing factions. The referee, Frank Stevenson, accepting that matters had gone beyond his control, called a halt. He declared the fight a draw, adding that all bets were off. While the few neutrals in the crowd felt that Carney was robbed of the world title by the actions of McAuliffe's unruly followers, they conceded that the Englishman might have been disqualified for his rough tactics. Thus ended the attempt to clear up the issue of who was world lightweight champion. There was no re-match.

McAuliffe had two contests of widely contrasting duration in February 1889. Against Billy Myer he showed too much respect for his opponent's vaunted right hand and had to be content with a draw after 64 rounds. Five days later he needed only two punches to flatten Billy Baltz in the opening round. McAuliffe bet his entire purse of $10,000 from a return match with Myer on John L. Sullivan beating James J. Corbett. Though he had the satisfaction of beating Myer in 15 rounds, he was distraught over Sullivan's loss. 'I'm stone broke,' he wailed to his friend and backer Dick Roche, 'you'll have to lend me my fare back to New York from New Orleans.' But Roche grinned and handed him back his money. He had been convinced Corbett would beat a paunchy Sullivan and refused to gamble McAuliffe's purse.

McAuliffe preferred the good life to the rigours of training and fighting. Apart from exhibition tours, he had only one serious contest in

1893 and that was only a four-rounder which he won on points after suffering a cut eye and being floored in the third round. When he stepped into the ring for a six-round tie with Jem Ryan of Australia in January 1894 his round figure drew laughter and hisses from the crowd. Puffing and blowing, he still managed to win handily on points. His poor condition was even more pronounced when he engaged the Australian wizard Young Griffo over ten rounds. Griffo, one of the most gifted of boxing's practitioners, clearly outboxed the cumbersome Irishman, but it was McAuliffe's hand that was raised at the finish. The verdict met with a storm of protest from the audience at the Seaside Athletic Club on Coney Island.

Realising he was nearing the end of the line, McAuliffe elected for one more defence of his title. To his credit, he picked no 'pushover' in Owen Zeigler, who had beaten some of the best lightweights around. Jack got himself into the best possible condition but the years of indolence had taken their toll. He was lying helpless against the ropes in the third round, his left hand broken after crashing it against Zeigler's elbow, when a police inspector insisted on calling a halt. Amazingly, referee Johnny Eckhart declared it a draw.

McAuliffe announced his retirement from the ring but came back two years later to notch up three more wins before quitting for good in September 1897. That last success in his remarkable unbeaten career came very near to being marked up as his first setback. Many pre-fight arrangements were made in that period and it had been agreed that McAuliffe would not try to knock out his opponent, Philadelphia Tommy Ryan, and that at the end of the ten rounds a draw would be rendered. Jack floored his rival in the second round but allowed him to recover in compliance with the arrangement. The referee, however, believed that the pact was that if Ryan was still standing at the end of the contest he should get the decision. When he announced Ryan as the winner he was surrounded by a furious McAuliffe and his cornermen. The referee then altered his verdict and, instead of calling it a draw, named McAuliffe as the victor.

His years of high living and reckless gambling left McAuliffe with no 'nest egg' to fall back on when he hung up his gloves. He was able to earn an adequate living, however, reciting monologues on stage, mainly humorous boxing stories. His interest in the turf never slackened and he was a familiar figure in his bowler hat, fashionable suit, white spats and jauntily swinging cane, either as a bookmaker, horse owner or plain punter. He continued to give occasional boxing exhibitions, despite his advancing years and his far from athletic appearance. In 1914 he made a trip to England to spar three rounds apiece with Dick Burge and Jem Carney at the National Sporting Club in London, before taking a holiday with relatives in County Cork. On Memorial Day 1919 McAuliffe, now 53, sparred two rounds with the future world lightweight champion Benny Leonard at Madison Square Gardens, New York. He enjoyed good health until the last few years of his life, when he developed throat cancer. He died, aged 71, at his home in Forest Hills, New York, on 5 November 1937.

'The Belfast Spider' - from Armagh!

Several well-known boxers have picked up the nickname 'Spider'. Jim and Billy Kelly, the father and son from Derry who both won the British featherweight title, and Ellsworth Webb, a talented American middleweight during the 1950-60s, are among those who carried the tag. It is easy to see how Webb came to be called 'Spider', while in the Kellys' case the appendage related to their cunningness in luring unwary opponents into deadly traps. The original of the species was Ike O'Neill Weir, known in America as 'the Belfast Spider' even though he came from Lurgan, in County Armagh. He earned the nickname because of his peculiar style of wriggling his body and keeping his left hand and shoulder in constant motion. He was also known as 'the Master Mechanic of Pugilism'.

Some ring historians credit Weir as being the first featherweight champion of the world. He was not. He fought three times for the crown, drawing twice and losing the other. In his youth in Northern Ireland, Ike enjoyed quite an array of talents. A useful jockey, he was also noted as a crack clay-pigeon shooter, a step-dancer, fiddler, pianist and comic singer. His father had wanted him to be a priest but the youngster ran away to England where he discovered he could box a bit. After winning some minor boxing competitions he went to the United States and ran up an impressive tally of 20 contests without defeat. He threw out a challenge to the world featherweight champion Dal Hawkins, but Hawkins forfeited the title when he could no longer make the weight limit of 118 pounds. Harry Gilmore staked his claim and offered to defend it against Weir, but only if he would agree to a new limit of 122 pounds. The Irishman declined, reasoning it would be too much of a disadvantage.

When Gilmore outgrew the division the way was clear for Weir to meet Englishman Frank Murphy for the vacant world title. The second floor of Mike O'Brien's general store in the remote Indiana town of Kouts was the venue for the fight in March 1889. A purse of $1,500 was the prize. Wearing skin-tight gloves, the boxers waged a long, bitter battle. Weir had the better of the early rounds and by the 18th both of Murphy's eyes were almost swollen shut. Ike tried hard to finish it but the Englishman rallied gamely. 'Spider' was too wily to be caught by Murphy's desperate swings and continued to pound his opponent's sorry features. Murphy could scarcely see, so puffed up were his eyes. One of his seconds, before the start of the 49th round, sliced open the skin to reduce the swelling. The merciless Weir quickly closed them up again. It was four o'clock on the Sunday morning as the weary fighters waited for the bell for round 80. There was no next round. The referee called the boxers together and told them, 'Gentlemen, the fight is over, I declare it a draw'.

Another Murphy, 'Torpedo' Billy from New Zealand, next encountered Weir in a bout advertised for the world featherweight title. As well as $2,500 prize-money there was the additional incentive for the winner of a championship belt donated by Richard K. Fox, publisher of the *Police Gazette,* the most widely-read publication covering boxing at the time. The Americans refused to recognise the fight between two foreigners as being for the world title. It didn't matter to Weir, for he was knocked out in the 14th round. Ike had one more try for the world title, but the police intervened in the fourth round of his meeting with Johnny Griffen and he had to be content with a draw. Weir retired after losing to Young Griffo in 1894 and no more was heard of him until his death was reported in 1908.

The forgotten world champion

In any recollection of Irishmen who won world titles, almost invariably the name of Dave Sullivan is omitted. Very little is known about the little Corkman who fought between 1894 and 1905 and held the world featherweight championship for a mere 46 days, the shortest reign of any title-holder in that division. All of Sullivan's ring career took place in the United States, with the sole exception of a London appearance to meet Pedlar Palmer, the British bantamweight champion, in 1897. Sullivan could not fathom the brilliant Palmer, known as 'the Box o' Tricks', and was clearly outpointed over 20 rounds. It was his first defeat in 24 contests.

Fortune smiled on Sullivan when he challenged Solly Smith for the world featherweight title at Coney Island in September 1898. Smith had taken the crown from the veteran black wizard George Dixon a year earlier and he did not look on the Irishman as a serious threat. But the champion broke his arm during the fifth round and was compelled to retire. Waiting in the wings for a chance to regain his old title was George Dixon. Sullivan agreed to defend his newly won championship against Dixon at the Lenox Athletic Club, New York. Dixon was much too good for the Irishman and was giving him a fearful beating in the tenth round when one of Sullivan's seconds entered the ring, thus earning Dave's disqualification. It saved him from the inevitability of a knockout. Two other world champions who beat Sullivan in non-title fights were Terry McGovern and Young Corbett. Dave did well to survive 15 rounds against 'Terrible' Terry, a ferocious hitter, but he was knocked out in 11 rounds by Corbett. He retired after being halted in nine rounds by Kid Herman in 1905. He died in 1929.

Knockout specialist with a 'glass chin'

Some brilliant prospects for top honours in the fight game have been plagued by what is known in the trade as a 'glass chin'. They simply couldn't take it as well as they handed it out. A perfect example of this none-too-rare breed was Irish heavyweight Peter Maher. He liked to show off his punching power by slamming his fist through a sack of oatmeal. He seemed to have a similar devastating effect on many of the world's best heavyweights around the turn of the century and was touted as a certainty to bring that world title to Ireland for the first time. The trouble was that he was too often beaten to the punch. His record is marred with 'KO by' blotches. In a career that spanned 20 years only two of his fights went more than ten rounds. His motto was 'Get the other guy before he gets me'.

Born in the townland of Gunnode, near Tuam in County Galway, in 1869, Maher left home for Dublin at the age of ten. He grew into a sturdy young man of just under six feet tall and 190 pounds in weight and was persuaded by his workmates at the Phoenix Brewery to enter for a boxing competition, for which he picked up a silver cup. The reward was even greater (£50) when he beat Belfastman John Seenan for the Irish middleweight title and then added the heavyweight crown by hammering Harvey du Cross. Obviously the Irish had discovered a fine prospect, but his handlers got carried away in their enthusiasm when they allowed the still raw youngster in the ring with the great Peter Jackson. It was a shameful mismatch. West Indies-born Jackson had fought in Australia, Britain and the United States and was blatantly shunned by world champion John L. Sullivan, ostensibly because of his colour but more likely for fear of defeat. Two years after meeting Maher, Jackson fought an epic 61-round draw with James J. Corbett, who praised him as 'the greatest boxer I ever saw'.

Major professional tournaments were a rarity in Ireland and the Jackson *v* Maher clash aroused great excitement. The strange choice of Christmas Day for the promotion in 1889 was something of a box office gamble, but plenty of Dubliners were tempted to forego the seasonal festivities to pack into the Leinster Hall in Hawkins Street, later the site of the Theatre Royal. They would have been better off staying at home by the comfort of their firesides. Jackson was in no charitable mood as he effortlessly dispatched Maher inside two rounds.

Maher redeemed himself somewhat with his fans by knocking out Alf Bowman in another Dublin promotion, then scored a first round knockout over Gus Lambert in London before taking up an offer from American manager Billy Madden, who promised to guide him to the world heavyweight title. Met by a brass band on his arrival in the United States, Maher fulfilled his manager's faith in him by bowling over a succession of useful rivals. Madden issued a challenge on his fighter's behalf to John L. Sullivan. But there were other eyes cast in that same direction.

Bob Fitzsimmons, who had taken the world middleweight title from Maher's compatriot, Nonpareil Jack Dempsey, wanted the heavyweight crown. He saw Maher as a likely stepping-stone to that ambition. It was an intriguing match, as Fitzsimmons, though conceding 13 pounds in weight, could punch as hard as the Irishman. On the night of the fight, 2 March 1892, the Olympic Club in New Orleans had to extend its normal capacity to accommodate the 9,000 fans who paid in. Fitzsimmons was favoured by those who had seen him demolish Dempsey but two top heavyweights, Peter Jackson and Charlie Mitchell, said they fancied the Irishman to win. The winner was promised nine-tenths of the $10,000 purse.

Maher began by storming from his corner and the surprised Fitzsimmons was almost swept out of the ring. But the Irishman's eagerness nearly proved his undoing. He left himself open to a left hand counter-punch which landed him flat on his back. The blood seeped from Maher's lower lip as he scrambled to his feet. Now it was the Englishman's turn to be over-anxious. Lashing out with both hands in a bid to end it quickly, he caught a terrific left hook to the jaw, causing him to sink to his knees. The Irishman's supporters, crestfallen a moment earlier, whooped with delight. Fitzsimmons was still dazed as he rose and was an easy target for a right that spun him against the ropes. Only his sheer defensive instinct kept him aloft. Poised for victory, Maher was cheated by Fitzsimmons' second, Joe Choynski, who scrambled onto the ring apron and 'accidentally' kicked the bell to end the sensational opening round. Fitzsimmons managed to back-pedal and stall throughout the second round as he regained his senses. Once recovered, he proceeded to give Maher a boxing lesson for round after round, repeatedly catching the oncoming Irishman with stinging straight lefts to the face. One of these broke Maher's nose. By the 11th round Maher was in so much distress and pain that he wanted to quit. His manager talked him into having 'one more go'. But it was more of the same. Peter made valiant efforts to catch Fitzsimmons with big punches but the middleweight champion was too smart to be caught. When he went back to his corner, Maher told his seconds to throw in the towel.

Despite his broken nose Maher was back in action 19 days later, scoring a one-round knockout over Mike Monahan. Disaster struck in his next outing, when he was flattened by Joe Goddard. His manager maintained that Peter could have scaled greater heights had he overcome his aversion to training, but it was Maher's basic philosophy that 'If you're going to lose, you'll lose and that's all there is to it'. Whatever his weaknesses, he gathered some impressive 'scalps', of men like Peter Courtney, Joe Choynski and George Godfrey, one of the numerous black heavyweights who had the odious colour bar thrown up against them when they went title-hunting.

When James J. Corbett, who had taken the world title from John L. Sullivan, announced his retirement, his manager William A. Brady staged a match between Maher and New Zealander Steve O'Donnell at the Empire Athletic Club, Long Island, in September 1895 and declared that the winner would be the new world heavyweight king. 'Gentleman Jim' would be there in person to crown his successor. The fight was scheduled for 25 rounds, but all the customers got was 63 seconds of action. Maher, after a few seconds sizing up his opponent, shot across a right that sent the shocked O'Donnell crashing. He rolled over, struggled to his feet, only to be sent back down again by another powerful right. Again he managed to get up before the count reached ten. Maher finished the job with a left hook. When Corbett climbed into the ring to congratulate the 'new champion', he was met by an unappreciative Maher, who growled, 'It's you I want and I'll do you just as quickly as I did O'Donnell'. It was clear to Maher that he would not be recognised as the genuine world heavyweight champion unless he beat Corbett, who shortly afterwards announced his comeback and reclaimed his title. As for Steve O'Donnell, he seemed reluctant to accept that Maher was his master. They met five times, with Maher winning every one. On three of these occasions, it resulted in a first-round knockout for the Irishman.

One of the first challengers for Maher's synthetic world title was his old rival Bob Fitzsimmons, who fancied he could do a quicker demolition job than the 12 rounds it had previously taken him. Maher was equally intent on revenge. The build-up to the fight was bizarre. Out of the blue came an invitation from a notorious self-styled lawman, 'Judge' Roy Bean, to put on the bout in a tiny shanty-town called Langtry in Texas. Bean (Paul Newman played him in a film based on his life) succeeded in getting the boxers' agreement, but not the approval of the Governor of Texas. He would have none of it and ordered a troop of the famous Texas Rangers to stay posted in the area to make sure the fight did not take place on Texan soil. So Bean switched the action across the Rio Grande river onto Mexican territory.

There were so many gamblers, gunmen and other undesirables flooding into El Paso, the nearest town, for the three-day carnival that preceded the fight that Bean engaged the services of Bat Masterson, the famous western marshall, who arrived with a dozen hand-picked gunmen to keep an eye on troublemakers. Admission to the ringside seats was $20, but as there was a hill close by most of the spectators perched there free of charge. Only 182 actually paid to watch. Unknown to the boxers, the promoter planned to make a film of the contest, using Thomas Edison's newly-invented Kinetoscope, one of the first moving picture cameras, for showing to the public later. Fitzsimmons was particularly angry when he learned that he would get nothing from the filming of the event. Unable to get satisfaction from his last-minute pleas for a cut of the action, Fitzsimmons had the last laugh. He stiffened Maher in 95 seconds. The cameramen hadn't time to get their contraption working properly before it was all over. Three days later the boxers agreed to spar three rounds for the film company, which hardly made up for missing the

Fight between Peter Maher and Bob Fitzsimmons on the banks of the Rio Grande

real thing. And this time the fighters had to be paid for their efforts.

One of Mahers' best wins was over the highly-rated Joe Choynski: and he had none other than Theodore Roosevelt to thank for this success. The future US president was at the ringside when a police inspector, watching Maher taking a drubbing, was just about to call on the referee to stop the fight. But Roosevelt, then Commissioner of Police of New York, restrained the inspector, saying, 'No, this man isn't beaten yet'. Maher repaid the favour by stretching Choynski with what Roosevelt described as 'the hardest punch I ever saw'. In two subsequent meetings with Choynski, Maher came out on the losing end.

One of boxing's most despicable characters, even if he was a masterful boxer, was Kid McCoy. He would stoop to any low trick to gain an advantage. McCoy had relinquished the world middleweight title to chase the more lucrative heavyweight crown when he came up against Maher on New Year's Day 1900. Just before he entered the ring, Maher received a cable to say there had been a sudden death in the family. Naturally upset, though not wishing to call off the fight at the last minute, his concentration was badly lacking and he was easily beaten in five rounds. He did not know until later that the 'bereavement' was a hoax perpetrated by McCoy. Not until the last bout of his career, in July 1908, did Peter get a chance to avenge his unfair defeat, but he was too far gone and McCoy won in two rounds.

The last six years of Maher's fighting life are a chronicle of knockout defeats, with only the odd success to keep him going. Among those who put him away in the opening round was George Gardner, the Irishman who was world champion in the newly formed light-heavyweight division. After his retirement Maher spent some years working as a night watchman in New York. He died at 71 in Baltimore, Maryland.

The toughest nut of them all

Tom Sharkey stood only 5' 11" and weighed no more than 12st 12lbs (180lbs) but he packed enormous power in his squat frame. His massive chest, decorated with tattoos of a sailing ship and a large star, was topped by broad shoulders, a bull-like neck and a solid, square jaw that took the hardest punches from some of the world's best heavyweights without adverse effect. Crowning his rugged appearance was a magnificent specimen of a cauliflower ear. He was anything but proud of the mis-shapen protuberance and, after his retirement, he offered $5,000 to anyone who could restore his ear to normality. A noted specialist undertook to do the job, but Sharkey pulled out of the operation at the last minute and kept his grotesque ring 'souvenir' for the rest of his days.

Although he never won a championship title Sharkey must certainly rank as the toughest Irish battler of all time. He made no pretences to being a fancy boxer, but made up for any technical deficiencies with his great fighting heart, his powerful punching, his ruggedness, his unlimited courage and an unshakeable belief in himself. He defied the best efforts of the mighty 'California Grizzly Bear' James J. Jeffries to put him away in two battles lasting a total of 45 rounds. Sharkey listed two other world heavyweight champions, James J. Corbett and Bob Fitzsimmons, among his victims, albeit in each case on a disqualification, but he suffered his most comprehensive defeat in a return with Fitzsimmons, who knocked him out in the second round.

As a kid Tom liked nothing better than the rough-and-tumble street scraps that were a daily occurrence around his home in Hill Street, Dundalk, County Louth. A yearning for adventure took him to sea and he spent almost a decade sailing the world. As well as surviving typhoons, hurricanes and four shipwrecks, he learned how to handle himself in many no-holds-barred batt'es on board ship and ashore. While stationed in Honolulu he had 14 fights and won them all by knockouts. He continued his career in California and one witness who was impressed with the Irish sailor's durability was Joe Choynski, one of the leading contenders for the world heavyweight title. Choynski made him an unusual offer: 'Fight me, and if you're still standing at the end of eight rounds you will be the winner'. Sharkey absorbed plenty of punishment from the vastly more experienced Choynski, but he was still on his feet at the final bell. As per the agreement, Tom got the verdict. Among the audience was James J. Corbett, who stepped up and offered Sharkey a fight.

'Gentleman Jim' had been out of action since giving up his world title the previous year and he was now embarking on a comeback aimed at re-establishing himself as title-holder. Out of condition after months of theatrical and personal appearances, Corbett insisted on the bout being limited to four rounds. It was just as well he did. He was able to outbox the clumsy Irishman for the first two rounds, but then he ran out of steam and Sharkey was able to rough him around for the remaining two. The referee's decision was a draw, which Corbett claimed was ridiculous, although he did admit that he took his opponent too lightly and he was so exhausted he could not leave his corner for half and hour. In his autobiography *The Roar of the Crowd*, a masterpiece of self-glorification, Corbett claimed that Sharkey 'did not hit me once in the whole fight'.

With Corbett now reclaiming the world title, a match was made between Sharkey and Bob Fitzsimmons to find his first challenger. The eliminator, scheduled for 2 December 1896 at the Mechanics Stadium in San Francisco, was riddled with controversy from the start. Sharkey's manager turned down several suggested referees, instead coming up with the startling choice of Wyatt Earp, the notorious gunslinger, who was in town with some of his horses for a race meeting. Earp had been a deputy marshall in such boisterous Wild West towns as Dodge City in Kansas and Tombstone in Arizona. He was alleged to have shot dead ten men, including his brother-in-law Ike Clanton. What his qualifications were as a boxing referee is hard to fathom. Fitzsimmons' manager objected to Earp as he had heard the lawman was friendly towards Sharkey. But Fitzsimmons said he didn't care who acted as third man in the ring: his fists would make it elementary. Another row broke out when Sharkey entered the ring wearing bandages on his fists. He removed them after Fitzsimmons objected to their use. Both boxers received a rapturous welcome from the crowd, while Wyatt Earp's arrival was roundly booed. The jeers turned to gasps when the ex-marshall took off his long-tailed coat to reveal a holster bearing his trusty six-shooter. A police captain insisted that Earp hand over his gun, which he did under protest. Then, waving a cheque under the policeman's nose, he sneered, 'Do you want to inspect this too? It's the $10,000 purse money, which I'm going to hand over to the winner'.

Sharkey, 20 pounds the heavier although three inches shorter, took the initiative right away, only to find his rushes playing right into the Englishman's hands. Fitzsimmons peppered him with sharp left jabs. Sharkey missed with a wild right swing and fell flat on his face. He jumped up immediately, only to be met with a perfectly timed right to the jaw that almost downed him. The bell came to his rescue. Fitzsimmons continued to dominate the action until the sensational finish in the eighth round. Sharkey was hanging onto his opponent and ignoring the referee's command to break. Fitzsimmons pulled himself free with much difficulty, then shot a terrific right to the Irishman's jaw. As his legs buckled Sharkey took a solid left dig to the stomach, the same 'solar plexus' punch that was to win Fitzsimmons the world heavyweight title from Corbett three months later. Sharkey sank to the floor, clutching his midriff. Earp started to count, then changed his mind and announced that he was disqualifying Fitzsimmons for hitting low. The English camp howled 'robbery' and alleged that Earp had been bribed to make sure Sharkey won. The referee denied this charge vehemently, claiming that he had never done anything dishonest in his life and that a foul blow had definitely been struck. Fitzsimmons obtained a court order holding up Sharkey's purse pending an investigation, but the court later decided in Tom's favour. Although it went on record as a win for Sharkey, public sympathy was with Fitzsimmons and it was he who got the crack at the title.

Another stormy occasion was the night Sharkey met his fellow countryman Peter Maher in June 1897. Sharkey had Maher down and almost out in the sixth round, but it was his turn to hit the canvas in the next. Corbett, who was reporting the fight for the *Chicago Tribune*, wrote:

I thought the fight was over but, to my amazement, Sharkey bounced up as though he were made of rubber. Tom was a raving maniac. He was slamming away at Maher when the bell rang and he didn't stop even when the referee tried to pull him away. The ring was filled with policemen and still Sharkey fought on. He hurt Joe Choynski, his own cornerman, when Joe tried to soothe him. A rope was thrown round the enraged sailor, but before they had him secured he bashed one of Maher's seconds in the face and opened a deep gash in his head.

The wild affray ended with a draw being declared.

Obviously in need of a calming holiday, Sharkey took a trip back to Ireland, fitting in fights in Belfast and his native Dundalk which he won by quick knockouts. Back in the United States after his five months' break he found the fight scene buzzing with excitement about a burly young Californian named James J. Jeffries. Although he had fought only ten times to date Jeffries had held two of the main contenders for the world title, Joe Choynski and Gus Ruhlin, to 20-round draws and had knocked out Peter Jackson in three rounds. He had also been a regular sparring partner to James J. Corbett. Jeffries' handlers put their young prospect to the test in a 20-rounder with Sharkey in May 1898. Both men boasted unbeaten records. It was Sharkey who learned what it was like to be a loser, for the first time in 34 contests. Outweighed by 35 pounds and six inches the shorter man, Tom found the powerful Jeffries just too much to handle, although he kept it close right to the end of a dour, punishing battle.

A great one-round knockout of Gus Ruhlin got Sharkey back into contention for the heavyweight title, now in the hands of Bob Fitzsimmons. But first came a return with James J. Corbett, who was seeking a re-match with his conqueror, Fitzsimmons. Corbett was the vastly superior boxer, but he was floored by a Sharkey haymaker in the second round. In his autobiography Corbett claimed that there had been a pre-fight agreement that there would be no in-fighting, an extraordinary pact if true. But Sharkey disregarded any such 'understanding' and belted 'Gentleman Jim' around the ribs and generally roughed him up whenever he got close enough. Corbett, warned for hitting too low, was looking tired and very dejected in the ninth round when Jim McVey, one of his seconds, jumped into the ring and earned his man's disqualification, thus cheating Sharkey of a more decisive win.

In his next outing Sharkey overcame the guile and tricks of Kid McCoy, the former middleweight king now trying his luck as a heavyweight, but the Irishman had to climb off the floor twice before finishing off the much lighter McCoy with a right to the body in the tenth round. The world heavyweight crown passed from Fitzsimmons to Jeffries and the Californian fulfilled his promise to give Sharkey the first crack at the title. Twenty-five thousand dollars, winner-take-all, was at stake when Jeffries and Sharkey squared off for their return encounter at the Coney Island Athletic Club, New York, on 3 November 1899. The fans who paid from five to $35 expected a long gruelling contest, just like the first match, and they got their money's worth. The gutsy Irishman made light of his physical disadvantages as he adopted an attacking role, shaking off the big man's hammer blows and hitting back

Tom Sharkey, complete with cauliflower ear and tattoo

with his own punishing digs. He shook Jeffries with a mighty left hook in the sixth and the champion finished the round bleeding from the mouth and ear. Sharkey, too, shed blood from the ear in the eighth round. The Irishman seemed to be marginally ahead going into the 20th round, but he appeared to lose heart when he put every ounce of power behind a right that caught Jeffries square on, only to find the rock-like champion kept coming at him. Jeffries tried with all his might to finish off the weary challenger, but he was still there at the end of the 25 rounds. Referee George Siler gave his points verdict to Jeffries, to yells of protest from the Irishman's supporters who felt he deserved at least a draw.

Many years later, in an interview with Nat Fleischer for *The Ring,* Jeffries professed his enduring regard for Sharkey.

> They came no greater. If ever there was a game and desperate fighter Sharkey was the man. I split his eye open with a blow and his ear started to swell until it was almost as big as my fist. When I landed on that ear it was like hitting a big wet sponge. Yet he wouldn't think of quitting. I also broke two of his ribs and still he kept coming at me. He was as game a fighter as I've ever seen.

Sharkey seemed to have fully recovered from the war with Jeffries as he came back to win six in a row by knockouts, including a second-round stoppage of Joe Choynski. But the years of gruelling battles were taking their toll. He lost to his former victim Gus Ruhlin on points and finished that match with his dodgy ear swollen like a balloon. Never a man to pick the easy ones, Sharkey gave Bob Fitzsimmons a return match. Fitzsimmons, still smarting from the Wyatt Earp disqualification, was intent on a quick finish, but it was he who walked into a big swipe that left him sitting dazed on the canvas. He was in the act of rising when the bell rang. Sharkey came out swinging for the second round, anxious to finish what he had started. Fitzsimmons met him half-way and the crowd was treated to a fine old punch-up. It was Fitzsimmons's punches, however, which had the more telling effect. A left hook made Sharkey sag at the knees and a sizzling right dropped him for a count of eight. He was an easy target for a relentless Fitzsimmons, who smashed home a left to the chin to put Tom down for the full count.

It was the end of the big time for Sharkey. He fought only twice in 1901 and twice again the following year. He quit the ring after being knocked out in 11 rounds by his old rival Gus Ruhlin during a gala boxing carnival staged in London in June 1902 as part of the celebrations for the coronation of King Edward VII. Tom came back two years later to box a six-round 'no decision' bout with Jack Munroe, finishing the encounter barely able to see through badly-swollen eyes. That was it, although he did don the gloves at the ripe old age of 61 to box an exhibition with Jack Johnson at the 1934 Chicago World Fair. Sharkey startled the former world heavyweight champion by charging at him in his old familiar style. 'Hey Tom,' laughed the great Johnson as he pinned the belligerent Irishman's arms, 'what are you trying to do to me?'

A thrifty man, Sharkey had saved an estimated $100,000 when he retired. He bought a palatial home in the Sheepshead section of Brooklyn, owned a stable of trotting horses and ran a saloon on East 14th Street, when Union Square was the heart of the New York entertainment world. For some years his bar did a lively trade as a popular spot for stage and sporting crowds, but it later became infested with undesirables and, after several scrapes with the police, Sharkey's licence was revoked. The loss of his prized saloon, together with some poor investments, saw him fall on hard times. He went back to California and teamed up with James J. Jeffries for a series of vaudeville and personal appearance tours. The two old rivals became great friends and Sharkey spent a lot of time on Jeffries' ranch in Burbank, California. After their variety act folded Tom worked as a guard at various race tracks in California. When Jeffries died in March 1953, Sharkey said softly, with a glint in his eye, 'It took a long time but I beat him after all'. Within a month Tom, too, was dead. He was in his 80th year.

A new weight division and an Irish champion

Before 1903 any boxer over 11st 4lbs (158lbs), which was the middleweight limit, had to compete against men of unlimited weight in the heavyweight division. There was nothing in between. Lou Houseman, a Chicago journalist and boxing manager, was one of the prime instigators of a new weight category. Backed by promoter James Coffroth, the new light-heavyweight division was born. The British liked the idea, but they didn't like the name, which they thought was confusing, so they called it cruiserweight. The Australians gave it yet another tag, mid-heavyweight. It was not mere co-incidence that Lou Houseman was so keen on the new division, for he looked after the affairs of one Jack Root, who was too big to be a middleweight and too small to be a heavyweight. In the first contest for the world light-heavyweight title, with an upper limit of 12st 7lbs (175lbs), Root outpointed Kid McCoy, the former middleweight champion.

Waiting patiently for the outcome was a dark-haired Irishman, George Gardner, who felt entitled to first crack at the new champion as, a year earlier, he had been the first man to defeat Root. Austrian-born Root was only ten weeks a title-holder when he put it on the line against Gardner at Fort Erie, Ontario, Canada, on 4 July 1903. The Irishman was an overwhelming winner. According to the *Police Gazette* report:

> While Root landed many times and more than one of his blows hurt, Gardner was hitting harder all the time. He was more aggressive and he had speed, all of which is an invincible combination.

When Gardner scored a knockdown in the 12th round Root got up but was too weak to continue. The dethroned champion took his defeat badly. He was still bitter when, aged 87, he told an interviewer in 1963:

That man Gardner was my Waterloo. Of my 55 fights I lost only three, one to Marvin Hart and two to George Gardner. He was a tough, vicious puncher. People say I was a clever boxer. Well, believe me, I tried every trick in and out of the book to save my crown, but he still kayoed me. I didn't like Gardner. He had a mean, rotten streak in him. He would taunt me about being an ex-champ whenever we met.

Gardner's accession to the world throne was a source of great joy to his father Pat, a former bare-knuckle battler, and his two younger brothers, Billy and Jimmy, both of whom were worthy fighters of the period. Jimmy won a claim to the world welterweight title after beating Jimmy Clabby in 1908, but the division was in disarray at the time and his claim was not taken seriously. Earlier that year he was outpointed by Mike 'Twin' Sullivan in an official title fight. The third Gardner brother, Billy, drew with Sullivan, but he never fought for a world title.

The Gardners left their birthplace of Ballinslacken, near Lisdoonvarna, County Clare, to settle at Lowell in Massachusetts. George, born on St Patrick's Day 1877, was 20 when he had his first professional fight. He lost only once in his first four years' campaigning, a defeat he later avenged. A trip to England in 1900 saw him score an impressive fourth round knockout over Frank Craig, known as 'the Coffee Cooler'. Unlike many white boxers of his time, Gardner had no objection to meeting black men. The Irishman learned the hard way why so many avoided the likes of Joe Walcott, 'the Barbados Demon', when the future world welterweight champion outsmarted him over 20 rounds. Gardner picked up enough to be able to turn the tables on Walcott the following year. In 1902 Gardner faced the most formidable black fighter of them all, Jack Johnson. Rated by many experts to be the best heavyweight in history, Johnson was still six years away from ruling the world when he met Gardner. A master boxer with a cast-iron defence, he was content during the early rounds to slip Gardner's punches and pick up points with a whiplash left and occasional right cross or uppercut. Way ahead on the referee's scorecard, Johnson decided it had gone far enough by the 12th round. He made the Irishman miss with a big right, then moved in to bury a vicious blow in Gardner's side. George winced with pain but he didn't go down. He managed somehow to survive the 20 rounds, but Johnson was a thoroughly convincing points winner. Gardner candidly admitted later that he considered himself lucky 'to finish with a head on my shoulders'. In *Jack Johnson and His Times*, by Denzil Batchelor, the author paid a colourful tribute to Gardner:

He did not pack a prodigious punch, but his feet skipped like the little hills in the Psalms, and that long left hand of his poked out at the most inconvenient angle and with the speed of a humming bird in its dart for a midge.

1903 was Gardner's year of glory, short-lived as it was. He poleaxed Peter Maher in the first round, outpointed top-rated heavyweight

Marvin Hart, who had beaten Johnson, and then took the world light-heavyweight title from Jack Root. George looked around for a not-too-difficult opponent for his first championship defence. Most unwisely, he settled for that scourge of Irish fighters, Bob Fitzsimmons. Had he bothered to ask Nonpareil Jack Dempsey, Peter Maher or Tom Sharkey for their opinions, he would have been strongly advised to give Fitzsimmons a wide berth. But Gardner didn't think he had anything to fear. The Englishman was now in his 41st year and his once-destructive hitting power was a thing of the past. He had been twice knocked out by James J. Jeffries in heavyweight title fights and it had been 12 years since he had won the middleweight crown from Dempsey. But Fitzsimmons was not finished collecting championships yet.

The old man gave Gardner a lesson in the arts and crafts of boxing and, even with damaged hands, floored the Irishman twice in the fourth round, again in the fifth, cut him under the right eye in the sixth and generally outmanoeuvred the defending champion. Gardner did succeed in bringing blood from Fitzsimmons' mouth in the tenth, but he was back on the floor for short counts in the 13th and 14th rounds. The veteran challenger tired noticeably over the last five rounds and Gardner, gathering confidence, tried desperately for a knockout to save his title. One good right, his best of the fight, shook Fitzsimmons to his heels in the 17th round, but the English marvel defied all his efforts and was good value for his points win. The referee, Ed Graney, was scathing in his comments on Gardner's performance:

I think that anyone who bet on Gardner has a legitimate kick coming. I was tempted to call all wagers off. At times I wondered if the affair was on the square and more than once I was on the verge of calling it no contest. It was the worst exhibitions I have ever been called upon to referee.

The *San Francisco Chronicle* was equally dismissive of Gardner's showing:

Fitzsimmons was a slow old man whose fighting days have passed, but Gardner had hundreds of openings and took advantage of none. Fitz would duck and run into the ropes in an effort to get away. A man with a modicum of brains and the force of a ten-year-old boy should have been upon him with a stinging smash.

Gardner, dejected by the loss of his crown after only four months' reign and stung by the flood of criticism, had an indifferent 1904, winning four and drawing four of his nine appearances. His one defeat was a six-round points verdict against Jack Root. It was the fifth time they met, with the final score even: two wins each and a draw. In the last four years of his career Gardner managed only one win in nine outings. He was stopped by Mike Schreck, Al Kaufman, Jim Flynn, Terry Mustain and Tony Ross, finally hanging up his gloves in 1908. He married a wealthy woman and lived in comfort until his 77th year.

Four

On the Home Front

WHILE AMERICA CONTINUED to be the land of hope and opportunity for Irish boxers, there were healthy signs of increasing ring activity on the domestic front. Those ringmen who chose to pursue their careers in Ireland found plenty of work, at least up to the outbreak of World War I. Many of them elected to fight for King and Country (all of Ireland then being part of the United Kingdom), but their active service did not preclude them from the less hazardous occupation of fighting with the gloves. Boxing servicemen often bore their rank alongside their name, as in the case of Bombardier Billy Wells, the British heavyweight champion. Among the Irish heavyweights were Petty Officer Matt Curran and Private Dan Voyles. Among the civilians who featured on regular boxing promotions in Ireland were the Wexford blacksmith Jem Roche, Corkman Pakey Mahoney and the only black man ever to win an Irish championship, 'Cyclone' Billy Warren.

The period reached an historic landmark when, on St Patrick's Day 1908, the heavyweight championship of the world was contested for the first - and only - time on Irish soil. Some of the more sensitive fans would prefer that the occasion be quietly forgotten, for the contest marked another record in the boxing annals. Jem Roche's bid to take the title from Canadian Tommy Burns lasted exactly 88 seconds, and that included the time it took the referee to count him out. It remained on the list as the shortest world heavyweight title fight in history for 74 years, until Michael Dokes beat Mike Weaver in 63 seconds of their World Boxing Association title fight in 1982.

By right Roche had no place in the ring with a world champion. He had scored 14 knockouts in 19 bouts to date, with only two losses, but all his activity had been at home and none of his opponents were world-ranked. He just happened to be the right man in the right place as Burns picked up some handy money on a world tour while avoiding his most legitimate challenger, Jack Johnson, the brilliant black Texan who finally caught up with him in Australia and made him pay for his snub. Burns was tempted to Ireland by a £1,500 purse offer from promoter Martin Fitzgerald, backed by a syndicate that included Tammany Hall leader 'Boss' Croker. The announcement that the world title fight had been secured for the Theatre Royal in Hawkins Street, Dublin, really caught the public imagination. Little else was talked about for weeks beforehand and every one of the 3,000 tickets sold well in advance, with plenty of takers for the outrageously priced black market seats.

Modern fans used to huge heavyweights would find the sight of Burns and Roche as heavyweight title contestants an incongruous sight indeed. Burns, at 5' 7" and weighing 179 pounds, is the smallest holder of the title on record. Roche was only one inch taller and tipped the scales at 13st 7lbs (189lbs). Most of his poundage consisted of fat which hung in unsightly rolls over the top of his trunks. Yet he moved well for a man of his build, was considered tough and game and had developed a strong right-hand punch from working with hammer and anvil. Born at Killurin, near Kilmuckridge, County Wexford, Roche's first love was Gaelic football and he played for Wexford United during his teen years. He was then attracted to boxing and won the Wexford amateur championship before turning to the paid ranks in 1902. He won the Irish heavyweight title by knocking out Jack Fitzpatrick at the Ancient Concert Rooms in Dublin and followed up with wins over ex-Irish Champion Myler Keogh, British Army and Navy champion Private Harris and American Joe Hagan, brother of former world champion Philadelphia Jack O'Brien (his real named was Hagan). Jem lost his Irish title to 'Young' John L. Sullivan when he collapsed, exhausted and bloodied, a minute before the end of their 20-round battle. He got himself into better condition for the return with Sullivan and regained the title with an 18th round knockout. It was a decisive win in eight rounds over Charlie Wilson, the Englishman who had knocked out British champion Gunner Moir, that made Irish fans sit up and take notice of Roche's true worth. His backers issued a challenge to Moir for a British title fight but Moir had a more important date, a crack at Tommy Burns' world title in London. Burns disposed of the British title-holder in ten rounds, then turned his attention to Ireland and Jem Roche.

When the biggest fight night in Irish history was announced Roche became a national hero overnight. Even people with little interest in boxing became instant fans. Roche's rail journey from Wexford to Dublin was like a royal processsion. Cheering crowds lined the platforms at every station and wherever the train stopped he had to get out and make a speech. On arrival in the capital, well-wishers thronged the streets from Westland Row station to Prussia Street, where he had set up training quarters. 'Give it to him, Jem,' they shouted, 'let him have it good.' As the boxers neared the completion of their training, a national newspaper sent each man a telegram inquiring about their condition. 'Just fine,' replied Burns. Roche, who never managed to look trim no matter how hard he trained, sent the message, 'Fatter but fitter'.

The city centre was thronged with enthusiastic fans on the night of the fight. The police formed a cordon 30 yards from the entrance to the Theatre Royal and no one was allowed through without a ticket. Roche had great difficulty reaching the stage door in Poolbeg Street as supporters heaved and pushed in an effort to shake his hand and wish him good luck. Burns, too, was besieged as he tried to reach the theatre. 'I've never seen anything like this crowd before,' he remarked. For the benefit of those who couldn't gain admittance, coloured lights had been set up in the street. A red light would glow if Burns won a particular round, or a green light if it went Roche's way. Inside the arena the atmosphere was full of excitement as spectators babbled away during the preliminary bouts, swapping opinions on the likely outcome of 'the big one'. Although the more realistic appreciated the size of the Irish champion's task and put their money on the visitor, there were plenty of bets on Roche to become Ireland's first world heavyweight champion.

It was ten past ten when Roche emerged from his dressing room to make his way to the ring to the strains of 'The Boys ᴼf Wexford' from the orchestra pit. The Canadian was greeted with Yankee Doodle Dandy', in keeping with the Stars and Stripes silk he work around his waist; he was now an American citizen. In Roche's corner were his manager N.J. Tennant, Dan Kelly, a former Irish lightweight champion, and Bob Brown. There was a last-minute flurry when it was discovered that Jem had forgotten his hand bandages. A messenger returned with a packet of lint, which was angrily rejected by Roche's manager. Burns preferred finger-less doeskin gloves under his padded boxing gloves. The last word in Roche's ear just before the bell was to watch out for the world champion's left hook, which had accounted for most of his 29 knockout victims in 48 fights (he had lost three). The contest was scheduled for 20 rounds.

The Wexfordman moved out warily at the bell, keeping his left arm extended while guarding his chin with his right. Burns fought from a crouch, making him look even smaller than he was. He snapped out a left but Roche skipped smartly out of range. Burns frowned at his clumsiness as the punch swept the smoky air. Roche saw his chance and tossed two quick punches, but this time it was Burns who danced away. Then, with dramatic suddenness, it was all over. Roche landed his only blow of the fight, a left jab that caught the world champion on the face and made him blink. Jem attempted a follow-up right, but Burns ducked inside it and moved forward to force his opponent against the ropes. The left hook that Roche had been told to watch came too quickly to avoid. It crashed against his jaw. Before he could grab or get away a perfectly timed right sent him tumbling to the floor. The challenger, his legs thrashing the canvas as he struggled to regain his shattered senses, managed to roll over and assume a kneeling position before jumping to his feet. But it was too late. The referee, Mr Watson, had counted him out. Roche pathetically followed the world champion to his corner and pleaded, 'Mr Burns, surely I'm not out'. The shocked silence of the fans gave way to sporting cheers as they acknowledged the precise execution job performed by Burns. There is a much-repeated story, now a part of boxing folklore, of how one member of the audience, quick off the mark, dashed out of the theatre as soon as the referee finished counting and announced to the milling throng, 'It's terrible in there. They're killing one another. There's blood everywhere. I can't stand any more of it. Who wants to buy my ticket?' After a mad scramble for the ticket, the delighted purchaser made his way in, only to be carried out on the tide of the emerging crowd.

The Australian heavyweight champion, Bill Squires, had come to Dublin to act as the world champion's sparring partner and he stayed on to meet Roche in the next tournament. Squires had also met Burns for the title, lasting a grand 41 seconds longer, so the pair were considered well matched. The Aussie proved too strong for Roche, however, and won in four rounds. Roche did have one more meritorious win, a knockout of 'the Harlem Coffee Cooler' Frank Craig, who was past his best. After his retirement Roche devoted most of his time to his first love, Gaelic football, and helped train the great Wexford team that became the first side to win four successive all-Ireland championships (1915-18). Jem was 56 when he died in 1934. A plaque in the Bull Ring, Wexford, erected by his admirers, perpetuates the memory of 'a great fighter, great sportsman, but greater still in his own simplicity and modesty'.

One of Roche's conquerors in his last year of fighting was Petty Officer Matt Curran from Lisdeen, Ennis, County Clare. Curran didn't manage a crack at the world title but he did enjoy a brief tenure as heavyweight champion of the British Empire. He might also be listed among the British title-holders for he knocked out the reigning champion 'Iron' Hague in 15 rounds at Plymouth. The snag was that only contests that took place at the London headquarters of the National Sporting Club, then the self-appointed governing body of the sport in Britain, were recognised as title fights. The NSC retained its powerful position until the formation of the British Boxing Board of Control in 1929. After his defeat of Hague, Curran was challenged by Gunner Moir, who had lost his British title to Hague. Moir reckoned that a win over Curran would entitle him to a chance to regain his crown. He punched the Irishman all around the ring but was so anxious to finish him off that he didn't hear the bell for the end of the second round. His protestations that the bell had been drowned out by the crowd's roars got little sympathy from the referee, who announced his disqualification and raised the hand of the bemused Curran. It was not the only occasion when one of Curran's fights ended in controversy.

He topped the bill at the Empire Theatre, Dublin, in July 1910 against

'Cyclone' Billy Warren in a farce of a contest that ended in the seventh round with both men being sent to their corners for 'not trying'. The referee declared it 'no contest'. Exactly the same thing happened when Currran met Englishman Dewey Smith but, amazingly, the fans turned out to see them in a return. This time Curran produced his best form to win by a third round knockout, even though Smith complained the finishing blow was below the belt. In a violent clash with Gunner Hewitt, Royal Navy heavyweight champion, Curran won in three rounds, but not before the ring had collapsed and the boxers had to sit it out at the ringside until the damage was repaired.

It was another controversial contest that saw Curran enthroned as British Empire champion in 1911. His challenge was to the Australian holder of the title, Bill Lang. The champion was a hot favourite, due to his more impressive record. He had dropped Tommy Burns in the first round of a world title fight before being flattened himself in the sixth. He had lost in nine rounds to Jack Johnson, which was no disgrace, and had stopped Bob Fitzsimmons in the old-timer's last contest. It looked like the odds were justified when Lang downed Curran in the opening seconds, but his follow-up blow struck the Irishman while he was on the canvas. Under the rules, the referee had no option but to disqualify the Australian. Curran lost the Empire title when disqualified for 'misuse of head' in the 20th round against American-based Irishman Dan 'Porky' Flynn.

Gunner Moir, still smarting over his loss on a foul against Curran two years earlier, got his chance of revenge in 1912. He found the Irishman at the peak of his form and the former British champion was left floundering at Curran's feet to be counted out after only 85 seconds. Curran tried to capitalise on his victory by taking a trip to Paris to take on the wily old trickster Kid McCoy. The American, though in his 40th year, knew too much for the Irishman and was good value for his points win after 20 rounds. Curran made another sojourn to Paris to take on another American legend, Sam Langford. The great Langford, considered by many to be the best non-champion in history, swept Curran to defeat in just 17 seconds, one of the shortest fights on record. When Curran got a crack at a British heavyweight champion, Bombardier Billy Wells, it was not recognised by the NSC as it took place in Plymouth. It mattered little to the Irishman, as it transpired. He lost all interest in the proceedings in the fifth round after coming into contact with Wells' dynamite right hand.

The most unusual of the 'Irish' heavyweight stars of the pre-World War I era, and a rival of Jem Roche, was 'Cyclone' Billy Warren, who was, in fact, a black Australian whose world travels took him to Dublin. He married an Irish girl and settled in the Nelson Street area of the city. A huge man, he was a familiar character with his bowler hat, cane and faded crombie overcoat as he stood every day outside the GPO in O'Connell Street right up to the time of his death in 1951. Warren won

'Cyclone' Billy Warren

the Irish title from Jem Roche in Belfast but lost it back to Jem shortly afterwards. 'Cyclone', who was still boxing at 50, was the last opponent of the once-formidable Peter Jackson. They fought a 25-round draw in Melbourne in 1899 when Jackson was 38.

Champion of the world - or was he?

Fight fans in the County Louth coastal town of Dundalk, baulked in their hopes of a world championship through Tom Sharkey, gained compensation - of a sort - in the rise of Tom McCormick, a gifted welterweight who was in Australia in 1914 when he staked his claim to the world title. The trouble was that he was just one of several boxers who aspired to the honour and his claim never won world-wide acceptance. Even his entry in the lists of British champions is shrouded in doubt, for the title fight took place 'down under' and not at the National Sporting Club in London. Only his right to the British Empire title would appear to be free from dispute.

McCormick, who as a boy left Ireland for England, was billed throughout most of his career as being from Plymouth, where he was based during his British Army service and was a regular performer there at the Cosmopolitan Club. In his first paid contest he amazed spectators with the skill he displayed in stopping Bill Mansell in three rounds. Queried as to where he picked up such precise moves and punches, he explained that he had made an intense study of a boxing textbook written by Jim Driscoll and he had practised the old master's instructions before a full-length mirror until he had them perfected. Tom made such rapid progress that by his second year in the ring he had beaten two former British champions, Young Joseph and Arthur Evernden, as well as holding the classy Welshman Johnny Basham to a draw. Later victims were Jack Goldswain, a one-time lightweight king, Gus Platts, future middleweight champion, and Eddie Beattie, a leading welterweight contender.

McCormick was unbeaten in 30 contests before he dropped a home town decision to Gus Platts in Sheffield. Angling for a British title fight, he was disappointed when champion Johnny Summers took off for a tour of Australia. Rather than hang around waiting for his return, the Irishman followed him 'down under'. An Australian promoter, spotting the attraction, matched McCormick and Summers over 20 rounds at Sydney Stadium in January 1914. Although it was billed for the British and Empire titles, the NSC back in London refused to give its approval. Summers, a strong, two-fisted scrapper, was expected to be too good for McCormick, but the Irishman surprised him by slipping his heavy blows and using his skills to score a convincing points win. Summers insisted his defeat was a fluke and demanded a return match.

The promoter, however, fixed up McCormick to meet the Dane Waldemar Holberg, a claimant to the world championship. Only a fortnight after beating Summers, McCormick stepped into the Melbourne

Stadium ring to tackle the bustling, determined Dane. Once again Tom's brilliant science frustrated his opponent and it was a plainly desperate Holberg who lashed out with a wild blow in the sixth round that landed well below the belt. The Dane was disqualified and McCormick was declared the new world champion. Anxious to cash in on his success, Tom agreed to defend his three 'titles' against Johnny Summers at Sydney Stadium. Summers, eager to catch the elusive Irishman before he settled into his immaculate stride, came charging from his corner like an express train. McCormick was forced into a corner, but cleverly slipped out to regain the centre of the ring. Summers leaped in again. Timing his arrival perfectly, McCormick pulled him up smartly with a left and right to the body. Tom switched quickly to the head and caught the Englishman with several short, sharp punches to the jaw. Summers pitched forward to the floor, face down, and he remained in that position to be counted out. His challenge had lasted two minutes and 20 seconds. McCormick might have been better advised to rest on his laurels, but he was committed to a series of fights for the Australian promoters. He agreed to put his claims to the world, British and Empire titles at stake against the experienced Englishman Matt Wells. This time he met a man with even greater skills than himself and lost a clear points decision over 20 rounds. Now a champion of nowhere, McCormick recklessly re-entered the ring seven days later and was again beaten, by American Fritz Holland. Another US visitor, Milburn Saylor, gave him a sound trouncing and McCormick was in a helpless condition when his seconds threw in the towel during the tenth round. This completed his contract with the Australian promoters and he sailed back to England, richer in pocket and experience, but minus his hard-won honours.

The Great War was now in full spate and McCormick rejoined his old Manchester Regiment, with whom he had served as a boy bandsman. He was sent to Aldershot as a sergeant physical training instuctor. In spite of the war, boxing continued in Britain, though obviously to a more limited degree. McCormick put his name down as a contender for the British welterweight championship, now held by Johnny Basham. The Irishman had kept himself in good physical trim while training soldiers, but he was short of genuine ring practice when he stepped into the NSC ring for his first officially recognised British title fight in May 1915. A mere shadow of his old self, McCormick never seriously worried Basham. Way behind on points, he was in trouble just as the bell rang to end the 12th round. A left hook had him down for two in the next and he was so weak on rising that he staggered and fell without taking another punch. This time he stayed down for eight seconds. Basham looked at the referee to see if he wanted to call a halt but he was motioned to carry on. A couple of well-timed uppercuts and the helpless challenger was on the floor again. One of McCormick's seconds jumped into the ring, prompting the referee to declare Basham the winner.

Tom felt like quitting the ring, but he was pursuaded to appear in a big tournament at Chelsea football ground in aid of war charities. He returned to the winning trail by knocking out Harry Paddon but lost in his next outing to the Swiss boxer Albert Badoud. He was counted out for the first and only time in his career when decked in the 14th round by Eddie Beattie. He was not to know it, but it was his last ring appearance and within a year he lost his life on the battlefields of France. He could have stayed in England as a PT instructor but volunteered for overseas service in 1916. He was in the trenches for the big push of that July. The Manchesters were ordered 'over the top' and, in spite of a heavy shell barrage and withering fire from the Germans, they ploughed through the mud of No Man's Land and sent the enemy into retreat. Crossing a strip of land between two lines of trenches, McCormick joked with his friend and old sparring partner, Colonel Jim Winspear, to be careful where he trod. A shell burst between them. Winspear suffered injuries that put an end to any ambitions he might have on the boxing scene. Sergeant Tom McCormick was killed instantly, at the age of 26.

Ireland's 'great white hope'

Black heavyweights have so monopolised the world fight scene ever since the coming of the fabulous Joe Louis in the late 1930s that it is hard to imagine how the sport would have survived without them. Dark-skinned boxers were not always so acceptable. Racial bigotry was so intense during the reign of the first black world heavyweight champion, Jack Johnson, from 1908 to 1915, that frantic efforts were made to find a white challenger capable of dislodging him. So desperate were the anti-Johnson brigade that a ludicrous campaign, led by writer Jack London, was initiated to bring James J. Jeffries out of peaceful retirement 'to regain the title for the white race'. Big Jeff foolishly answered the call and returned after a six-year layoff to suffer total humiliation at the expert hands of Johnson. The film of the fight caused race riots when it was shown in the United States and it was banned in Britain for fear of similar disturbances there. Interestingly, the film was shown at the Rotunda Cinema in Dublin without noticeable objection from any quarter, probably because of the almost total absence of black residents in Ireland.

Jeffries' downfall only served to intensify the hunt for a white heavyweight to dethrone Johnson. Numerous 'white hope' tournaments were staged throughout the United States. Among those who emerged was a sturdy young Irishman, Jim Coffey, who stood an impressive 6' 3" and weighed 210 pounds. He was nicknamed 'the Roscommon Giant'. Coffey's record bears excellent comparison with any of the other 'great white hopes' of the Johnson era. During a six-year career, he won most of his 62 fights inside the distance and was beaten only four times. A lethal right-hand puncher, he was shrewdly managed by Billy Gibson, who later handled ring immortals Gene Tunney and Benny Leonard. Gibson beat the ballyhoo drums successfully on Coffey's climb up the fistic ladder, although the Irish boxer just failed to reach the top rungs.

Born at Loughglynn, County Roscommon, on 4 July 1891, Coffey emigrated to America as a young man and settled in New York. While working as a motor mechanic he was enticed, mainly because of his size, to try his luck as a boxer. He quickly made a reputation as a stunning hitter and his manager boasted that Jim would become the hero, not only of the American Irish but of the entire white race. A temporary hiccup hit Gibson's plans when Soldier Kearns ignored this script and flattened the big Irishman in one round. The setback by Kearns was soon pushed into the background as Coffey strung together a fine collection of heavyweight scalps, among them that of Soldier Kearns in a one-round demolition job. Fireman Jim Flynn, who had gone nine rounds with Johnson in a world title bout and bowled over Jack Dempsey in one round, was twice on the losing end against Coffey, in four rounds and in nine. Jack 'Twin' Sullivan was stiffened in five. Arthur Pelkey lasted less than two and Terry Kellar, a one-round conqueror of British champion Frank Goddard, was halted in six.

Coffey really appeared to be going places until he tangled with the formidable Frank Moran, an outstanding 'white hope' who had lasted 20 rounds with Johnson in a title scrap. The old Madison Square Garden in New York was packed solid for the Coffey versus Moran duel on 19 October 1915. There was a last-minute hitch when Moran demanded his purse money in advance. He couldn't really be blamed, for the promoter of his last fight had absconded during the action leaving Moran with only his cuts and bruises to count. 'No money, no fight,' he declared. No amount of pleading or threatening could budge him. Coffey's manager, learning of the reason for the delay, stormed into Moran's dressing room and told him, 'Hurry up and get in the ring, Moran, so that Coffey can put you where you belong: on the floor'. Moran snorted in reply, 'Go back and tell that big man that when I kiss him with my little sweetheart Mary Ann,' and here he kissed his right fist, 'he won't know what it's all about until tomorrow.' The reporters crowded into the dressing room loved the pet name for Moran's right hand and, the next day, described how 'Mary Ann' had caressed Coffey to sleep in the third round.

It was a stunning setback to Coffey's hopes for a crack at Johnson's title, but his backers maintained that Moran had landed a lucky punch and wouldn't do it a second time. While arrangements were being made for the return, Coffey redeemed himself by sinking Gunboat Smith in four rounds. In the return match with Moran, Coffey's superior boxing ability had him ahead up to the eighth round but Moran was getting through with too many big rights for comfort. Gradually, the punches took their toll on the Irishman. He absorbed some heavy punishment before Moran's faithful 'Mary Ann' had him draped across the ropes in the ninth when the referee, seeing his helpless condition, stopped the fight in the American's favour. It was the end of Coffey as a serious 'white hope'.

He fought 'no decision' contests with capable men like Carl Morris,

Battling Levinsky and Bill Brennan, while continuing to knock over lesser rivals. The final curtain fell on his career in 1917 when he was halted in seven rounds by Bartley Madden, from Connemara, at Providence, Rhode Island. Coffey was one of those more fortunate ringmen who held onto his earnings and fulfilled his ambition to return home to Ireland on retirement. He bought a farm at The Glebe, Loughglynn, in his native County Roscommon. Few would now associate the big, quiet farmer with the feverish quest for a 'great white hope' to dethrone Jack Johnson. Coffey was 68 when he died five days before Christmas 1959.

Mike McTigue's championship homecoming

Boxing historians are unanimous in their choice of Battling Siki as the greatest optimist in the sport's nearly 300-year existence. For the African to risk his world title against an Irishman in Dublin on St Patrick's Day and expect to keep it...one can only marvel at his innocence. With the sole exception of Siki himself, no one was surprised when the referee raised the hand of the Irish challenger, Mike McTigue, after 20 closely contested rounds and proclaimed him the new light-heavyweight champion of the world. To add to the strangeness of the circumstances, the 1923 contest took place to the echo of bombs and bullets as civil war raged in the streets around the venue, La Scala Opera House in Prince's Street, off the capital's main thoroughfare, Sackville Street (now O'Connell Street). The 'troubles' were temporarily ignored as 1,500 spectators inside the theatre merged jubilant voices with the thousands gathered outside awaiting news of the outcome. The announcement that McTigue had become the first Irishman to win a world title on native soil caused an explosion of cheers to rival the mine blast that had rocked the city centre shortly before the fight.

For Michael Francis McTigue, fate had brought him home from the United States to an unexpected crack at the world title. To his credit - and the eternal gratitude of the Irish - he didn't let the opportunity slip. Mike was born on a farm in the parish of Kilnamona, near Ennis, County Clare, on 26 November 1892. He shared work on the farm with his twelve brothers and one sister until he was 16 when he took a job with a local blacksmith to raise the fare for his emigration to the United States. It was while working as a beef handler on New York's West Side that Mike proved himself useful with his fists. His foreman was attacked by a drunken bully and McTigue intervened to flatten the aggressor with a single punch. So impressed was his boss that he encouraged the young Irishman to take up boxing. Mike took lessons from a respected former ringman, George 'Elbows' McFadden, and got his first public try-out in a four-rounder at the New York Athletic Club in 1909. His barely noticed winning debut set him off on a ring career that was to last 21 years and bring him into combat with many of the most famous fighters of that era.

Billed as the Irish middleweight champion, he fought regularly around the New York area, winning most and losing some, all the time picking up invaluable experience and honing the ring-craft that was to sustain him throughout his long career. Many of his appearances were ten-round 'no decision' contests, which were unsatisfactory in that, under the Frawley Law operating in New York State between 1911 and 1920, all bouts were meant to be exhibitions with no verdict given at the end. The only way a boxer could win in these bouts was by a knockout. If a fight went the full distance, a poll of ringside reporters would produce a 'popular decision', also termed a 'newspaper verdict'. It was common for champions to avoid hard-hitting opponents in 'no decision' contests, knowing that only a knockout could deprive them of their title. Among the quality ringmen that McTigue met during this period were Harry Greb, Battling Levinsky, Tommy Loughran and Augie Ratner. 'Tough nut' Galwayman Mike Farrell went ten rounds with him in one of these no-win clashes.

While well established on the American circuit, McTigue was not a spectacular performer. He was a fair hitter, but tended to rely more on his clever boxing to win rather than go all-out for a knockout. Consequently, he was not a box office attraction. In 1922, with his career already 13 years old and no nearer to a world title shot, Mike decided to take a break and enjoy a holiday back home. To supplement the cost of his trip to Ireland he had four fights in England en route, winning them all inside four rounds. Irish promoter Tom Singleton was at the ringside in Liverpool to see him beat Jack Reeves and a delighted McTigue was told that he could have a world title fight with Battling Siki in Dublin on the following St Patrick's Day. The promoter's main worry was getting Siki to travel by sea as the world champion was terrified of water.

The problem was overcome by filling Siki with wine and spirits before the journey. One of boxing's most bizarre characters, Siki (he was born Louis Phal in the French West African colony of Senegal) startled Parisians by parading along the fashionable boulevards with a young lion on a leash. Constantly in trouble with the law for his boisterous behaviour, he was banned by the French Boxing Federation for bringing discredit to the sport and he was refused entry to Britain by the Home Office. He had won the world title in a startling upset over the immensely popular Frenchman 'Gorgeous' Georges Carpentier. Despite the terrible stories that preceded his arrival in Dublin, Siki proved highly popular with the Irish, most of whom had never even seen a black person before.

Siki set up training camp at Howth, while the Irish challenger had his quarters just beyond the Phoenix Park at Lucan. Every day the newspapers carried reports of how fit both men were. They rounded off their training with public sessions at the Rotunda Cinema (now the Ambassador) in Parnell Street, each going through his paces on alternate days. Naturally, all Ireland hoped that McTigue would put up a better

Mike McTigue in Dublin in 1923 signing autographs during a break from training

Battling Siki in Dublin in 1923

showing then the last world title challenger, Jem Roche, whose 88-second eclipse 14 years earlier still brought a blush to Irish cheeks. The £2,000 purse for the fight was to be split 75% for the winner and 25% for the loser. The scheduled distance was 20 rounds and the referee was Jack Smith from Manchester.

The fight was not a great spectacle, but as long as McTigue kept his nose in front the home fans were happy. It was a case of Siki's strength and aggression against the Clareman's more polished skills, especially his fine defensive work. The champion always looked the more menacing with his vicious hooks from both hands, but McTigue never gave him a chance to land the haymakers that had destroyed Carpentier. He slipped under Siki's punches, ducked and dodged out of trouble spots and punished the champion with a steady left jab. There was a scare for the Irishman in the fourth round when he caught Siki on the top of the head and broke his right thumb. He had to be sparing with his right hand from then on. Brittle hands had given him trouble in the past. His concern was eased when his cornerman Ted Broadribb told him, 'You can beat this guy with one hand'. Mike foxed his way through until the 11th round, when he suffered further damage. A barrage of punches from a desperate Siki left him with a badly gashed left eyebrow. Things looked bad for McTigue when the referee visited his corner at the end of the round, but Broadribb covered the injury with a towel and convinced the official he could deal with it.

Siki, inspired by his opponent's obvious discomfort and not wanting the fight to go to a points decision, went all-out for summary execution. McTigue managed to ride the storm, although rocked by a right in the 16th round and nearly floored in the last. He had to back-pedal furiously at times to escape the champion's wild lunges, but he never lost his composure, all the time picking up points with his accurate left jab. The referee had no hesitation in raising the Irishman's hand at the end, to the disgust of Siki and his handlers and the wild delight of McTigue and the audience. McTigue dismissed Siki's protests over the decision when he told reporters, 'I was always the master. Let's be honest, Siki didn't hit me with 20 solid punches during the 20 rounds.' Referee Smith said he had no doubt about the winner, who was consistently scoring, even when he was on the retreat. McTigue's was one of the greatest displays of ring generalship he had ever seen.

While Siki continued his downward slide until his body was found in the gutter of the notorious Hell's Kitchen area of New York after being shot, McTigue quietly enjoyed the feeling of being a world champion. On his return to the United States he found no great demand for his services; promoters still regarding him as a dull, careful boxer who didn't bring the crowds flocking to see him in action. Mike's manager, Joe Jacobs, urged him to put more spark into his work but Mike reasoned that as long as he won without getting hurt, he saw no reason to change his style. His first bout as champion was an eight-round 'no decision' affair with Tommy

Loughran. The newspapermen present thought Loughran had the better of it, but in a return match McTigue had the edge. Mike signed for a ten-round 'no decision' contest with Young Stribling in Columbus, Georgia, but was startled to discover it billed as a world title fight, with a decision being rendered if it went the distance. Unable to pull out, the Irishman fought badly and was relieved when referee Harry Ertle declared it a draw, thus ensuring him of retaining his crown. Stribling's supporters threatened a riot and the referee, under duress, anounced that he had made a mistake and that Stribling was the winner. But once he got out of town he telephoned the news agencies and the Georgia newspapers to say that his original verdict stood. It was a draw. Five months later McTigue and Stribling met again, with Stribling proving the better man, but it was a 'no decision' match.

The absence of a points verdict saved McTigue when he was given a sound beating by little Mickey Walker, the reigning world welterweight champion, who frequently made light of his physical disavantages to tackle much bigger men. After the bout, McTigue revealed that he had broken both his hands. He took a four months' rest before putting his world title on the line for the second time. He picked no pushover in Paul Berlenbach, a strong, hard-hitting New Yorker who had won an Olympic Games wrestling title before switching to boxing. Berlenbach had an impressive record of knockout wins and was the bookmakers' favourite to relieve McTigue of his championship. The odds proved justified. He gave the Irishman a relentless hiding over fifteen rounds. Mike gallantly refused to be knocked out, but the decision for Berlenbach was a mere formality. McTigue took the loss of his precious title after a two-year tenure badly. He had very little money to show for his years of ring toil and his efforts to find a job outside boxing, the only 'trade' at which he was qualified, proved fruitless. Disheartened, he began to drink heavily. After a heart-searching talk with his wife he decided to take the family back to Ireland and settle there.

A chance meeting with well-known boxing manager Jimmy Johnston, however, convinced him that his future lay in the United States; and in the ring. Johnson expressed his faith in McTigue if only he changed his style. The Irishman agreed to give it a try. In a ten-rounder with Tiger Flowers he attempted to match his opponent punch for punch, but failed. McTigue managed to stave off his opponent's attempts to floor him, but was as surprised as anyone to find himself declared the winner on points. Stopped in four rounds by Canadian Jack Delaney, McTigue's comeback hopes seemed to be at an end. But he persisted. He astonished the experts who had written him off by beating Johnny Risko, one of the most durable heavyweights around at the time. Maintaining his new, aggressive style, Mike notched up four knockouts before landing his long-awaited return with Paul Berlenbach. The only drawback was that Berlenbach had lost the world title to Jack Delaney by then. McTigue wasn't all that bothered. He just wanted to avenge his title loss to the

German-American.   The knowledgeable fight fraternity didn't share McTigue's optimism.   The Irishman was now 35 years of age and his best fighting days were considered long past.   Mike put up the best performance of his career, notwithstanding his title win over Siki, by smashing Berlenbach to the floor several times and causing the referee's intervention in the fourth round.   The cheers as he left the ring were an unfamiliar sound to a boxer known for his negative performances in the past.

McTigue seemed to have found a new lease of life and his manager lost no time in laying his claim to a crack at the title.   Champion Jack Delaney relinquished the crown to take part in eliminators for the more lucrative world heavyweight championship, vacated by Gene Tunney. McTigue, too, joined the chase for the big prize.   Though giving away 15 pounds in weight and ten years the older man, McTigue was a revelation as he outboxed Jack Sharkey who was to win the heavyweight title on a controversial verdict over Max Schmeling, and even matched Sharkey in exciting punch-for-punch exchanges.   With the crowd loving this all-action McTigue, he seemed set for victory until the disastrous ninth round.   A right swing caught him on the cheek, driving his teeth through the flesh and rupturing a blood vessel.   He swallowed blood so quickly that it almost sickened him.   Nothing could be done to stop the flow and the referee called a halt in the 12th round.   Despite his unlucky defeat, McTigue was now the promoters' pet.   The chance he had been awaiting for so long came in October 1927, a match with Irish-American Tommy Loughran for the vacant world light-heavyweight title in New York. They had already met three times in 'no decision' contests and knew each other's strengths and weaknesses.   It was a meeting of master craftsmen. The real difference was their ages.   Loughran, at 25, had a ten-year advantage.   It proved significant over 15 gruelling rounds.   Even before the referee raised the new champion's arm, McTigue sportingly walked across the ring to congratulate Loughran and acknowledge that he had met his master.

It was downhill all the way for Mike after that.   He was put away in the opening round by Mickey Walker, world middleweight king, a month after losing to Loughran.   He managed a draw with Canadian heavyweight champion Larry Gains in Toronto, but in 1928 he fought seven times and did not win once.   The best he could secure was two draws.   His last fight of the year saw him halted in one round by Tuffey Griffiths, a journeyman fighter.   He fared somewhat better the following year, winning three, boxing one 'no contest' and losing two by the short route.   The boxing authorities withdrew his licence in 1930 after he won only one of his last six contests.   He was now aged 38 and had been an active professional for 21 of those years.

After his retirement Mike ran a successful bar on Long Island, New York, until the late 1940s.   He then succumbed to poverty and ill health. He was confined to various hospitals around New York for the last ten years of his life. Unable to recall anything of his long career in the ring, he finally gave up the fight on 12 August 1966 at the age of 74.

'Baby Face' with a killer punch

No novelist or Hollywood script writer could ever have dreamed up as drama-packed and heart-warming a story as the true-life adventures of Jimmy McLarnin. And far from being the hackneyed yarn of handsome boxer being exploited by greedy manager and then dumped in the gutter when he's no longer useful, McLarnin's relationship with Pop Foster is more that of father and son than manager and fighter. Foster, an English-born, battle-scarred veteran of some 200 fights in fairground booths, taught his young protégé all he knew, expertly guided him to the welterweight championship of the world, then advised him to quit while he still had his good looks and his comfortable retirement assured. The remarkable bond remained intact right up to Pop's death at the age of 83. In his will he left his entire fortune of a quarter of a million dollars to Jimmy McLarnin.

At first glance, McLarnin's record of 77 contests, with 63 wins, three draws and 11 defeats, does not appear to justify his ranking as one of boxing's all-time greats. Nor does his modest 20 inside-the-distance wins seem to support claims that he was an outstanding puncher. But closer scrutiny bears out just how good he really was. No less then 13 of his victims were former, current or future world champions, which serves to underline the exceptionally high quality of those he met. Neither Jimmy nor his manager believed in 'easy touches' and they shrewdly picked matches against boxers they knew would draw in the customers and thus enhance his purse money. Recurring hand trouble, a handicap that afflicts many hard hitters, also helped to reduce McLarnin's knockout average.

Jimmy's birthplace has often been disputed. Most of the boxing record books list Belfast as where he was born, but McLarnin has been quoted as saying he came from Inchicore, in Dublin, where his father worked on the railways. Relatives still living in Belfast are adamant that he was from the Sandy Row area of the Northern Ireland capital. A check with the Registry of Births and Deaths in Dublin, however, reveals the facts. Jimmy was born at Hillsborough, 12 miles from Belfast, on 19 December 1907. He was less then three years old when the family emigrated to Canada to join his father's sister. One of 12 children, Jimmy did his bit to supplement the family income by selling newspapers on a street corner. Often he had to defend his pitch against covetous rivals and that was how he first learned to use his fists.

He joined a boxing club and had his first fateful meeting with Pop Foster, who ran the gym. The veteran tutor saw the boy's natural ability and spent hour after hour teaching him the tricks of the trade. By the time he was 16, McLarnin was considered ready for his first bout. He outpointed George Ainsworth over four rounds. Many years later Jimmy told Pete Heller, author of *In This Corner*, 'For my first fight I got $1 and for my last fight I got $60,000. But between the one and the 60, boy, there was a lot of hard work'.

After serving his apprenticeship in Canadian rings, McLarnin ventured as far as Los Angeles for his first 'name' opponent. Fidel La Barba had just returned from Paris with an Olympic Games gold medal and had turned professional. The young flyweights buzzed around and stung each other for four lively rounds, with McLarnin getting the referee's nod. A return was inevitable and this time it ended in a draw. A third clash was arranged, this time over ten rounds, and La Barba had to reluctantly admit he had met his master. Now a popular performer for the movie set which patronised Los Angeles fight cards, the Irishman notched up several more impressive wins before Pop Foster made his first mistake. He let Jimmy into the ring with rugged Bud Taylor, a vicious body puncher who had considerably more experience and was to go on to win the world bantamweight title. Taylor inflicted on McLarnin his first defeat in 32 outings. Jimmy stuck it out for the full ten rounds, but his reddened ribs bore testimony to the constant bombardment of Taylor's fists.

His manager was sufficiently confident of Jimmy's ability to match him with the current world flyweight champion, Pancho Villa, in a non-title ten-rounder. McLarnin didn't let him down. He scored a decisive points win over the Filipino, who had beaten the legendary Welshman Jimmy Wilde for the title two years earlier. But the fight had a tragic aftermath. Villa had entered the ring against McLarnin with badly infected gums following the removal of a wisdom tooth. He contracted blood poisoning and died ten days after the fight.

Another man destined for world title honours, Jackie Fields, was pitted against McLarnin. The Irishman revealed hitherto unsuspected hitting power by breaking his rival's jaw while knocking him out in the second round. The win marked the opening of a remarkable series of successes against Jewish boxers, so much so that he became known as 'the Scourge of Jewry'. Great Jewish fighters like Sid Terris, Louis 'Kid' Kaplan, Al Singer, Joe Glick, Ruby Goldstein (later a top referee) and Benny Leonard all fell before him. Only Barney Ross, in two of their three meetings, managed to reverse the pattern. No one could blame Pop Foster for exploiting the situation. It was a profitable success for all concerned. The Irish-Americans came to see McLarnin win and the Jewish fans to see him beaten. No lasting bitterness was engendered between the rival factions and the promoters certainly didn't complain.

McLarnin was promised a world title bout with lightweight champion Sammy Mandell if he could dispose of the leading contender, Sid Terris. The Irishman didn't let the chance go by. A wicked right crashed against Terris' jaw after one minute, 47 seconds of the first round and he was out to the world. Champion Mandell was as good as his word and gave Jimmy a crack at the world title in May 1928. The problem was that McLarnin had grown into a welterweight. Rather than pass up the chance, however, he sweated off the necessary pounds to make the weight limit. But it left him considerably weakened and he was well beaten over 15 rounds.

From then on McLarnin wisely concentrated on the welterweight division. After a couple of quick wins, he suffered the only inside-the-distance loss of his career against Ray Miller. Miller, a vicious left-hooker, sliced open Jimmy's eye and stopped him in the eighth round. McLarnin later got his revenge by outscoring Miller and also wiped out another defeat by beating Sammy Mandell in a non-title bout. Exciting short-route victories over Ruby Goldstein and world lightweight champion Al Singer, plus points wins over Sammy Mandell (again) and Young Jack Thompson had Jimmy among the leading contenders for the world welterweight crown. But there was one major obstacle: Billy Petrolle. Nicknamed 'the Fargo Express', Petrolle was one of those talented ringmen who were probably too good to entice world champions to share a ring with them. Petrolle never got a chance at the title, even though he was handled by one of boxing's shrewdest managers, Jack Hurley. Petrolle and his mentor devised a plan to beat McLarnin. He would come 'inside' McLarnin's powerful right with his own left hook. The scheme worked to perfection. All the Irishmen showed that night was his great heart. Nat Fleischer, in his book *Fifty Years at the Ringside*, wrote:

McLarnin displayed fighting courage that many thought beyond reason. I recall the smashed, bloody figure of Jimmy, reeling under the terrific impact of Petrolle's merciless wallops; yet as he stood in the ring, bathed in his own gore, hardly strong enough to keep his hands up in defence, he wouldn't give in. Referee Patsy Hagate moved over to Jimmy and begged him to quit. 'No, no, please don't stop it. Don't ask me to quit,' he pleaded. Weak, but still defiant, he staggered through to the finish of the tenth round.

So endowed with raw courage was McLarnin that, after a six months' break, he was back in the ring again to face Petrolle. And this time the Irishman was the victor after ten rounds. Good fighters learn from setbacks and McLarnin emphasised how good a pupil he was by again beating Petrolle in a third meeting. After that series of hard battles Jimmy took a well-earned rest for a year. But his lay-off affected his timing in a ten-rounder with Lou Brouillard, an awkward southpaw who had won and lost the world welterweight title and was on his way to collecting the New York version of the middleweight title. Brouillard won on points. A six-round stoppage of the once great Benny Leonard, now 36 and attempting a comeback, re-established McLarnin as a top attraction and, on 29 May 1933, he got his long-awaited chance to lift the world welterweight championship.

The champion, Young Corbett the Third (born Ralph Capabianca Giordano in Naples, Italy) was a southpaw and the experts always reckoned that the best way to beat a right-hand-forward boxer was to catch him with a right hand. There was no better right-hand puncher around than Jimmy McLarnin. It took him less than three minutes to put Corbett down for the full count. Pop Foster embraced his new champion and together they shed tears of joy at the realisation of a dream that had begun so many years before.

Jimmy rested on his laurels, enjoying the fruits of being champion of the world for a full year, less a day, before accepting the challenge of Barney Ross, a Jewish boy from Chicago who was the reigning world lightweight champion and had designs on the welterweight prize. Jimmy and Pop had agreed that, if he beat Ross, the champion would retire from boxing. He had looked after his earnings wisely, with Pop's help, and there were no worries about his future. But Ross forced them to shelve their plans. A brilliant boxer, he edged out McLarnin to take a split decision after 15 evenly contested rounds. Immediate arrangements were made for a return encounter, and this time a razor-sharp McLarnin walked out of the arena as world champion again. As in the first meeting, it had proved a fascinating duel of skilful moves and exciting punch exchanges between two of the great welterweights. Again the decision was the subject of much argument and there was an obvious need for a 'decider'.

An eager crowd of 26,599 paid $140,480 to witness the third meeting between McLarnin and Ross at the Polo Grounds, New York, on 28 May 1935. Former world heavyweight champ Jack Dempsey was appointed as referee, which didn't please Pop Foster. But once they were inside the ring Pop shook hands with Dempsey and assured him of his trust. Ross was first in the ring, wearing a striped dressing gown of Turkish towelling. Seconds later came McLarnin in his familiar green satin robe with the Harp of Erin emblazoned on the back. Jimmy, usually a fast starter, began quietly. Ross peppered him with swift jabs and caught him with snappy left hooks. The challenger won the first three rounds and McLarnin's left eye was swollen from the steady attention of Barney's jabs. McLarnin split Ross' nose with a long left and gained the upper hand for a spell. As in each of their previous meetings it was nip and tuck all the way, with no quarter asked or given. McLarnin, though cut over the right eye in the 11th round, rocked the challenger with smashing right hooks as he strove for a knockout. The audience loved the action, passing comment on the clever manoeuvring for position, the nimble footwork and the superb craftsmanship of both men. It was so close going into the 15th round that most people thought this last round would decide it. McLarnin appeared to shade the final three minutes and to have done enough to retain his crown. But the judges thought differently: Abe Goldstein marked it eight rounds for Ross, six for McLarnin and one even. George Le Cron gave it to Ross nine-four-two. Referee Jack Dempsey had seven rounds even, but gave Ross five of the remaining rounds and McLarnin three. So it was unanimous. Ross was welterweight champion of the world for the second time; and McLarnin was back in the number one contender spot.

Jimmy was so annoyed at what he felt was raw justice that he wanted to quit right away, but Foster convinced him he should go for one more big pay-day. He ended up having three more big pay-days. There were no more title fights, but each was against a reigning world champion. Tony Canzoneri, the lightweight title-holder, was the Irishman's first opponent in his farewell year of 1936. It was constantly argued that Foster protected his charge by matching him against smaller, lighter men. But they were quality opponents, every one of them, as was proved when Canzoneri, after a shaky first round, recovered to outpoint McLarnin over ten rounds. Canzoneri lost his title to Lou Ambers in his next fight and then agreed to meet McLarnin in a return. True to form the Irishman showed he had learned from his defeat and won convincingly on points. For his last contest McLarnin faced the new lightweight champion Lou Ambers. Jimmy employed all the skill and experience at his command to hand out a boxing lesson to Ambers. It was a good note to bow out on.

Still only 29, McLarnin took his family back to live on the Pacific coast, with more than half a million dollars saved from his ring exploits. He opened a machine shop in Los Angeles and during World War II it grew into a highly profitable concern. After the war he sold out for a handsome figure and invested the profits. Always a dapper dresser, he enjoyed playing golf in celebrity tournaments such as the one with his friend Bing Crosby. Life was comfortable for Jimmy, his wife Lillian and their son, Jimmy junior, and three daughters. For many years he ran a successful tool-and-dye business, operated a travel agency in Hollywood and, in 1970, formed McLarnin Sales to represent firms. Now aged 80, Jimmy enjoys the comforts of his luxurious home in Glendale, California, and stays in trim by playing golf and taking brisk walks.

Assessing McLarnin's status among the best Irish boxers is difficult, as any man's ranking comes down largely to a matter of opinion. But there is ample evidence to put him way up there with the pick of the bunch. Barney Ross, once asked how he thought McLarnin would have fared against Sugar Ray Robinson, many experts' choice as the greatest welterweight of them all, said that 'McLarnin would have knocked him out. Robinson carried his left hand too low. I know he was fast enough to do that and still beat an opponent to the punch, but no fighter who ever lived could do that against McLarnin's right hand.'

Jimmy McLarnin (right) and Tony Canzoneri

Sophia Loren, Marlon Brando, 'Butty' Sugrue and Jack Doyle

Five

The Great Pretenders

WHENEVER THERE IS a discussion among Irish fight fans on the merits of the country's outstanding ringmen, there is bound to be one who will curtly dismiss the McLarnins, the McTigues, the McAuliffes, the Sharkeys, the Monaghans and the McGuigans and insist that not one of them could match Jack Doyle. When the howls of derision have died down, the Doyle supporter will qualify his remark by stating that what he meant was that Doyle could have been the greatest of them all, if only...

In those last two words rest the case for Jack Doyle. He was certainly a gifted boxer with a dynamite right hand, but he lacked totally the dedication and self-discipline which are a vital part of the make-up of any aspiring champion. As in all walks of life, having the talent is less than half the battle. Unless one is prepared to back it up with hard work and the will to overcome setbacks and obstacles, success will remain just a dream. Old film newsreels bear out the claims of the Doyle backers that he had the potential to go all the way to the top. They also reveal his greatest flaw: an inability to absorb a solid whack on the chin. His record tells the whole story. Of his total of 23 professional contests, only one went the full distance, when Doyle surprised everyone by jabbing the head off American King Levinsky for a decisive points win. Most of his 16 knockout wins were scored in the first few rounds. Just as significantly, three of his six losses were on first round knockouts and another was in the second round. His two remaining defeats were on disqualifications.

It was the possibility that anything might happen when Doyle climbed between the ropes that brought the crowds flocking to his fights and made him one of the biggest earners of his time. His outside-the-ring exploits as a singer, actor, womaniser and international playboy served to add to his charisma. The gods certainly dealt him all the natural attractions any man could ask for. A magnificently proportioned 6' 4" and weighing 15 stone (217lbs), he was strikingly handsome and had a plentiful supply of what the Americans call 'Irish blarney'. He also had a fine tenor voice, which enabled him to pick up ready cash when the boxing ring lost its appeal for him, which was frequently. During the height of his fame in the 1930s and 40s he picked up nicknames such as 'The Gorgeous Gael', 'The Singing Thrush', 'The Fighting Nightingale' and 'The Pugilistic Playboy of the Western World'. There were other, less complimentary, names. He earned an estimated quarter of a million pounds in his heyday: and spent it as quickly as he got it. Right up to the time he died, aged 65, alone if not completely forgotten, in a dingy basement flat at Notting Hill Gate, London, he maintained he had no regrets about the way he had lived. Perhaps he meant it. How many men wouldn't give up a life of dull security for just a taste of the devil-may-care lifestyle Doyle enjoyed?

There were none of the trappings of easy living when Joseph Alphonsus Doyle was born, one of six children of a hard-working quarryman, at Queenstown (now Cobh), County Cork, on 31 August 1913. Already a strapping six-footer at 16, Jack lied about his age and joined the Irish Guards (the minimum recruiting age was 18). Entered for his battalion's boxing championships against his wishes, he proceeded to dispatch each of his three opponents in one round apiece to win the cup. Bitten by the boxing bug, he hung around the gymnasium above the Star and Garter pub in Windsor while off duty and pestered the British middleweight champion Len Harvey to spar with him. When he did consent to the sparring session Harvey was so impressed with the youngster that he advised his manager, Dan Sullivan, to buy Doyle out of the army and launch him on a professional career. Jack first insisted on competing in the Brigade of Guards championships, which he won in a series of quick knockouts. He turned to the paid ranks with a fine amateur record of 28 wins and no defeats. Garda Gerry Mulligan, twice Irish heavyweight champion, was the only man to last the distance with the hard-hitting teenager as an amateur.

Doyle's professional debut at the Crystal Palace in April 1932 set the pattern for many of his subsequent bouts. In trouble in the opening seconds, he recovered to flatten Chris Goulding in the first round. His mighty right accounted for six more jig-time victims before he got his first real test. The match with big Jack Pettifer was a natural box-office winner. Pettifer, a giant of 6' 6" and 17½ stone (245lbs) was, like Doyle, unbeaten as a professional. More than half his 15 wins had been inside schedule. Some 12,000 fans packed the glass-domed Crystal Palace to see less than two rounds of action; but what action it was!

Doyle, showing scant respect for the towering Pettifer, sailed straight in and planted a huge right on his jaw. Though badly shaken, Pettifer hit back with his own right and it was the Irishman's turn to go wobbly at the knees. Instead of following up his advantage, Pettifer allowed Doyle to recover. Doyle came surging back in and the crowd was treated to a rare exhibition of wild slugging, with each man hurt in turn. The bell for the second round saw the Irishman charge forward and send Pettifer reeling into the ropes with a right swing. There he hung, helpless, while Doyle pounded punches at his body. Pettifer slid slowly to the canvas and lay dangling over the bottom rope. The noise of the crowd was so great that the referee couldn't hear the timekeeper's count. By the time Pettifer heard the seconds being tolled over him it was too late. He rose just as the referee got to ten.

Doyle's sensational win put him to the forefront of challengers for Jack Petersen's British heavyweight title. But he was still only 19 and the public adulation showered on his handsome head proved very hard to handle for a lad who enjoyed life as he did. He was invited to dine in London's most fashionable restaurants and there was hardly a big party that didn't have Jack Doyle's name on the guest list. Nevertheless he trained diligently for the big chance of his boxing life, his attempt to take the British title. Promoter Jeff Dickson couldn't go wrong with this one. Every one of the 70,000 seats was sold out at the open-air White City Stadium in London on 12 July 1933. Champion Petersen had won all his 23 contests, 13 inside the distance, while Doyle had disposed of each of his ten opponents inside two rounds. Someone's record was about to fall, and it turned out to be the Irishman's. Had he kept a cool head, Jack might well have become British heavyweight champion that night. His aggressive style had knocked the stylish Welshman out of his stride and a right swing near the end of the first round had Petersen in real trouble. But Doyle was so intent on winning quickly that he threw away his chance with wild punching. A left hook that sunk well below the champion's waistline early in the second round earned Doyle a caution from the referee, C.H. 'Pickles' Douglas. As Petersen stung him with punches to the head, Doyle incurred another warning, this time for holding. Several more times he struck Petersen low and, finally, the exasperated referee sent him to his corner.

His disqualification not only cost Doyle his great chance of winning the British title, but earned him a fine of £2,740 out of his £3,000 purse. He was also suspended for six months by the British Boxing Board of Control. He took the board to court and won but, on appeal, the original fine and suspension stood. In later years Jack admitted that he lost all real interest in boxing after what he termed that injustice. He fought only once in 1934, scoring a first round knockout over Frank Borrington, but found he could pick up £200 a week singing on the stage without risking his good looks. He celebrated his 21st birthday with a party in a Dublin hotel for hundreds of guests who got through a hundred gallons of champagne.

Hollywood beckoned and Jack made a couple of forgettable films, married starlet Judith Allen in a Mexican registry office, and prepared to make his American ring debut. The boxing ballyhoo merchants had a field-day as Doyle flattened Phil Donato in one round and followed up with knockouts over Jack Redmond and Bob Morton. He was then pitched in against Buddy Baer, the 6' 6" younger brother of former world heavyweight champion Max Baer, at Madison Square Garden, New York. It was another one-round sensation, only this time it was the Irishman who finished stretched out on the canvas. Doyle had blown a kiss to Judith at the ringside and turned around to see the massive American bearing down on him. A right caught Doyle low, but before he could complain to the referee a further right to the jaw dropped him. He rose unsteadily at three and was promptly put down again for five. He again struggled to his feet but the referee mercifully called a halt after two minutes and 38 seconds. It was the end of Jack Doyle as a would-be world title contender. He had entered the United States bearing the publicity legend 'He can box like Dempsey and sing like John McCormack'. After his brief outing against Baer, the critics said the ballyhoo boys had got it wrong. He sang like Dempsey and boxed like McCormack!

Jack forgot his troubles by returning to England and finding comfort in the welcoming arms of Delphine Dodge-Godde, heiress to the motor-car millions. A proposed fight with Tommy Farr fell through and Doyle returned to America: and more trouble. Judith served a lawsuit on Mrs Dodge-Godde 'for alienation of my husband's affections' and, at the same time, asked Jack for a divorce. The marriage had lasted four years. Meanwhile, Mrs Dodge-Godde's father offered Doyle $50,000, plus a monthly payment of £100 for the rest of his life, if he would leave his daughter alone. Jack accepted. Free of his romantic entanglements, he announced his intention of picking up his boxing career. He was still only 26 and could make the grade, he reasoned.

His London comeback proved another fiasco. He had Alf Robinson down inside the opening minute but was so anxious to finish matters that he hit Robinson while he was down and was disqualified. Undaunted, he stopped Dutchman Harry Staal in six rounds and then came that strange points victory over King Levinsky. Jack attributed his 'new' style to an injury to his right hand, necessitating his reliance on his left, but there was a persistent rumour that one of his rich supporters had promised him £1 for every left he landed on the American's face, which would have netted him a handy little bonus over the 12 rounds. On paper, at least, it was a win of some merit for the Irishman, as Levinsky had beaten four one-time world champions, Tommy Loughran, Jimmy Slattery, Jack Sharkey and Primo Carnera.

Inspired to try his luck again in the United States, 'the Gorgeous Gael' got involved in an argument at a party with the fiery Mexican actress Movita and ended up marrying her in a civil ceremony three days later. It was a stormy liaison from the word go. Mr and Mrs Doyle teamed up for a variety tour of the US, Britain and Ireland. Their theme song was 'South of the Border' and their duet always brought the house down

Jack Doyle

wherever they appeared. The more puritanical Irish did not take quite so readily to the couple. They were booed and jeered when they took the stage at Dublin's Olympia Theatre, but by the end of their performance the abuse had turned to cheers. As if to cement their acceptance by the Irish, they decided to get married in a Catholic ceremony at St Andrew's Church in Westland Row, an occasion that bought Dublin city centre traffic to a stand still. But all was not bliss in the Doyle household. Their stage earnings were not enough to sustain their high lifestyle and the tension led to rows. Jack candidly admitted that his tiny 'Mexican spitfire' gave him more punishment than most of his heavyweight opponents.

At times of financial trouble, Doyle always turned back to boxing. His name was still a crowd-puller, even if those who paid for tickets often regretted their rashness. For instance, there was the time he fought Eddie Phillips: and knocked himself out! Doyle rushed the former British light-heavyweight champion to the ropes in the second round, missed with a lunging right and sailed through the ropes onto the floor of the arena. By the time he scrambled back into the ring he was counted out. He complained that Phillips' manager had stood on his foot to stop him getting back in time.

Ten months later he was back in action, and again faced Eddie Phillips. An indication of the Irishman's faith in his own drawing power was his gamble on taking a percentage of the 'gate'. He earned £40,000, whereas the top-of-the-bill contestants for the British light-heavyweight title, Len Harvey and Jock McAvoy, lost out by accepting fixed payments. Doyle's wages for his night's work were especially outrageous when he confined his 'activity' to 144 seconds. That was how long it took Phillips to find Doyle's vulnerable chin with a right. Peter Wilson, the famed Fleet Street journalist, described the scene graphically in his book *Ringside Seat:*

No doubt you've seen those rather outmoded comic drawings in which a man falls backwards, stiff as a plank, with a dotted line indicating his collapse. I can't describe Doyle's transformation from the perpendicular to the horizontal better than that. What's more, his early Guards training reasserted itself in this crisis, for he lay rigidly to attention while he was being counted out!

His double disaster against Phillips finished Doyle as a box office attraction in Britain. The crowds, or the promoters, were no longer prepared to put up with his unpredictability. The Irish were more forgiving. Now 30 and with more than a suspicion of a 'spare tyre' around his middle, Doyle topped the bill at Dalymount Park, Dublin, in June 1943 against Chris Cole from Mullingar. All approach roads to the ground were jammed as 16,000 fans made their way to the scene of Jack's latest comeback. The big Corkman repaid their warm reception with a smile and a wave as he walked across the turf to the ring. His cheerfulness didn't last long. He was hanging helplessly on the ropes taking a fierce pounding from Cole, who was little more than a light-heavyweight, when referee Harry Hanley stopped the slaughter after two minutes and 35 seconds. There was just one more bout for Doyle, but at least he made it a winning farewell. Cork's Butcher Howell was his third round victim at Tolka Park, Dublin. Despite regular talk of further comebacks, with Jack pouring scorn on the current crop of heavyweights, his only subsequent ring appearances were as an all-in wrestler.

Gone forever were the champagne parties, the luxury hotels and limousines, the array of Savile Row suits. Gone, too, was Movita. After seven stormy years of marriage she walked out on him in 1945. He didn't hear from her again for ten years until, out of the blue, she wrote saying she wanted a divorce to marry actor Marlon Brando. Doyle replied that there could be no divorce as they had married in a Catholic church. That was the end of it, as far as he was concerned. Not even a personal visit by Brando could change his mind. But he did hear later that Movita and Brando had married and later divorced.

In his later years life had more downs than ups for the one-time playboy. He divided his days mostly between the local public house near his London flat and the bookies, buying drinks for his cronies when he had the cash, accepting their charity when he hadn't. He hit rock bottom in 1966 when he was fined £5 for stealing a packet of cheese from a supermarket. He could still earn a few pounds singing in pub cabarets or telling his story, generously embellished, to newspapers. After his death on 13 December 1978 his body was taken home to Cobh for burial. Over a thousand people attended his funeral and a wreath in the shape of a boxing glove was laid on his grave by the Cork ex-boxers' association.

Uncrowned champion of the world

Belfast has produced many a great fighting man in the lower weight divisions, but none was as unrewarded for his talents as Jimmy Warnock. He twice beat the great Benny Lynch when the hard-hitting Scot was world flyweight champion, but on neither occasion was Lynch's title at stake. When he took part in a final eliminator to decide Lynch's opponent in a title fight, Warnock was so weakened making the weight limit that he was stopped in four rounds by Peter Kane. He never even got a crack at the British title. In fact, the only honour the Belfast southpaw had to show for 17 years' hard scrapping was a *Boxing News* Certificate of Merit for knocking out the Japanese Katsumi Morioka in Belfast in 1937.

Jimmy was one of four brothers, all of whom boxed as professionals. One of his brothers, Billy, also fought Benny Lynch in a non-title fight and was knocked out in 11 rounds. A more remarkable feat was that claimed by Belfastman Jackie Quinn, who fought all four Warnocks between 1929 and 1935. Quinn outpointed Johnny and Billy, drew with Freddie, and won and lost on points against Jimmy.

A real 'home bird' (only eight of his 84 fights took place outside Belfast) Jimmy's loyal supporters saved the day for him when he appeared in the first boxing tournament at the newly built King's Hall in 1935. Warnock was knocked down and in danger of being counted out in his contest with former French champion Maurice Huguenin when the lights suddenly went out. Someone had pulled the master switch. When the lights came on Warnock was sitting on his stool, fully recovered. He went on to win on points.

A second-round knockout of Tommy Pardoe, who had lasted 14 rounds with Benny Lynch, put him in line for a try at Lynch's world and British flyweight titles. Lynch was agreeable to meeting Warnock in Belfast for a generous purse of £300, but he insisted that the match be made a couple of pounds over the flyweight limit to protect his title. Lynch, beaten only once in 52 previous outings, was hot favourite, but the Northern Irishman refused to be overawed by his reputation and frequently beat the Scot to the punch with stinging right jabs and left crosses. At close quarters Lynch's heavy digs were effective, so Warnock elected to keep the exchanges at long range. His nifty footwork and sniping jabs frustrated Lynch's best efforts to get close enough to unload his heavy artillery. As the rounds sped by, Warnock forged further ahead and the world champion became more and more desperate. A couple of cracking body blows caused Jimmy some distress in the 11th round, but he managed to steer away from further trouble. When Lynch came out of his corner for the 12th and last round he knew he had to score a knockout to win. To his surprise, and the crowd's delight, Warnock met him half-way and the fight ended to a crescendo of cheers. Lynch, anticipating the referee's verdict, beat him to it by sportingly lifting Warnock's hand.

While awaiting his deserved return with Lynch for the world title, Warnock kept busy. In fourteen outings, he slipped up only once, losing on points to Pat Palmer in London. Finally came news of a second meeting with Lynch, but this time he would have to travel to the world champion's home town of Glasgow for the fight. Promoter George Dingley made the match for 2 June 1937 over the championship regulation distance of 15 rounds. But fate still frowned on the Irishman. The British Boxing Board of Control refused to sanction it as a title fight. The board insisted that Warnock must meet the winner of an eliminator between Peter Kane and Phil Milligan, who had outpointed Warnock two years earlier, before he could challenge for the British and world titles. Lynch and Warnock both stated their willingness to waive the customary six months' grace allowed after a title fight and meet the Kane v Milligan winner, but the board stayed adamant. Lynch and Warnock could fight as planned, but the Scot's titles would not be at stake. It was especially heartbreaking for Warnock as he had undergone a course of special training at Bangor, in County Down, and declared himself 100% fit and confident of proving himself the best flyweight in the world.

Jimmy Warnock

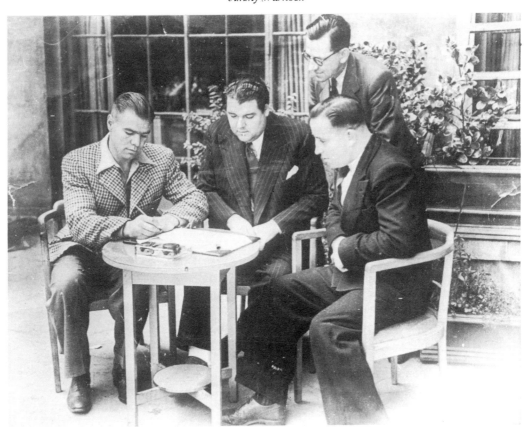

Jimmy Ingle (left) signs the contract for a fight with Spike McCormack under the

watchful eyes of Gerald Egan, the promoter, and Watty Meehan (standing),

McCormack's manager.

Parkhead, the headquarters of Glasgow Celtic football club, was the venue for the fight. Threatening rain and unseasonal cold kept the attendance down to a disappointing 16,000. The contest was arranged at 8st 4lbs (116lbs) to avoid its being labelled as a world title fight, but Lynch caused a surprise by weighing-in at 8st 6bs (118lbs). He had to agree to pay £150 forfeit to his opponent, but this did not satisfy the Irish party and the promoter had to increase Warnock's purse by £200. Warnock's case for extra cash was beyond reproach. Conceding six pounds to an opponent is a major disadvantage to a flyweight, particularly when the man he was opposing was champion of the world.

With the rain pelting down, Lynch tried his best to get it over with quickly. A vicious left hook and a right cross caught the Irishman cold and sent him tumbling half-through the ropes. Warnock bobbed and weaved and back-pedalled desperately to avoid his would-be avenger until the bell brought relief. Jimmy settled down in the second round to spear the champion with long rights and occasional lefts. Lynch bided his time, waiting for an opportunity to repeat his opening barrage. It came in the fifth round. Warnock had been piling up points with his hit-and-run tactics, but he got a little careless and left himself open to a fast combination of lefts and rights. Knocked off his feet, the Belfastman was up before the referee could start counting and delighted his fans by mixing it with the aggressive Scot. Warnock was in trouble again in the eighth round from a body bombardment. Only his pluck and his nimble footwork earned his survival. Jimmy's stylish boxing won him the next five rounds in a row. What was more, by the 12th round it was clear that Warnock no longer had to fight a retreating campaign, but was actually the stronger of the pair. Lynch's heavy drinking habit and generally careless attitude to training was taking its toll. Realising he was behind, the Scot made a desperate effort in the 14th round. Employing a favourite trick, he backed off, lay against the ropes and then bounced back with a terrific right to Warnock's jaw. To his dismay, Lynch saw the Irishman shrug it off and come right back at him. As the world champion tried with all his might to land a pay-off punch, Warnock ducked and swayed to make him miss. *Boxing News* takes up the story for the 15th round:

> Spectators gripped their seats as the lads came together for the last. A rare punching mill had them on their feet. Lynch went out to storm his way to a snatch victory. Warnock, as game as a pebble, met him half-way. Left after left they planted on each other's chin. Neither would yield an inch.

There was a tense hush as referee Arthur Myers, the sole arbiter, totted up his scorecard. He then walked to Warnock's corner to raise the Irishman's hand. Lynch looked dumbfounded and his supporters booed loudly, while the Irish fans whooped with joy. Now, surely, Jimmy had earned the right to a chance at Lynch's world crown, having beaten him twice. The ruling body disagreed. He must first meet Peter Kane who had won his eliminator against Phil Milligan, to decide who should go forward to challenge Lynch for his world and British flyweight titles. Kane, winner of all his 40 professional fights to date, with only eight opponents lasting the distance, would obviously be a formidable opponent for the Belfastman, but Warnock was fully confident of earning the belated right to a title bout. Nevertheless, he turned down Kane's offer to make it a winner-take-all encounter. Both men were guaranteed £1,000, a record purse for a non-title fight in Britain at the time, and 40,000 fans flocked to Anfield, the home of Liverpool football club, for the eagerly awaited showdown in August 1937. Warnock had a pre-match fright when a cut eye suffered in training threatened a postponement, but a doctor told him it wasn't bad enough to put off the bout. More worrying for Jimmy was the weight he had to work off in several days to make the limit of eight stone. The effort left him weak.

Warnock took the worst beating of his long career from the Lancashire blacksmith. One of the hardest punching flyweights in history, Kane ripped through the Irishman's usually sound defence with his punches and Warnock was dropped for eight in the opening round. He was down three times for lengthy counts in the third. In the fourth round, a powerful right sent Warnock down for the fifth time. He struggled gamely aloft, only to meet a merciless Kane, who knocked him down again. He was in the act of rising when the referee ended the slaughter. When Lynch failed to make the flyweight limit for a title fight with American Jackie Jurich and forfeited his crown, Kane became world champion by outpointing Jurich.

Amazingly, Warnock carried on boxing for another eleven years after his conclusive defeat by Kane. Never again did he get within range of a title fight. Indeed he made only one more excursion out of Belfast, to Scotland in 1938, when Johnny McManus knocked him out in three rounds. On the home front, Jimmy still reigned supreme, with only two cut eye defeats to mar his clean scorecard up to the outbreak of World War II, when he joined the Royal Ulster Rifles. He was discharged after four years with ear trouble. When regular boxing resumed in Belfast in 1945, Warnock took up the threads of his career but his best days were clearly behind him. He carried on until 1948 when, aged 35 and after reducing his weight by nearly two stones, he was easily beaten in four rounds by Jackie Briers in an eliminator for the Northern Ireland flyweight title. When his betting business failed, he went to work on the roads with Belfast Corporation. The cheery workman always had a wave and a smile for his townsfolk who knew him as the 'uncrowned champion of the world'.

Boxing boom in the Irish Free State

The period of 'The Emergency', as World War II was quaintly termed by the government of the Irish Free State, proved a boom time for professional boxing in the 26 counties that remained neutral during the global conflict. Not so happy with the exodus to the moneyed game was the Irish Amateur Boxing Association, which looked on helplessly as many of its top stars were tempted by professional managers and promoters. Dire warnings by the amateur body of exploitation and the dangers of long, tough battles to boxers' health failed to stem the flow to professionalism. Money was not the only reason for the best amateurs making the switch, although it was obviously the prime motivator. Because of the war, all international amateur competition was suspended, which included the Olympic Games and the European championships. There was very little attraction in merely competing in club tournaments and trying for the national senior titles once a year. Free travel abroad has always been one of the main perks for amateur internationals and this avenue had now been cut off. It also made common sense to cash in on whatever talents one had. Former European amateur flyweight champion Jimmy Ingle was given £100 to join the professional ranks in 1942, plus a guarantee of four contests at £25 a time. That was more than he could earn in 18 months at the Dublin sawmill where he worked.

The 40s were especially prolific in coming up with talented Irish middleweights. Cork had Pat O'Connor and Pat Mulcahy, each of whom also ventured into the light-heavyweight class, plus Paddy Roche. Galway offered Freddie Price, who had boxed as an amateur under his real name of Frank Parsons, and Kildare had Frank Hayes. Dublin, as well as having Jimmy Ingle, prided itself on two other exciting middleweights in Bert Hyland and Spike McCormack. All of these ringmen performed with credit in England during and after the war, with the sole exception of McCormack. He was prevented from appearing in Britain or Northern Ireland because he had come home on leave from the British Army and forgotten to go back! Spike was a product of Dublin's famous 'street of champions', Gardiner Street, which claimed some of the great names of Irish boxing during the 30s and 40s among its residents; men like Peter Glennon, Paddy Hughes, 'Blackman' Doyle and Willie 'Blinky' Gifford. Lauded by promoter Gerald Egan as the best fighter he featured on any of his bills, McCormack got plenty of work on the Dublin shows so as not to worry unduly about his travel restrictions. Not surprisingly, the same boxers were inclined to crop up in opposition to each other quite frequently. McCormack met Ingle four times, winning twice, drawing once and losing the last encounter. Spike retired in 1948 as undefeated Irish middleweight champion and he was a proud man during the 60s when two of his sons, John and Pat, won British titles.

The most naturally gifted of the home-based middleweights was Jimmy Ingle, one of nine boxing brothers from Ringsend, Dublin. Winner of the European amateur flyweight title at the tender age of 17, on a memorable night that saw Paddy Dowdall also take the featherweight title at a rapturous National Stadium in 1939, Ingle had blossomed into a welterweight by the time he turned professional and later moved up another division. Undoubtedly the highlight of his paid career was the draw he fought with Ernie Roderick, the British welter and middleweight champion, at Dublin's Theatre Royal in 1946. Big-time London promoter Jack Solomons topped the bill with a non-title match between world flyweight champion Jackie Paterson, from Scotland, and Bunty Doran, from Belfast. Ingle was ahead by the half-way stage until an old eye scar re-opened. Roderick made up much of the leeway as the Dubliner struggled under his handicap, but a grandstand finish by Ingle seemed to be enough to merit the points verdict. The crowd reacted angrily to the referee's drawn decision.

Ingle travelled to Jersey to take on Vince Hawkins, who had beaten Roderick for the British title, and lost narrowly on points. Three other British title-holders who proved too good for the Irishman were Albert Finch (twice), Randolph Turpin and Alex Buxton. Ingle retired after his first-round defeat by Buxton in 1950 and now lives in Luton, Bedfordshire.

A great rival for the affections of Dublin fight fans during the 40s and early 50s was red-haired Bert Hyland, who never failed to give the customers value for money. Although he was considered a lucky points winner over Ingle in their Irish middleweight title eliminator at Dalymount Park, Dublin, in 1949, Hyland did achieve something Ingle never did; he beat a British champion. Indeed, he defeated two of them. Ernie Roderick was outscored in a London eight-rounder and Albert Finch, who had beaten Bert in their first two encounters, lost a close decision in a rousing battle, also in London. Another outstanding Hyland performance was his first-round knockout of classy Jimmy Davis, who had earlier outpointed him. But Bert came a cropper when he met young Randolph Turpin in 1947. The brilliant Turpin, having only his seventh professional bout, swept through the Dubliner's guard with his sledge-hammer punches to score a first round knockout. Hyland's only consolation was that he wasn't Turpin's quickest Irish victim. Freddie Price received that unwanted distinction. He was floored five times before being counted out after exactly 60 seconds. Turpin, who beat the great Sugar Ray Robinson for the world middleweight title in one of boxing's greatest upsets, renewed acquaintances with Hyland in 1952, when Turpin boxed an exhibition at Tolka Park, Dublin. Hyland, now boxing as a light-heavyweight, lost on points to Wally Beckett on the same bill.

If the middleweights supplied most of the real talent in Ireland during the 40s, it was the heavyweights who caught most of the headlines, often for the worst reasons. Flamboyant Gerald Egan was the main boxing promoter of the period and his shows usually reflected his larger-than-life personality. Egan always had a keen eye for a publicity angle and was not shy about advertising a forthcoming match as 'the Fight of the Century', even if the participants hardly matched up to the billing and invariably provided a major let-down for gullible ticket-buyers. An example of Egan's taste for the bizarre was his promotion of the genial giant from Tipperary, Jimmy Cully. Billed as 'Ireland's Carnera', Cully was the tallest man in Ireland at 7' 2" and weighed 18 stone, but he was never a serious boxer. It was his freakish size that brought him into the business as a kind of curiosity. A couple of useful-looking knockout wins over Corkman Butcher Howell and Belfast's Joe O' Neill led to a match with Chris Cole in Dublin in 1942 for the vacant Irish heavyweight title. One of boxing's oldest and truest axioms is 'the bigger they are, the harder they fall'. It proved especially apt as Cole, dwarfed by over a foot and outweighed by four stone, chopped the giant down like a lumberjack axing a tall pine. It was all over inside two rounds. Cully later tried his luck in the United States, where there was an equal demand for boxing oddities, but he was badly beaten by Red Burman, a one-time challenger for Joe Louis' world title, and had his nose broken by Earl Pierce. His licence to box was then revoked by the New York State Athletic Commission. Only one man, American John Rankin, who stood 7' 4" and fought briefly during the 1960s, nudges Cully out of being the tallest boxer in history.

But the heavyweight that most long-time Irish fans remember with a kind of grudging affection is Martin Thornton, whose extraordinary showing against British champion Bruce Woodcock at the Theatre Royal, Dublin, in 1945, still provides a controversial talking point. Right up to the time he died after suffering a heart attack while thatching the roof of a cottage near his native Connemara village of Spiddal in 1982, Thornton would take delight in spinning the yarn for customers at his public house of how he 'threw' the fight against Woodcock for a bribe of £4,000. The more knowledgeable patrons of the *Droighnean Donn* would smile quietly to themselves as Martin told of how he made an extra £10,000 from the fight by betting on his opponent!

He insisted that Woodcock knew nothing of the 'bribe'. Nor would he confess as to who was behind it. The promoter of the fiasco, Jack Solomons, admitted that he allowed the Irishman to blackmail him into paying him his £800 purse before the fight, but that was only because Thornton made his demand at the last minute and refused to enter the ring unless he had the cash in hand. Solomons, however, laughingly dismissed the allegations of a bribe. Why would he have been so foolish as to shell out £4,000 to a man who stood no real chance of halting the unbeaten run of Woodcock, who had already beaten Thornton in two rounds at Manchester a couple of years earlier?

Prior to that initial Woodcock setback, Thornton had strung together quite an impressive winning streak, including knockouts of Al Hayes, 'Cast Iron' Casey, Tom Reddington and Ben Valentine, the Jamaican champion. Labelled 'the Connemara Crusher', he won the Irish heavyweight title from Paddy O'Sullivan in three rounds and, in a re-match, stiffened the Corkman in 77 seconds of the opening round. So his supporters were hopeful of a revenge victory over Woodcock. With that hurdle overcome, all that remained was a challenge to Joe Louis for

Martin Thornton

the world title, they reasoned. Caught up in the euphoria, they flocked to book out the Theatre Royal weeks in advance. Black market tickets were in high demand.

A huge outburst of cheers greeted Thornton's arrival into the ring, but it was obvious to ringsiders that all was not well with 'the Connemara Crusher'. He fidgeted nervously during the introductions, in contrast to the cool, confident British and Empire title-holder. This was how the *Irish Press* reported the event the following morning:

Thornton, generally a human volcano at the start of a fight, came out of his corner like a well-beaten man. With his chin tucked tightly into his shoulder, he concentrated upon avoiding punishment rather than handing it out. Woodcock, with a lightning left, played upon Thornton's only exposed spot - his left eye - and, before the first round was over, he had drawn blood and raised a swelling. Now and again Woodcock brought over his right, but failed to find a vulnerable spot on which to land it. The fight was as good as over in the third round when Thornton, giving up all pretence to fighting, stood back and stuck out his tongue at his English opponent while the crowd yelled, 'Fight, Thornton, you're getting paid for it'. At the end of the round Thornton appealed to the referee (Andy Smyth from Belfast) to stop the fight, but the referee said 'I won't stop it'. Half a minute later his seconds threw in the towel.

Thornton ducked through the ropes and fled to his dressing room to the accompaniment of loud jeers, whistles and a couple of empty bottles, while Woodcock was given a rousing cheer. In his dressing room, the dejected Irishman said he was quitting the ring and added, 'It's all very well for the crowd to boo: they weren't facing a chunk of greased lightning like Woodcock'. The anonymous sports writer in the *Evening Herald* echoed the views of many when he asked:

What was wrong with Martin Thornton last night? Where was the fighting Irish blood, that dynamic energy and that 'killer' spirit that swept from the corner like a human volcano and demolished Paddy O'Sullivan and Butcher Howell almost before they had their gloves up?

Somewhat charitably, the writer suggested that Thornton was either over-trained or under-trained. Martin knew what he was doing when he made the promoter pay him in advance, for when the Eire Boxing Board of Control met to debate the fiasco, they could not order that his purse be withheld since it had already been paid out. All they could do was suspend him and relieve him of his Irish title. Thornton made a brief return to the ring four years later to face Ray Wilding, a young English prospect, at the Ulster Hall, Belfast. Ring-rusty and out of condition, he was no match for the sharp-hitting Wilding and the referee acted humanely in coming to his rescue in the third round.

On paper, Thornton's career record of 25 wins in 36 contests, with only two of his victims lastin the distance, looks quite respectable. But it was the Woodcock debacle that people remembered him for. They could afford to laugh about it afterwards, but the odious taint left on Irish professional boxing by performances such as his had the effect of permanently damaging the sport's image south of the border. Although the few professional shows in Dublin in recent years have been completely fair and above board, long memories and tales of sorrow linked to the likes of Jack Doyle, Jim Cully and Martin Thornton have left the southern Irish, whatever their great passion for the sport, wary of spending their hard-earned cash on professional tournaments.

Six

Northern Stars

BELFAST WAS LIKE a ghost town on the night of 20 October 1947. Cinemas and public houses were deserted. Anyone who had a radio was tuned into the BBC for the live commentary from Harringay Arena, London, where little Rinty Monaghan was carrying Irish hopes into battle against Dado Marino of Hawaii, in a 15-rounder billed as for the vacant world flyweight championship. In the northern capital's docks area, where Rinty lived, loudspeakers were erected to carry the progress of the fight to the crowds in the street. Thousands crammed around 32 Little George's Street, the Monaghan household. Rinty's wife Frances was not there. She was so nervous that she took her baby daughter to her sister's house in nearby Toome Street and spent the entire duration of the contest pacing up an down outside while the rest of the family sat glued to the wireless. Only when her sister rushed out to tell her that Rinty had won did she smile. And what celebrations there were. Bonfires were lit all along York Street, Corporation Street and on the Glenard Estate where the new champion's mother lived.

What did it matter that Rinty was recognised as world champion only by the National Boxing Association of America and the Eire Boxing Board of Control? Or what did his fans care if it was one of the dullest flyweight title fights in history, with many in the London audience calling for their money back? Marino, a smooth-moving boxer who later won the world title after Monaghan's retirement, had given the Irishman few chances to land his favourite right cross. He had even floored Rinty for seven in the 11th round. But all that was forgotten when Monaghan was awarded the verdict and then took the microphone to delight the 13,000 spectators and the listening radio audience with a rendition of 'Irish Eyes Are Smiling'. He had enough breath to give an encore of 'Patsy Fagan'. The drab contest was pushed into the background as the crowd broke into sustained cheering for the singing scrapper. It was a pattern that Rinty followed for all of his big fights; and the fans loved him for it.

Although the Monaghan-Marino fight had taken place under the jurisdiction of the British Boxing Board of Control, that body was unable to give it its stamp of approval as a world title bout. Jackie Paterson still claimed the crown he had won by knocking out Peter Kane in 1943. When Paterson failed to make the weight for a scheduled title defence against Marino, the British Board withdrew recognition of him as champion. Paterson, however, obtained a court injunction restraining the board from accepting any contest not involving himself as a title fight. Clearly, the only way to settle the issue now was for Paterson and Monaghan to meet in the only place it mattered: the ring.

It was Belfast promoter Bob Gardiner who pulled off the scoop by securing the fight for the King's Hall on 23 March 1948. As well as the undisputed world title, Paterson's British and Empire titles were at stake. The widespread rumours that the Scot would not make the eight stone weight limit were heightened when he failed to show up at the Saturday afternoon weigh-in on time. With only minutes to go to the deadline, he arrived, looking pale and drawn, and made the weight with four ounces to spare. But what a price he had paid to achieve it. It later emerged that he had spent all of the previous night sweating in front of a roaring fire, smothered in sweaters, in a desperate bid to lose the excess poundage. He had left it to the very last minute before catching the plane to Belfast.

Frank McAloran, Monaghan's manager and a former Irish featherweight champion himself, knew Paterson would be weak after his ordeal, but he advised his man to be extremely cautious. The Scottish southpaw was a noted puncher, as Rinty was only too well aware, having suffered a fifth round knockout by Paterson back in 1938. He had since avenged that setback by stopping Paterson in seven rounds. Monaghan began the world title fight carefully, but saw an opening in the second round and clipped the Scot with a hard left hook. Paterson hit the deck and took a count of seven. He weathered the immediate storm and, in fact, had Monaghan back-pedalling in the next round after shaking him with a right hook. Paterson, realising his weight reducing ordeal would handicap him if the fight went a long distance, went all out to finish it. He hadn't come any nearer his objective by the seventh round, when the Irishman ripped through his guard with a great right and sent him crashing to the canvas. Paterson lurched up groggily at the count of eight, to be forced back into a corner by the fury of Monaghan's attack. Punches rained on the helpless Scotsman propped up by the ropes. Slowly, he sank to the floor where he sat, with one leg folded beneath him, while the referee counted him out. Paterson was carried to his corner, unable to appreciate the Irishman's victory song, 'Irish Eyes Are Smiling', or the joyful chorus of the thousands of King's Hall fans. No one could now dispute Rinty's right to be flyweight champion of the world. He was Ireland's first world champion since Jimmy McLarnin in

1934. What was more noteworthy was that he was the first home-based Irishman to become a world title-holder. All of his Irish-born predecessors were domiciled in the United States when they became champions.

His crowning as king of the world's flyweights was a fitting reward for a man who treated physical fitness as a way of life. When he worked in the Belfast shipyards he always asked for the hardest labouring jobs so he could help build up his strength. His spartan training routine was legendary. After a four mile run he would regularly climb the steep Cave Hill, overlooking Belfast, to chop down trees. He would then call to a local farmhouse, swallow a couple of raw eggs and wash them down with a pint of goat's milk. Then it was on to the gymnasium for a few hours' hard grind of skipping, exercising, bag punching and sparring.

The nickname 'Rinty' was picked up during his boyhood as his favourite screen star was the wonder dog Rin Tin Tin. Born John Joseph Monaghan on 21 August 1920, he was only 14 when he had his first fight for pay. That was a six-round draw with Sam Ramsey. In his next 30 contests he was held to a draw three times but only Jim Keery from Lisburn managed to get the better of him. After his shock defeat by Jackie Paterson, he was again beaten in his next outing, by a near-neighbour of his from York Road, Tommy Stewart. But Monaghan got his act together again with a revenge win over Stewart and a prestigious points victory over highly-rated Joe Curran from Liverpool. Things were looking bright for the perky little Belfastman when World War II interrupted his progress. From January 1940 to September 1946 he only drew on the gloves in earnest ten times. One of those occasions was a trip to Dublin to outpoint the pride of Engine Alley in the city's historic Liberties, Joe 'Boy' Collins. A fourth round knockout of Bunty Doran brought Rinty the Northern Ireland flyweight crown. Now punching with great power for an eight-stoner, he was most impressive in halting Terry Allen in one round in London. Allen was to meet him twice more and succeed him as world champion.

The trouble with Monaghan was that he could spoil the memory of a fine win by having the occasional 'stinker', like getting himself disqualified for persistent holding against Dado Marino. Then, after beating Marino and Paterson to conquer the world, he clowned his way through a non-title ten-rounder with Terry Allen and saw the referee raise the Londoner's arm at the close. When his precious world title was at stake, however, it was a different story. The ease with which he outscored the talented Frenchman Maurice Sandeyron at the King's Hall, Belfast, was the perfect answer to his critics. Not only did he keep his world title that night, but he picked up Sandeyron's European crown as well. But those who followed Rinty's career closely noticed that he tired considerably towards the end of the 15 rounds and seemed to be having trouble with his breathing. He gave no clue to his discomfort as he gave his customary 'Irish Eyes' party-piece, but his manager, Frank

Rinty Monaghan (left) v Terry Allen

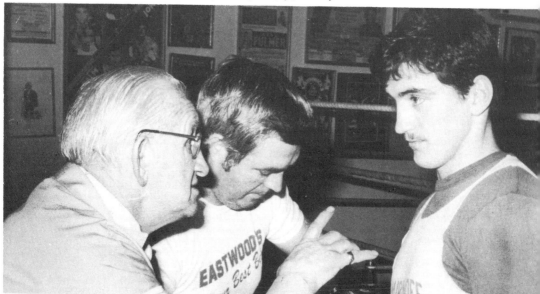

A word of advice for Barry McGuigan from Rinty Monaghan, with

trainer Eddie Shaw lending an ear

McAloran, and others close to him knew that his chest complaint ruled out a long reign as world title-holder. Yet few of the cheering crowd could have guessed that he was only two fights away from retirement.

After beating Italian Otello Belardinelli in a non-title bout, Monaghan put his world, European, British and Empire titles at stake against Terry Allen at the King's Hall on 30 September 1949. It was far from a memorable fight in which to make his exit. With each having a win over the other to his credit, they were understandably cautious. But challengers for a world title are expected to be a bit more enterprising than was Allen. He got off to a promising start by flooring the Irishman in the second round, but failed to follow up his advantage. Rinty fought well in patches, but his general performance was below par. He was clearly having difficulty with his breathing and regularly had to resort to holding and defensive tactics. Referee Sam Russell, from London, felt that neither man had done enough to deserve victory and called it a draw. The verdict didn't please the local fans and a potentially nasty situation was nipped in the bud when Rinty took the microphone and burst into song. The crowd, accepting that their hero was still champion, joined in the chorus, even though they felt he had deserved to win. The challenger and his handlers were equally adamant that Allen should have been crowned the new champion and vowed never to fight in Belfast again.

Six months later, with another title defence against Allen looming, Monaghan announced that he was through with the ring. He was aged 30 and had fought 66 times, with 51 wins, six draws and nine defeats. Sadly, the big purses he had earned did not ensure the life of ease that he deserved. Fast cars, slow greyhounds and a too-generous nature (he couldn't resist a hard-luck story) combined to leave him, like so many gifted Irish ringmen, having to work for a living. Not that his fate left him despondent. Throughout his life, whatever the circumstances, Rinty was always the same cheerful character. He worked as a taxi man and a lorry driver and could always fall back on his personality and singing talent to earn a crust in times of need. Not all his performing was done for cash either. He would not turn down a request to do a charity show or an old folks' concert. He took as huge a delight in performing on stage as he did in the ring. His Popeye and Olive Oyl impressions were guaranteed to bring the house down.

Failing health curtailed his cabaret work in his later years, but he was a familiar attender at Belfast fight nights. When he died on 3 March 1984, at the age of 63, his loyal fans turned out in their thousands to pay their final tribute. They lined the streets as the coffin was taken to St Patrick's Church in Donegal Street for the funeral Mass. During the service Father Myles Murray told the congregation, 'He brought good news. He was a gentleman, loved by many. That is what life is all about; touching people, bringing joy and happiness, making friends.'

Among the many written words of affection was this contribution from Fred Heatley in the *Irish News:*

In the death of John Joseph 'Rinty' Monaghan, Belfast has lost not only a former great boxer, but one of the outstanding citizens of our generation.   His ever-friendly welcome to both close friends and strangers never varied.   Always there was the cheery word and the wide grin over a face that bore the hallmarks of many a gloved fist, a smile that had its own radiance and made one want to smile with him. He was a small man, but one who made up in heart for what he lacked in height.

Top honours escaped the clouting Kellys

Of the abundant talented Northern Ireland boxers in the lower weight divisions, none topped the popularity during the 1950s of the two Kellys, John from Belfast and 'Spider' Billy from Derry. They were not related, but Billy's father preceded him as British featherweight champion in the first part of a remarkable father-son championship 'double'. It was John Kelly, however, who came closest to world title honours, only to have his hopes dashed in three rounds by Robert Cohen on one of the saddest nights in Irish boxing history. Entering the King's Hall ring on that occasion in 1954, Kelly was bantamweight champion of Europe and Britain and one of the leading contenders for the world crown. He was unbeaten in 20 contests since turning professional two years earlier after highlighting a fine amateur career with the winning of a European championships silver medal. Kelly's smooth skills and knockout punch carried him swiftly up the professional ladder and, in only his sixth outing, he outscored the rugged Nigerian Hogan 'Kid' Bassey over eight rounds. Refusing to be overawed by his opponent's reputation, Kelly earned frequent rounds of applause for the way he faded away from Bassey's attacks and made him miss with dangerous hooks. In the middle rounds Bassey stopped in the middle of the ring and shook his head in despair of catching the local lad with a decent punch. The merit of Kelly's victory can be gauged by the fact that the Nigerian later became world featherweight champion.

Kelly blasted out the number two contender for the British title, Tommy Proffitt, in two rounds, took the Northern Ireland crown from veteran Bunty Doran and gave a flawless exhibition of boxing to outpoint Peter Keenan and win the European and British bantamweight titles before a delirious King's Hall crowd. Not even Barry McGuigan's great support among the Belfast fight fraternity would outshine the acclaim that attached to John Kelly. *Irish Press* columnist Jim Davey, in an article headed 'How good is John Kelly?' confessed that some writers, himself included, might have gone overboard in their praise, but compared the Belfast southpaw to the great Freddie Miller, the former world featherweight champion.

Kelly has all the attributes of a world champion. He is beautifully balanced on his feet, carries a knockout in both hands and has a cunning defence. He feints, jabs, rides a punch as well as any fighter I have ever seen and, in addition, has the most important attribute of all - a boxer's instinct to do the right thing at the right moment.

Although Kelly was virtually unknown outside Ireland, where all his professional fights had taken place, word of his ability began to spread through the sporting media abroad. The reigning world bantamweight champion was the Australian Jimmy Carruthers and the publicity drums began to beat for a showdown between the two unbeaten southpaws. Before that could happen, however, there was a little matter of Kelly's European title defence against a swarthy, muscular French Algerian named Robert Cohen. Although Cohen had lost only once in 33 contests, there wasn't a man in the packed King's Hall, outside of the challenger and his cornermen, who anticipated the total humiliation facing the local hero. The crowd, who had given Kelly a rousing reception on his way to the ring, was stunned into silence and disbelief within seconds of the opening bell. Cohen came out slinging bombs and the Irishman's pale skin soon showed the effects of the aggressor's body blows. Kelly kept cool, however, and jabbed the shorter man with a right and followed up with a left cross to the jaw. Cohen shrugged off the punches and charged in again, incurring a warning from the Italian referee about careless headwork. Despite the menacing approach of Cohen in those opening three minutes, no one, least of all Kelly, was prepared for what happened in the second round. The French Algerian ducked under John's right lead and drove him back against the ropes with a bewildering barrage of punches from both hands. A left hook crashed against Kelly's jaw and sent him tumbling to the canvas. He hauled himself up at four, only to be dropped again for eight. A short right sent him down again, this time for six seconds. Gamely he rose, to meet a rain of punches. Kelly sank to the floor, took a count of nine and, just as the bell rang to end that disastrous round, caught a mighty right hook that felled him, face down. His frantic seconds leaped into the ring and dragged his limp form to the corner, an action that is now prohibited. (Boxers can no longer be 'saved by the bell', unless, of course, it signals the end of the contest. The referee must now continue his count over a downed boxer even after the bell has rung.)

No amount of massaging Kelly's tired limbs, slapping his face or dousing him with cold water could revive him as he slumped on his stool. His seconds acted unwisely in sending him out for the third round, seeing his helpless condition and knowing he faced further needless punishment. The Belfastman tried a couple of pathetic swipes which failed to connect. Cohen calmly measured his distance and crashed home a great right to the champion's jaw. Kelly went down for the seventh - and last - time. The count was a mere formality. The transition from world title hopeful to 'has been' was completed in less than seven minutes. Never has the finality of a boxer's fate been more graphically emhasised than on that sad occasion for Irish boxing followers.

Kelly's downfall was as rapid as his rise. After a short rest he came back to face Pierre Cossemyns of Belgium. He showed glimpses of his old form as he outboxed Cossemyns in the early rounds, but suddenly weakened and was knocked out in the ninth round by what did not appear to be a very hard blow. A further five months' rest was followed by a defence of his British title against Peter Keenan, from whom he had won it. The fight took place in Paisley, Scotland, the first time Kelly had fought outside Ireland as a pro. It was evident from the outset that he had lost his old brilliance and enthusiasm. Keenan regained the title by a sixth round knockout. An attempted comeback as a featherweight saw Kelly notch up a few meaningless wins over inferior opposition, but a first round knockout at the hands of Teddy Peckham convinced him to call it quits.

In his book *From the Ringside*, Terry Leigh-Lye wrote of Kelly's quite remarkable rise and decline:

Never in my 25 years' experience of the fight game can I remember a fighter so idolised by his fellow countrymen. Even experts appeared to lose their critical faculties and could only speak in superlatives, completely disregarding the obvious mistakes that Kelly and his advisors were making in the conduct of his affairs. I plead guilty to this as much as any of my colleagues. From the first moment I saw the little Irish southpaw, I became convinced that he was a world champion in embryo. I lauded his boxing capabilities in radio interviews before and after he won the championship from Peter Keenan and I tipped him to beat Robert Cohen in my column in *The Irish Times*. The story of John Kelly is a tragic one. It is full of warnings to boxers of outstanding potential ability and to the managers and handlers of such young men.

Derry's Billy 'Spider' Kelly never quite showed the potential of his Belfast namesake, although he made it to number six in the world featherweight ranking list and he enjoyed a considerably longer career than John. Billy was a delight to the boxing connoisseur with his almost uncanny knack of ducking or slipping an opponents's punches, his magical footwork and his ability to catch his rivals with surprise counter attacks. His trouble was that he tended to over-emphasise his evasive skills and lost contests he might have won with a bit more aggression. He was involved in more controversial points verdicts than any other boxer of his time. His supporters might be so entranced by his slippery style that a referee who favoured his more enterprising, if less talented, opponent would end up getting hounded from the ring. Two of Kelly's major championship fights in which the verdict went against him were followed by riots.

It was as a grinning, if slightly bewildered, six-year-old that Billy had his first experience of the famous 'King's Hall roar'. The youngster was

John Kelly

Jim 'Spider' Kelly

Billy 'Spider' Kelly

hoisted over the ropes on a memorable night in 1938 and ran to the out-stretched arms of his father Jim, who had just outpointed Billy Caplan for the vacant British and Empire featherweight titles. As little Billy gazed in wonder and admiration at the beautiful Lonsdale Belt that had been buckled around his dad's waist, not even his vivid childish imagination could have projected that, in that same ring 16 years later, he too would be proclaimed as British and Empire featherweight champion.

Unlike dad, Billy had to earn his British and Empire titles in separate bouts. Ghana's Roy Ankrah was tempted to Belfast to put his Empire crown at stake, confident that he could repeat an earlier win over Kelly. Ankrah's title had not been on the line in that first encounter, but Kelly made sure of his success in the one that mattered with a dazzling display of ring-craft and left-hand jabbing. And he wasn't afraid to stand his ground and mix it when the opportunity presented itself. Not even a broken bone in his right hand suffered in the third round proved too big a handicap on his way to a clear win over the 15 rounds. British champion Sammy McCarthy was next to rue his bowing to pressure to defend his crown against Kelly in Belfast. The Londoner, though favoured to keep his title, won only two of the 15 rounds, according to ringsider Terry Leigh-Lye, who wrote in *The Irish Times*:

> I had expected Kelly's style to puzzle the Londoner, but even in my most optimistic moments I never believed that the Irishman would completely outclass the champion in all departments of boxing skill. Kelly, from the very first round, took command of the fight. He would draw McCarthy's left lead, avoid the punch by clever evasive tactics, and then spring back into counter action with lightning left jabs to the face. All through the contest Kelly's left hand was superior to McCarthy's and the fact that he was able to out-jab the Englishman completely upset the calculation of the McCarthy plan of campaign, for this was the first time in the Londoner's career that he had met a boxer capable of beating him to the punch with left leads.

Young 'Spider' aimed to go one better than his father by challenging for the European featherweight title in 1955. The title was in the grasp of the gifted Ray Famechon, at 31 a veteran of 11 years boxing, but a master technician who could match every clever trick of Kelly's. The Frenchman had tried for the world championship, but had met his master in Willie Pep and was soundly outpointed over 15 rounds. London impresario Jack Solomons outbid Belfast's Bob Gardiner for the right to stage the European title fight and he sprang a surprise by electing to put it on in Dublin, at the unlikely venue of Donnybrook bus garage. Had he known anything about the history of the site, Solomons would have steered well clear of it. The bus depot stood on the site of the infamous Donnybrook Fair, where wild drinking and fighting often marked the annual event until it was finally abolished in 1855. Americans often refer to a free-for-all brawl as 'a Donnybrook'. The setting proved extraordinarily apt, for the contest ended in a disgraceful exhibition of hooliganism by a section of the 6,700 crowd protesting over the decision in favour of Famechon.

Seconds after the announcement that the Dutch referee, Barend Bergstroem, had Famechon three points ahead at the close of the 15 rounds, programmes, orange peels, bottles, chairs and anything else the rioters could lay their hands on came flying towards the ring. Pressmen dived for cover under the ring though a BBC commentator wasn't quick enough and had his head gashed by a flying bottle. Promoter Solomons, who had nothing to do with the referee's decision, had a bucket of water poured over his head. The referee himself was punched on the jaw and threatened with lynching as he was escorted to the comparative safety of the bus depot office by police. Nat Fleischer, editor of *The Ring* and much respected as a boxing expert, was besieged by Kelly supporters seeking confirmation that the Irishman had won 'by a mile'. In fact, Fleischer revealed later that he had given it to the Famechon by a single point, but he wasn't going to risk his neck by telling that to the mob.

In the next issue of *The Ring*, Fleischer wrote:

Talk about a kid being popular. Kelly is *it* in Ireland. And well he deserves the support, for he is one of the classiest little feathers I've seen in a long time. Unfortunately he lacks a solid punch. If he possessed it, he would be tops in the division. He lost the fight due to the continued aggressiveness from start to finish by Famechon. Several times Ray was jarred when one of Kelly's counter punches landed on the jaw as the defending champion came tearing in, but Famechon carried the fight to his adversary, landed the harder punches, was the aggressor and, because of that, he gained a hairline decision.

Tommy Farr, the Welshman who went 15 rounds with Joe Louis in a heroic bid for the world heavyweight crown, was among the many ringside reporters who thought Kelly deserved to win. But it was A.J. Liebling, one of the greatest American writers on boxing, who aptly summed up the Irishman's weakness. In his book *The Sweet Science*, he wrote:

When Famechon started a punch, Kelly would be going in another direction. Usually when the Frenchman got close to him, Kelly would cease trying to do harm and concentrate on escape, as if he were fighting a middleweight instead of a gaffer his own size. He was good at ducking and slipping away, but nobody was ever hurt by being ducked away from.

Billy had another flaw. He would often drop his left hand while awaiting the opportunity to jump in with a left hook. In a defence of his British Empire title against Hogan 'Kid' Bassey in Belfast, Kelly outclassed the Nigerian up to the eighth round, when he left his chin unguarded for one split second. That was all the challenger needed. Bassey smashed him with a terrific right and it was several minutes before Kelly regained his senses, to find he was no longer champion of the Empire. Within three more months his British title had gone too. Scot Charlie Hill was adjudged by referee Tommy Little to have outpointed the Derryman in their King's Hall encounter, and the verdict was the trigger to another outburst of crowd violence. *Irish Independent* reporter Michael Cogley, although in agreement that Kelly was 'robbed', was struck on the head by a chair as he phoned his account of the proceedings to his Dublin office. A cameraman was felled by a bottle and the MC, taking the microphone in a vain bid to restore order, was struck by a chair. Eventually the Royal Ulster Constabulary quelled the disturbance with their truncheons.

Kelly tried again as a lightweight and got as far as twice fighting final eliminators for the British title, only to lose them to Ron Hinson and David 'Darkie' Hughes. He did enter the ring with British champion Dave Charnley in 1959, but Charnley's title was not on offer. The Irishman gave a good account of himself against one of the best lightweights in British boxing history, only to get disqualified in the sixth round for 'persistently ducking below the waistline'. It seems a petty interpretation of the rules, but Scots referee Frank Wilson had warned him several times for the offence.

Billy gave former Empire champion Willie Toweel a hard tussle over ten rounds and drew with Frenchman Guy Gracia, the scourge of British lightweights at the time, but six defeats in his last eight fights convinced him that the old sparkle had gone forever. He was 31 when he made his farewell appearance, an eight rounds draw with another master craftsman, Belfast's Jim 'Spike' McCormack (no relation to the Dublin 'Spike' McCormack) in March 1962.

Gilroy v Caldwell, the epic encounter

Great home-grown ringmen are rare enough in Ireland, but when two come along together and in the same weight division as did bantamweight rivals Freddie Gilroy and John Caldwell, it is fair reason for the fans to get excited. These two Belfast-men blazed a trail together as amateurs, won bronze medals in the 1956 Olympics at Melbourne (Gilroy at bantamweight and Caldwell at flyweight) and moved on to further success as professionals. When increasing weight forced Caldwell into the bantamweight division, the propect of him meeting Gilroy in the ring was inevitable. Sometimes expected classic encounters between local rivals turn out to be damp squibs, but not the 1962 showdown between Gilroy and Caldwell at the King's Hall. It remains indelibly etched in the memories of those lucky enough to be there as one of the most exciting ring battles ever waged in Ireland, or anywhere else.

Gilroy, from the Ardoyne district of Belfast, was a southpaw with a wicked punch in either hand. Pound for pound, there has never been a harder hitter in Irish boxing history. Caldwell, nicknamed 'the Cold-eyed Killer' because of his icy stare, was from Cyprus Street, just off the city's Falls Road. He was probably a better box-fighter than Gilroy, but it is a matter of personal preference as to which was the superior fighter. Caldwell was British champion at flyweight and bantamweight and held a version of the world title. He won 29 of his 35 fights, 15 inside the distance, lost five and drew one. Gilroy won 28 out of 31, with three losses. Eighteen of his wins were scored inside the distance, with ten of them on count-outs, a remarkably high knockout total for a man weighing around 8st 7lbs (118lbs).

Gilroy turned professional in 1957 after an honour-laden amateur career. Resisting the tempting offers from cross-Channel managers to sign with them, he remained faithful to his amateur trainer, Jimmy McAree, who guided him throughout his professional campaign. The baby-faced destroyer swept through the bantamweight ranks to earn a shot at Peter Keenan's British and Empire titles after only 13 contests. Keenan went the way of all the others, floored seven times before being rescued by the referee in the 11th round. A fine points win over former world champion Mario D'Agata in London led to a crack at another Italian, Piero Rollo, for the European championship. 'Win this one,' promoter Jack Solomons told Gilroy, 'and I'll do everything in my power to get you a world title fight.' The Irishman duly obliged, although he had a hard tussle with the tough veteran before emerging the winner on points. World title-holder Joe Becerra, however, was in no hurry to accommodate Gilroy or Solomons. Freddie kept busy by defending his British Empire title in Belfast against South African Bernie Taylor, who was counted out in the fifth round, and then putting his three titles at stake against Glaswegian Billy Rafferty. The Scot gave him an unexpectedly hard battle, absorbing everything the Belfastman threw at him and closing Gilroy's right eye with the fury of his counter attacks. But Rafferty was surviving on sheer grit when the referee called a halt because of the Scot's badly cut eye in the 13th round.

While waiting for Becerra to make up his mind about defending his world title, Gilroy took on a 'warm up' bout against a little-known Mexican, Ignacio Pina. As sometimes happens, the 'sacrificial lamb' decided he was nothing of the kind and proceeded to hand the Irishman a boxing lesson. Not only did Gilroy suffer his first loss in 22 outings, but he was put on the floor for the first time by a sharp right in the opening round. His disappointment was quickly forgotten when Joe Becerra announced his retirement and the world bantamweight scene was thrown into confusion. The National Boxing Association of America paired Eloy Sanchez of Mexico, whose knockout defeat of Becerra in a non-title fight had prompted his abdication, with Eder Jofre of Brazil for the vacant title. The European Boxing Union and the British Boxing Board of Control disagreed with the NBA and chose to recognise the winner of a match between Gilroy and Alphonse Halimi of France as the world title-holder.

The record books show that Halimi outpointed Gilroy over 15 rounds at the Empire Pool, Wembley, on 25 October 1960. The cold statistic does not reveal that there was hardly a person in the arena, outside of the French party, who agreed with the verdict of the Belgian referee Philippe de Backer. Though floored in the 13th round (the bell rang at three) Gilroy seemed to have been in command most of the way. He constantly slipped under the Frenchman's guard to pound away at his mid-section and trapped him on the ropes time after time. Halimi had more success when he stayed in the centre of the ring and scored with jabs and hooks. The Irishman was in some trouble in the 14th round, but he threw everything into the last round and appeared to be a clear winner. It was the first time a neutral referee had handled a world title fight in Britain (at Halimi's insistence), although this is now standard practice. The ringside pressmen were unanimous in their opinion that Gilroy was the better man. *Boxing News*, the British trade paper, devoted its front page to a picture of the contest under the heading, 'Shock verdict robs Gilroy of world title'.

Perhaps it was the depression following his unlucky 'world title' setback that caused Freddie to lose again next time out, a shock stoppage in nine rounds by Pierre Cossemyns in Brussels. The Irishman had already knocked out Cossemyns in four rounds on his way to the top and may have dismissed his rival too lightly. He should have remembered what happened to another Belfast idol, John Kelly, when he tangled with the dangerous Belgian. Gilroy was floored three times in the fourth round of the return encounter, but fought his way back and had Cossemyns in trouble in the eighth. As he attempted to apply the finisher, he walked straight into a smashing right that dropped him for eight. Down three more times before the bell saved him, he was battered to the canvas again in the next round and his seconds threw in the towel. It was the only time he lost inside the course. Gilroy took ten months off, then beat Scot Billy Rafferty for the second time. His successful defence of the British title earned him the Lonsdale Belt outright, the first Irishman to achieve that distinction. The stage was now set for the local showdown with John Caldwell.

Caldwell had turned professional in 1958, a year after Gilroy, with a fine amateur record of only seven defeats in 250 contests. Ever since he first pulled on a pair of boxing gloves at the age of ten, the tiny youngster's natural ability to jab, hook and uppercut with the skill of a veteran had onlookers enraptured. His capture of the Ulster junior and senior titles, plus the national junior and senior honours, in the 1955-6 season was the first time any boxer had won that cluster of crowns in one period. Clearly an exceptional talent, Caldwell was snapped up by Scottish promoter/manager Sammy Docherty. Most of his early professional appearances were reserved for Glasgow and London audiences, who saw him brilliantly outscore the British Empire flyweight Dennis Adams in only his fifth contest and chop down former European title-holder Young Martin of Spain seven times on the way to a great third round knockout. After 17 straight victories, John's hometown fans, who had seen only three of those bouts, were adequately compensated when his challenge for Frankie Jones' British flyweight title was arranged for the King's Hall on 8 October 1960. The Scot's three-year reign came to an abrupt halt in the third round as he lay crumpled, face downwards, on the canvas after taking two precision rights to the jaw.

Increasing weight forced Caldwell to give up his flyweight title. But after only three outings as a bantamweight, all inside-the-distance wins, he found himself in with Alphonse Halimi, Gilroy's 'conqueror', for the European version of the world championship. He reached the peak of his career that 1961 night at the Wembley Pool, London, to trounce the Frenchman over 15 rounds. Halimi was never in with a chance and he was very nearly knocked out in the last round. Caldwell, as cool as ice, scored repeatedly with sharp jabs, hooks and crosses and neatly ducked or skipped away from his rival's desperate attempts to nail him. Halimi's left eye, nicked in the second round, spurted blood after a hard exchange in the seventh. He brought out every trick he knew to try to turn the tide, but the Belfastman trumped everything. Halimi knew as he emerged from his corner for the last round that only a knockout could save his title. He threw everything he had at his opponent, only to find it returned with vigour. Caldwell's cornermen almost choked with fright as they watched him engaging the still threatening Frenchman in a final punch-up. All John had to do was stay on his feet to win, but here he was risking all in a crazy late attack. Their fears were dispelled when Caldwell dug a left to the body, followed up with a right to the jaw, a left and another right and Halimi was down. It was nearly impossible to hear the count, such was the crowd's din, but the champion crawled up at five. Caldwell rushed in to finish the job, but the referee restrained him and continued to count to eight. Only by clinging on like a limpet did Halimi survive until the final bell. In notching up his 22nd consecutive victory, Caldwell was now bantamweight champion of the world, at least according to the European Boxing Union and the British Board of Control. He gave Halimi a chance to regain the honour five months later, again in London, but the Hallowe'en night clash failed to produce any fireworks. Caldwell was a clear points winner, but it was a boring affair punctuated with outbreaks of slow hand-clapping from the disappointed crowd.

The Brazilian Eder Jofre was recognised as world champion by the National Boxing Association of America and the eagerly awaited showdown with Caldwell for the undisputed title was finally set for 18 January 1962. It was unfortunate for the Irishman that he had to enter enemy territory and face a hostile crowd of 20,000 wildly enthusiastic Jofre supporters who booed and jeered Caldwell all the way to the ring at the Ibirapuera Stadium in Sao Paulo. As if that was not enough to tear at his confidence, he had to face the fact that he was meeting one of boxing's all-time greats. In a magnificent 20-year career, Jofre was

world champion at bantamweight and featherweight and only lost two
contests, each to the same man, Fighting Harada of Japan. Going into
the Caldwell fight he boasted an unbeaten run of 43 bouts, with 30 wins
by the short route. He had drawn three times. Caldwell had won all his
25 contests, 13 inside schedule. But records count for little in the ring.
As Sammy Docherty hammered frantically on the ring apron to signal his
man's retirement, referee Willie Pep, himself a former ring great, threw
his arms around the gallant Irishman and led him to his corner. The little
Belfastman had fought with commendable bravery, but he was on a
mission without hope. Downed by a body blow in the fifth round for a
count of nine, Caldwell already knew who was the real world champion;
and it wasn't him. Reg Gutteridge, reporting for the London *Evening
News*, wrote:

> Caldwell, at times, boxed intelligently and always defiantly, yet the
> harsh and sad truth is that he looked a dainty pretender to the throne in
> comparison with the Brazilian. Before Pep finally acted in two
> minutes, 45 seconds of the tenth round, Caldwell's only challenge lay
> in raw courage, fitness and Irish pride, but these, historically, are the
> possession of losers.

Nine months later Caldwell climbed into a Belfast ring for the first
time in two years, to meet Freddie Gilroy in one of the most natural
pairings in Irish boxing history. Local promoter George Connell teamed
up with his big-time London counterpart, Jack Solomons, to put on the
fight, in which Gilroy's British and Empire bantamweight titles were at
stake. The Fleet Street boys had to dig deep into their dictionaries to
lavish the superlatives on two boxers who fought the fight of their lives.
Frank McGhee wrote in the *Daily Mirror:*

> Whenever men meet to argue about the great fights of all time, the
> night Freddie Gilroy, the baby-faced bantamweight, kept his British
> and Empire titles against the pale-eyed little challenger, John
> Caldwell, will be lived again. This is how murderously, memorably
> wonderful it was to be in Belfast on Saturday night - this battle of two
> local boys who never pretended to like each other and who proceeded
> to make that the understatement of any year in the nine bitter,
> bruising, bloodstained rounds of raw hate it lasted. Not that the
> arguments are over. Caldwell's retirement, forced by a cut the length
> of his right eyebrow, has left him still unconvinced that but for this he
> would have won against a man who was weakening visibly. Gilroy,
> slamming the suggestions that if he made the weight he would be a
> burnt-out shell of a man, is equally certain he could have kept and
> increased a desperately slender points lead.

The fight began at a tremendous pace and never faltered. The punch-
for-punch exchanges in the opening three minutes set the pattern for the
rest of the bout and even though Caldwell was on the floor within the
sound of the first bell, he stormed back to win the second round with
lightning-fast, strength-sapping hooks to the body. It was Gilroy

ripping in punches with little regard for his personal safety, then Caldwell swinging the fight his way with bewildering clusters of blows, and all the time the crowd roaring itself hoarse with excitement. First blood to Caldwell in the sixth round, when a red trickle appeared by the champion's eye. Gilroy's seconds did an excellent job of patching up the injury. In the eighth, two searing left hooks to the body had Caldwell doubled over in pain. His mouth hung open as he gasped for air. Gilroy showed him no mercy. 'Before a fight I go into a church and pray,' Caldwell had once said. 'I pray for myself and I pray that my opponent will not be seriously injured. Then I go into the ring and try to hurt him as much as I can.' The man they called 'the Cold-eyed Killer' was giving an honest assessment of what boxing is all about. He gave no quarter and expected none. In a torrid ninth round both boxers were covered in blood, most of it coming from Caldwell's eyebrows. He looked dejected as he went back to his corner. His chief second, Danny Holland, an expert 'cuts man' who looked after Henry Cooper in many such crises, had a brief consultation with Sammy Docherty and then called over the referee, Belfastman Andy Smyth, to tell him Caldwell could not go on.

Inevitably, there was public demand for a return match, but it was not to be. Gilroy, in fact, never fought again. He did sign a contract with Jack Solomons for another bout with Caldwell, but a dispute over the terms caused long delays and ended in Gilroy and his manager being fined £1,000 for breach of contract. They were given six months to pay by the British Board of Control. When the time expired and the fine had not been paid, the board withdrew the licences of Gilroy and Jimmy McAree. It was a sad way to end what had been a short but memorable career. But Gilroy seemed content to spend more time with his family and, from his ring earnings, he bought the Tivoli bar in Donaghadee, County Down, as well as a nice house in the hills overlooking his native city. Life was good until the violence of the early 1970s reached the normally peaceful fishing port. Gilroy's pub was bombed and anti-Catholic slogans were daubed on the walls. He sold out and took his family to Australia. Three years later, after a short sojourn as a barman in Dublin, he returned to Belfast to work for a furniture firm along with Jimmy McAree, the man who had 'discovered' him as an eager nine-year-old and who had guided him throughout his amateur and professional careers. But even that job was not to last.

Gilroy's disappearance from the boxing scene gave Caldwell a clear run at the now vacant British and Empire bantamweight titles, which he duly collected at the expense of England's George Bowes, who was outboxed, outfought and forced to retire with a badly cut eye in the seventh round. History was made in that 1964 contest, as Caldwell became the first Irishman to win British championships at two different weights. But recurring rows with his manager and an obviously growing disenchantment with the fight game spoiled any hopes his fans cherished of his renewing his world title quest. Though still only 27, he looked like a battle-weary veteran as he lost his titles at the first defence to Liverpudlian Alan Rudkin. Under pressure from the start, Caldwell was bleeding heavily from the nose by the sixth round and his eye was cut in the ninth. Rudkin's body blows were taking a further toll. When the Irishman fell against the ropes in the tenth round after another sustained attack, Scottish referee George Smith called off the action. John blamed his defeat on his nose injury, claiming he could not breathe properly from the third round. An operation, the second on his nose, seemed to correct the trouble, but he suffered further complications in his comeback bout against Monty Laud. He looked impressive at the start as he scored with good combinations, but his performance deteriorated as the bout progressed. He suffered a cut on his nose in the ninth round and lost the points verdict to a strong, bustling opponent. He saw there was no point in carrying on boxing.

Sadly, little remained of the substantial purses he earned during his seven-year campaign (he was reckoned to have received £10,000 for each of his world title fights with Halimi and Jofre) and he drove a taxi around Belfast for some time after his retirement. After an unrewarding spell in Canada, he returned to join the lengthy dole queues that haunt his home town.

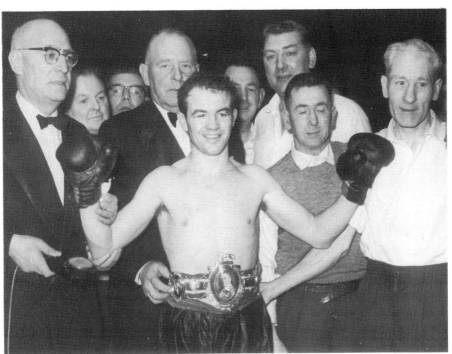

Freddie Gilroy after knocking out Billy Rafferty at the King's Hall,

Belfast

Mick Leahy (left) v Brian Curvis

Seven

A New Stepping Stone

MICK LEAHY, A fiery, red-headed battler from the Spangle Hill area of Cork, demolished the barriers that had stopped boxers from Southern Ireland making progress via the British championship. He successfully campaigned for British citizenship and pursuaded an initially reluctant British Boxing Board of Control to include him in an eliminator for the British welterweight title in 1961. This precedent opened the way for other ringmen from the Irish Republic to follow suit; the McCormack brothers, 'Young' John and Pat; Derry Treanor and Barry McGuigan. Before this, when for example Dundalk's Tom McCormick won the British welterweight title in 1914, all of Ireland was part of the United Kingdom. By the time Jack Doyle had a go at the heavyweight crown in 1933, the southern 26 counties formed the Irish Free State but retained Commonwealth status within the UK. It was not until 1949, when it became the Irish Republic, that southern Irish citizens grew totally independent of Britain, and boxers from that part of the country were no longer eligible to fight for a British title. Boxers from Northern Ireland, which has remained part of the UK, have enjoyed the best of both worlds. They have always been allowed to contest both Irish and British championships. Yet in amateur boxing the sport takes an all-Ireland stance, with Northern ringmen appearing in the green vest in international competition, while not being eligible to box for Britain. They can, however, take part in the British Commonwealth championships.

Leahy's history-making assault on the British welterweight crown proved fruitless when Welshman Brian Curvis stretched him out cold with a perfect left hook in the eighth round. Never one to give up easily, the Irishman moved up to middleweight and earned the right to challenge British champion George Aldridge by narrowly outpointing Wally Swift. Leahy made no mistake in his bid for the middleweight crown in May

1963. He leapt from his corner and smothered the astonished Aldridge with a barrage of punches to the head and body. The champion was forced into a corner and battered to the canvas for a count of five. He was offering no resistance when the referee, Ike Powell of Wales, stopped the slaughter. It had taken Leahy just one minute and 45 seconds to capture the British title. Five months later Mick tried to add the British Commonwealth crown to his collection, but he was adjudged to have lost on points to Gomeo Brennan from the Bahamas, a verdict that did not meet with the approval of most of the Wembley Pool, London, audience.

An inveterate globe-trotter, Coventry-based Leahy was a highly popular performer wherever he appeared with his bustling, all-action style. His brave losing battle against Irish-American Joey Archer at Madison Square Garden, New York, was one of the most exciting encounters on British TV's 'Fight of the Week' series during the 60s. Downed twice and cut over an eye, the fighting Irishman stormed back to make the classy American fight every inch of the way for a points decision. Earlier, he had thrilled Australians in winning eight out of twelve contests 'down under', including a fine victory over Commonwealth welterweight champion George Barnes in a non-title clash.

A perusal of Leahy's 71-bout record over nine years confirms that he ducked no one. In 1964 he fought, in close succession, two of boxing's immortals, Sugar Ray Robinson and the legendary Hungarian Laszlo Papp. And he beat Robinson on points over ten rounds. At least, that's what the record shows, though most of the spectators at the Paisley Ice Rink in Scotland didn't see it the same way as referee Ike Powell of Wales. At 44, the sleek American was no longer the magnificent fighting machine who had won the world welterweight championship once and the middleweight title an unmatched five times, but he seemed to have retained enough of his ebbing skills to have earned the verdict. The London *Evening Standard*'s ace correspondent, George Whiting, reported that:

> Robinson's once immaculate left jab is now a reminiscent slap, his hooking a memory, and his rib-bending right cross has become a wild swipe that more often than not finishes up as an illegal kidney punch. The slim brown arms that once whipped swift destruction out of the air are now artfully at anchor under an opponent's shoulders. At times they tied the eager, but ungainly, Leahy into knots and tangles of sheer frustration. Leahy badgered and bustled like an Irish terrier, finished strongly and, outside of one palpable kidney punch, was never in any great physical danger. In my view Robinson's less frequent but cleaner punching, plus a three-second knockdown in round two, might well have gained him the decision.

Donald Saunders of the *Daily Telegraph* gave Leahy full marks for endeavour

> for he never stopped trying to wear down a man 14 years his senior and infinitely the better craftsman. He knew he must make Robinson

fight for every minute of every round if he wanted to sap the energy from the ex-champion's ageing legs. In my view he failed to do so and consequently lost the fight.

A month later Leahy was in Vienna to tackle Laszlo Papp for the European middleweight title. Jack Solomons, who accompanied the Irishman to the Austrian capital, had promised him a match with Dick Tiger, the Nigerian ex-world champion, should he beat Papp. Then, if things went according to plan, the London promoter would try to lure world champion Joey Giardello over from the United States for a defence against Leahy. But, realistically, Leahy had little chance of getting over the first hurdle. Papp, though slowed up at 38, was still a master of his craft. Easily the most outstanding boxer ever produced in Hungary, he was three times an Olympic Games gold medal winner and never lost as a professional. As professional boxing was banned in his native land, Papp's entire paid career was conducted outside Hungary. He might have gone on to fight for the world title but, after turning back Leahy's challenge, he was advised to retire as the Hungarian authorities thought 'a continuation of his career would not be compatible with socialist principles'.

Leahy gave his European title bid everything he had, as usual, but he was a thoroughly beaten man at the close of the 15 rounds. He did have the satisfaction of taking Papp all the way, something no one else had managed in the Hungarian's seven previous title defences. Mick realised his normal swarm-in tactics would be made to measure for the sharp counter-punches of Papp, so he chose to play a waiting game for a few rounds. Papp, a slow starter, did not contribute much and the boxers were about even after three rounds. In the fourth, the champion cut loose with a swift barrage to send Leahy down for seven. The Irishman was dropped again and suffered a nasty cut on his cheek before returning to his corner for repairs. He kept plugging away, but the Hungarian southpaw's hard, stabbing rights and whiplash left hooks left his face badly cut up. Mick made a valiant effort to make up the leeway with an all-out assault, but Papp came out strongly for the 13th round and had the challenger on the floor with a rapid burst of punches. Leahy never gave up and was still trying gamely, if hopelessly, when the final bell rang. There were no protests from the Irish corner when the champion's hand was raised. A trip to hospital revealed that a blood vessel in Leahy's throat had been burst as early as the third round. He had found it difficult to breathe, but kept the full extent of his troubles to himself lest his seconds would have forced him to quit.

His disappointment was compounded when his old rival Wally Swift relieved him of the British title. In this their fourth meeting the Corkman fought with grim determination, but he could never match the all-round craft of the Nottingham challenger. The points verdict in Swift's favour was never in serious doubt. In 1965, Leahy's last year in the ring, he fought only twice, each time on the continent and losing both on points.   The unbeaten Italian champion Nino Benvenuti, later to become world title-holder, beat him in Milan and Jupp Elze, the champion of Germany, outscored him in Cologne.   Though then aged 30, Mick might have carried on for a while longer had tragedy not struck one day while he was at the wheel of his car in Coventry. The vehicle struck a lorry and Mick's head went through the windscreen. It was several days before he recovered consciousness, to find he was blind in one eye and partially deaf. It obviously meant the end of his boxing career, but he was glad to be alive. His wife, who was expecting their fifth child at the time, was overwhelmed by the volume of sympathy and support they received.   'I never thought I had so many genuine friends,' said Mick, who still lives in Coventry.

Championship 'double' for the McCormacks

When Dubliner 'Young' John McCormack found himself in line for a crack at the British light-heavyweight title in 1967, he approached the necessity of taking out British citizenship papers with some trepidation. It wasn't the quality of his rival contenders he feared. It was what his father might say. For Dad was 'Spike' McCormack, Irish middleweight champion of the 1940s, and an avowed nationalist. But the youngster's caution proved unnecessary. 'Spike' might have no great affection for things British, but he was not going to stand in his son's way if he thought the British championship would advance his boxing career. And there was no prouder man than old 'Spike' the night John had the Lonsdale Belt clasped around his waist.   Within seven years, John's brother Pat completed a unique 'double' by winning the British light-welterweight crown.   'Spike' was so delighted that he celebrated by giving up the drink for good.

Just as 'Spike' never went by his real name of John, his eldest son was billed throughout his career as 'Young' McCormack. In olden times it was customary for sons of famous fighters to adopt the prefix 'Young', but in John's case it was more in deference to the wishes of the BBBC. There was another John McCormack campaigning at the same time, a Scot known as 'Cowboy' because of his bow legs, and it was thought there might be some confusion among fight followers.

Although a quieter personality than his extrovert father and younger brother, inside the ring John was a formidable battler. He wasn't a great hitter, but he was relentless in his pursuit of his quarry and he hacked away until his opponent finally wilted. He took a punch on the chin better than brother Pat, but suffered the bugbear of vulnerable eyebrows. At one stage he was being hailed as a serious world title contender, but he fell just short of that stature.   Though expertly managed by fellow Dubliner Paddy Byrne and trained by much-respected Frank Duffett, John never really lost the raw edges that stopped him fulfilling his early promise. Duffett summarised him as 'an able fighter, but always too nice a guy to be at his most effective. He needed a little of his brother Pat's ruthlessness.'

While most kids were growing up on nursery rhymes, John and his 11 brothers and sisters heard all about the exploits of the heroes of the ring from their father. When young John's fists were big enough to stay in a pair of boxing gloves he enlisted in the Consolata amateur club, which had been founded by 'Spike'. In 40 amateur contests, including many in different parts of the world while he served in the merchant navy, he lost only twice. The highlight of his unpaid career was his winning of the Irish junior light-heavyweight title in 1962. It was around this time that he met Paddy Byrne, who was to become his professional manager. Byrne, who was based in London, took the youngster to England, got him fixed up with a job as a painter and decorator, and launched him on the professional fight scene. His debut was an unnerving experience. It took place at the plush Napoleon Room of the National Sporting Club, in London's Regent Street, and his walk to the ring was on expensive, ankle-deep carpet. NSC members were dressed in dinner suits and bow-ties, smoked outsize cigars and drank brandy. They politely applauded the boxers' entry into the ring, but after that any shouting or hand-clapping was strictly forbidden. McCormack got used to the eerie silence quickly and put his Nigerian opponent Roy Burke away inside three rounds. Then the club members gave vent to their appreciation of his performance. Indeed, the Dubliner proved so popular that they kept asking him back again and again. His exciting wins earned him the accolade as the club's 'Best Young Boxer of 1964'.

By the end of 1965 McCormack was high in the queue for a chance at Chic Calderwood's British light-heavyweight title and *The Ring* noted him as a boxer 'destined for top honours'. Cut eyes had been responsible for his two defeats to date. Welshman Derek Richards had held him to a draw, but the other 19 outings were all wins; and only two of his opponents had stayed around to await the referees' points verdicts. His Irish debut at the Ulster Hall had the Belfast sports writers in raptures over his eighth round stoppage of English Southern Area champion Bob Nicolson. George Ace wrote in the *Newsletter:*

Chic Calderwood's reign as British champion will end just as soon as he can be persuaded to share a ring with McCormack. Jabs, hooks, uppercuts - you name the punches and McCormack had them all in his repertoire.'

Jack McGowan in the *Belfast Telegraph* was equally glowing:

This boy simply fizzes with belligerence, moving forward all the time and banging away with both hands to the head and body. He's like a wasp at a picnic - he just can't be discouraged.

But the adulation proved to be premature. In his next outing, against Lion Ven of Belgium, the raw edges were all too evident. The points decision for Ven was hotly disputed, but the Dubliner had shown an inability to master a back-pedalling, fast jabbing rival. The shock setback did not affect his British ranking and he overpowered his Scottish namesake, John 'Cowboy' McCormack, in an eliminator. A rather fortunate win over Derek Richards on a cut eye stoppage disposed of the other main challenger, but McCormack was much happier with his revenge victory over Lion Ven at the Ulster Hall. The Dubliner won nine out of ten rounds. Offers arrived from the United States for matches with former world middleweight champion Carl 'Bobo' Olsen and coming champion Bob Foster, but he wisely elected to stay and try for the British championship. The title had become vacant on the death of Chic Calderwood in a car crash. Welshman Eddie Avoth was chosen to contest the honour with McCormack. It was to the Irishman's delight that he heard that the National Sporting Club had secured the championship contest on 19 June 1967. But it was a strange mixture of joy and sadness with which he greeted his acquisition of the Lonsdale Belt. The same NSC members who had encouraged him so heartily when he started out as a professional now loudly booed the referee's decision to stop the contest in the seventh round. They did not feel that Avoth's cut eye was bad enough to warrant the stoppage at that point. The American monthly *Boxing Illustrated* was in no doubt that the best man lost.

A Dublin Boyo, Young John McCormack, is the latest in a long line of British pocket heavyweight champions. But he does not bear comparison with Len Harvey, Jock McAvoy, Freddie Mills, Randy Turpin or Don Cockell in the cruiser class. He was the luckiest winner of a title since Max Schmeling grabbed his protector and Jack Sharkey lost via a foul. Avoth, of the Howard Winstone camp, had exposed Mac as a willing trier without the champion class and seemed set for a certain win. Another few rounds might have settled it.

Lucky or not, McCormack was British champion and his Dublin fans clamoured for the chance to see him in action. Dublin bookmaker Terry Rogers teamed up with his Belfast counterpart Barney Eastwood to stage McCormack's first and only appearance in his home town. It was a Frenchman Daniel Leullier in two rounds. He was in equally devastating form three months later as he unleashed a classic 'one-two' to knock out persistent rival Derek Richards in defence of his British crown at Birmingham.

With Terry Rogers promising to do all he could to entice world light-heavyweight champion Dick Tiger to put his title at stake in Dublin, McCormack set off for Australia in confident mood to face Bob Dunlop for the British Commonwealth championship. But there were no more honours to be won. He cut Dunlop's lip with one of the first blows landed, but the Aussie made him pay for it. McCormack fought bravely but he was taking a fierce battering when referee Vic Patrick, a former noted fighter, stopped the one-way traffic in the seventh round. Back in London to defend his British title against Eddie Avoth, he suffered defeat in an odd reversal of their first encounter. This time it was the Irishman's cut eye which caused him to retire at the end of the 11th round. It had been a hard, evenly contested affair with the Welshman's smoother boxing perhaps giving him the edge.

After winning three and losing two of his next five fights, McCormack challenged Avoth for his old title at Nottingham Ice Rink in April 1970. No one could have thought beforehand that it would be the Dubliner's last contest. He quit the game in disgust at what he felt was unfair treatment by the referee, the late Wally Thom, a former British welterweight champion, who disqualified him in the eighth round for alleged butting. McCormack's head-down style of attacking often led to head clashes, but they were always accidental. Often he was the one who emerged with an eye injury. There was certainly an element of 'needle' between the boxers since their first clash and the referee was ever watchful for any hint of a foul. McCormack, especially, was frequently warned for even minor rule infringements which normally would have gone unchecked. When Thom finally sent the Irishman to his corner there were heated protests from McCormack's seconds, to no avail. Although only 25, John hung up his gloves for good. He spent some years in London after his retirement, but later returned to Dublin where he now works for an oil company and spends most of his spare time expertly coaching young boxers at St Saviour's amateur club in the old Dorset Street fire station.

Kid brother Pat, two years younger than John, was a reincarnation of the bare-knuckle, fight-to-the-finish pugilists of old. He earned good gladly have fought for nothing. 'When the punches are going in and the blood is flowing,' he told one reporter, 'you'll see me enjoying myself. I just love to fight.' There was no fancy stuff with Pat, no cautious probing for openings or waiting patiently for the other man to make mistakes. He just dug in his heels, bit into his gumshield and threw his leather-encased bombs. Like his brother, he was prone to cut eyes. Unlike John, he was not blessed with too sturdy a chin. He could be tagged and put down for the full count by good counter punches. His professional trainer, Frank Duffett, said of Pat: 'He was one of the strongest fighters I've known, short but with shoulders like a heavyweight and he had a heavyweight's punch. It could take him a little while to work his way in, and he could be caught as he moved forwards. But once he was in you were in real trouble.'

Pat was what his fellow Dubliners call a 'character', just like his father. Stories told about him are legendary. Like how he used to enjoy a few puffs of a carefully concealed cigarette when he returned to his corner during amateur bouts. And the time he appeared on American television and was asked what he did when he wasn't fighting. 'I paint,' replied Pat. Was that oils or water colours? 'Jaysus, no: houses!'

When he made his professional debut at the National Sporting Club in London he stopped Winson Thomas in five rounds but injured his hand in the process. He blamed the injury on the constriction of tight bandages.   When the trouble persisted after five more contests, he dispensed with hand bandages for the rest of his career.   He would probably have been even happier if he had been allowed do without gloves as well! He quickly won himself a reputation as one of the best value-for-money fighters in British rings and promoters clamoured for his services. Hardened ringmen like Ray Fallone and Lex Hunter fell before him, but the first signs of his vulnerability to facial cuts came in his eleventh outing, when he was stopped in two rounds by Ricky Porter. In his next fight he was knocked out in 55 seconds by Peter Quinn. Pat said later: 'I heard he was a good hitter, so I tore across the ring trying to flatten him. He must have beaten me to it, because I remembered nothing about what happened until the next day.'

On two trips to Denmark to twice beat former European lightweight champion Boerge Krogh in three rounds, McCormack made such an impression on promoter Mogens Palle that he wanted to 'adopt' him. If Pat would agree to settle in Denmark, Palle could promise him plenty of lucrative matches. The boxer was tempted but his wife Maureen was not keen to uproot her home in London. Unlike most fighter's wives, Mrs McCormack loved to watch her man boxing. They had actually met at a boxing tournament in Dublin.

Some of the overseas fighters imported to face McCormack in London proved too much for him. The lanky black American Johnny Gant pole-axed him in just 90 seconds with a couple of long, powerful right-handers, and he got himself into such a tangle with Italian Bruno Meggiolar that, in trying to wrench himself free, he wrestled his opponent to the canvas. The Italian claimed he had hurt his shoulder in the fall and could not continue, whereupon the referee disqualified McCormack. He was much happier with his trip back home to Dublin in July 1972, when he shared a bill at Croke Park with none other than Muhammad Ali, who beat fellow-American Al 'Blue' Lewis. Pat disposed of Frenchman David Pesenti in five rounds. It was quite an upsetting evening for McCormack's victim all round. When his gumshield was knocked out of his mouth in the third round and landed on the ring apron, a delighted youngster lurking at the ringside grabbed the 'souvenir' and disappeared into the crowd. And when he entered the ring Pesenti found he had only one glove! An appeal was made for the culprit to come forward, but he couldn't be found. Eventually a new pair of gloves was located and they were put on the Frenchman's hands by Paddy Byrne, McCormack's manager. As someone remarked, it could only happen in Ireland!

McCormack was a promoter's dream. He would fight anyone anywhere and could be guaranteed to provide the fans with value for money. His devil-may-care outlook obviously brought its dangers for he was often caught out by heavy punchers. In a trip to South Africa in 1973 he was halted in four rounds by Gielie Buitendag, whom he had already beaten on a previous visit, and moved on to Australia to suffer another fourth round loss to the Commonwealth light-welterweight

'Young' John McCormack

Pat McCormack with his shillelagh

Dan McAlinden (right) v Richard Dunn

champion Hector Thompson.   But unbeaten Danish prospect Erkki Meronen was summarily executed by a rampant McCormack in Copenhagen.   Promoter Mogens Palle had billed the Irishman as 'the Animal' and released photos of him being led around with a chain around his neck. He certainly lived up to his reputation on this occasion.

After six years of hard, bruising battles in many corners of the globe, McCormack was finally rewarded with a fight for the British light-welterweight championship in March 1974. With brother John lending vocal encouragement from the corner, Pat endured some rough passages before a left hook crumpled the exhausted champion, Jamaican-born Des Morrison, to the floor for the count-out in round eleven. McCormack was cut above and below the right eye, had another gash on his left eyebrow and suffered damage to his nose and mouth, but he had his heart set on winning the title. It was his sheer persistence and guts that carried him through to victory in a long, bruising battle. His championship tenure lasted only eight months. He went to challenger Joey Singleton's home town of Liverpool and came away minus his title. The Irishman looked set for an easy defence when he floored Singleton, who was having only his eighth contest, in the opening round. But the lanky challenger managed to survive and scored well on the retreat for the rest of the fight. The points verdict for Singleton was hotly disputed by McCormack.

Pat resumed his world travels, boxing with mixed fortunes in Denmark, Norway, the United States and South Africa before coming back for another crack at the British championship, this time at welterweight. Champion John H. Stracey had given up the crown to chase the world title, leaving McCormack and Pat Thomas to dispute the vacancy. As in almost all his fights, McCormack's title bid was a 'war' from start to finish. He managed to shake his West Indies-born rival several times, but was generally on the receiving end against a more accurate puncher. Pat was badly cut up facially and took two counts of six before a final flurry of blows put him down against the ropes in the 13th round. He tried to get up, but the effort was too much and referee Wally Thom, who had held the same title 20 years earlier, completed the count.   After a heart-to-heart talk with his manager, McCormack announced his retirement from boxing in January 1976. *Boxing News* editor Graham Houston paid him a farewell tribute:

> Pat was a fighter who scorned refinements. He slipped a few jabs but was always willing to take a blow to land one. He was a true, honest-to-goodness fighting Irishman with, as manager Paddy Byrne put it, the heart of ten men. He had a ripping left hook and was one of the most brutal body punchers of recent years. He tended to cut up and he could be tagged early, but he always came to fight.

Finally, a champion of the heavyweights

They called him 'Dangerous Dan' and 'Dynamite Dan' as he mowed down a succession of heavyweights, with just a few stumbles along the way, to become the first Irishman to win the British heavyweight championship. Then, as his career hit the skids and he made a series of disastrous comebacks, Dan McAlinden became known as 'Desperate Dan'. Unlike the comic-book character, McAlinden did not have a chin of steel. He could be tagged with alarming ease and he was knocked out or stopped eight times in 45 professional contests. On the credit side, his ability to dish out punishment is borne out by the fact that only three of his 31 victims were able to last the distance. He could hit all right, but he tended to lose confidence if his opponent failed to buckle quickly under fire. He lacked the right size (he stood 6' $1/2$") for a top heavyweight, tended to cut easily and never seemed to overcome his amateurish style of gambling on all-out aggression, which left him open to a good counter-puncher. Domestic and managerial troubles didn't help his concentration at the height of his career. Yet, for all his faults, McAlinden was a colourful, exciting performer. Anything could happen when he climbed between the ropes and he usually managed to give the customers value for their money.

An energetic youngster from Newry, County Down, Dan was only eleven when he discovered he had a fair punch in his right hand. He knocked out a school prefect who had caught him 'mitching'. Badly hit by the unemployment of the 1950s, the McAlinden family, led by Dan's father Patrick, emigrated to Coventry, where Dan joined the Edgewick amateur boxing club. Even then he found it hard to stay out of clashes with officialdom. After winning the Irish senior heavyweight title in 1967 and representing his country in the European championships in Rome, he by-passed the next Irish tests to try for the British amateur title. He qualified as he was domiciled in Coventry. McAlinden stormed through to the semi-finals, but got into a row with his club officials when he failed to show up for a tournament. The club promptly suspended him, a decision which was backed by the British Amateur Boxing Association, and that was the end of his quest for the British title. An angry McAlinden signed a professional contract with George Middleton, who had handled Mick Leahy as well as the three Turpin brothers. Jackie Turpin took on the job of trying to iron out some of the rougher aspects of the Irishman's style, but without too much success.

Dan certainly made an initial impact in the paid ranks by beating three opponents on the one night. The occasion was a novice heavyweight competition staged by Jack Solomons at the World Sporting Club in London in July 1969. He overwhelmed John Cullen in two rounds, Richard Dunn in one and Denis Avoth, also in the first. Solomons was so impressed with the fiery Irishman that he took a deep interest in his career and ended up as his manager when George Middleton stepped down a few years later. Despite his unhappy experience with Martin Thornton, Solomons had always cherished the hope of finding an Irish heavyweight contender. Perhaps he had found his man at last. With

Dan's first ten opponents all bowled over in less than five rounds, it looked as if he was heading for the top: until the giant American Jack O'Halloran spoiled the script by snatching a points win in an eight-rounder. The first seeds of self-doubt were sown in McAlinden's mind. To restore his confidence Solomons imported another American, Mose Harrell, who had gone the full route with Britain's latest 'golden boy', Joe Bugner. McAlinden smashed him down for the count in the first round. That was the pattern of the unpredictable Irishman's career. He could look great on one occasion, only to flop badly on the next.

After a rather fortunate draw against Ray Patterson, brother of former world heavyweight champion Floyd, Dan journeyed to New York to take on another brother of a famous heavyweight. His opponent at Madison Square Garden was Rahman Ali, whose brother Muhammad topped the bill in the first of his three epic encounters with Joe Frazier. It was the night the better known of the Alis had his self-proclaimed invincibility shattered by the pounding fists of Frazier. McAlinden made it an extra-black night for the Ali clan by convincingly outpointing Rahman. His bout was just before the main event and as he emerged from the ring he heard a shout: 'Just a minute, I want to see the man who just whupped my little brother'. The ex-world champion started clowning around and sparring up to McAlinden. Not sure of the Irishman's name, he snarled: 'I'm gonna whup you, Macmillan, for what you done to my brother'. McAlinden, cool as ice, retorted: 'I can beat you just as I did your brother'. The great one was struck dumb for once. Later Ali repeated his desire to teach the Irishman a lesson, because he considered him 'too cocky'. But their ringside battle of words was as close as they ever got to thrashing out their differences.

Jack Solomons' plan to force Joe Bugner into a showdown clash with McAlinden by matching the Irishman with men who had given Bugner trouble came unstuck when he faced American Larry Middleton. The tall, stylish Middleton, a points winner over Bugner, did an even more decisive job on McAlinden, stopping him in eight rounds. The setback was put to the back of Dan's mind as he began preparations for a crack at Jack Bodell's British and Commonwealth heavyweight titles in Birmingham in June 1972. This time Eddie Thomas, the former British and European welterweight champion and now a highly successful manager and trainer, was hired to get McAlinden into top condition. Bodell's habit of sticking out his chin and dropping his guard proved too inviting a target for the hard-hitting Irishman to miss. It was all over inside two rounds, with the champion lying face down on the canvas to be counted out as an ecstatic McAlinden was engulfed by a swarm of supporters.

What should have been an enjoyable and lucrative period for the new heavyweight champion turned out to be a sorry tale of missed chances, out-of-the-ring problems and good wins being wiped out by shock losses. He broke his thumb in losing to Irish Pat Duncan from Idaho and it took a one year absence from the ring for it to heal. His comeback bout was a defence of his British and Commonwealth titles against Bunny Johnson, a Birmingham-based Jamaican. During that long resting period he had split with Jack Solomons and had to pay the big fight mogul £10,000 to free himself from his contract. He then signed up with another well-known manager, Sam Burns, but that partnership did not last either.

On paper Dan looked liked he shouldn't have too much trouble with Johnson, who was really only a light-heavyweight. In fact, Johnson later moved down and won the light-heavyweight title. But many shrewd judges pointed out that McAlinden always had trouble with crafty boxers and Johnson fitted that category. They were proved right. The champion fought with little heart for the job. He looked tense and nervous and his fans were alarmed to see him sag at the knees after taking seemingly innocuous punches. In the ninth a left hook and a right uppercut sent him down for the second time in that round. Bemused and with blood seeping from his cheek, he sat it out on the canvas while the referee counted him out. So Britain had its first black heavyweight champion: and Ireland's first holder of the title had surrendered it in his first defence.

Three impressive comeback wins by McAlinden were followed by a stroke of luck that brought him an unexpected chance to regain his British and Commonwealth titles, which Bunny Johnson had since lost to Richard Dunn. Dunn was scheduled to meet Belgium's Jean-Pierre Coopman for the vacant European title at Wembley when Coopman was forced to pull out. Promoter Harry Levene switched McAlinden from a preliminary bout into the main event against Dunn, with the latter's two titles at stake. Dan was delighted with his apparent change of fortune and fancied his chances against a man he had already met twice. They had first clashed in an amateur international in Dublin, when Dunn came off the floor to knock out the Irishman. Then, when both men made their professional debuts in the same novice heavyweight competition, it was McAlinden's turn to score a knockout over the Englishman. Both men could hit, but neither took a whack on the chin too well. McAlinden, outweighed by 21 pounds and towered over by the 6' 4" Dunn, tried a big right in the second round. It missed, but Dunn's countering right didn't. Down went McAlinden with a thud. He jumped up before the count could begin, only to be sent down again for three. He tried to duck his way out of trouble, but a cluster of punches dropped him for the last time. He was in the act of rising when referee Harry Gibbs spread his arms to indicate he had been counted out.

Dan might sensibly have heeded the agonising lesson that his glory days, such as they were, were gone forever. But fight on he did, for another six years, in an amazing succession of retirements and fruitless comebacks. There were occasional glimpses of the old fire, but they were quickly doused when he would get his suspect chin or vulnerable eyebrows in the way of a wild hook. He did manage to win a championship during those twilight years, the Northern Ireland heavyweight title. The title fight with Sean 'Jumbo' McKenna from Downpatrick at the Templemore Sports Complex in Derry, promoted by Jack Solomons, was like a Wild West punch-up in the short while it lasted. The contestants slung blows with reckless abandon, with McAlinden, though repeatedly staggered, scoring two knockdowns in the opening round. The second round was only a minute old when McAlinden half-punched, half-wrestled his rival to the floor. McKenna's face hit the canvas hard and the blood oozed from his eyebrow. The injury was too bad for him to continue. McAlinden left the ring to a good round of applause, although he had been booed on entry. Part of the reason for the crowd's initial hostitity was undoubtedly Dan's widely publicised break-up with his wife Patricia. He had been fined £100 by Coventry magistrates after pleading guilty to maliciously wounding his wife and another man after tracing them to a night club.

So McAlinden was now heavyweight champion of Northern Ireland, but the title had a hollow ring to it. McKenna had only three previous fights and had been stopped in two of them. He was clearly no match for even a run-down former British and Commonwealth champion. McAlinden had six more contests spaced out between retirements over the next four years and only won one of them. He finally accepted his time had come to quit for good after being stopped in five rounds by Jamaican Denton Ruddock in March 1981.

That same month, by a strange co-incidence, saw another Northern Ireland boxer crowned British heavyweight champion. Gordon Ferris, a former Irish senior amateur champion and Commonwealth Games bronze medallist from Enniskillen, County Fermanagh, just edged out 35-year-old Billy Aird by one point in a dull 15-rounder for the championship vacated by John L. Gardner. Ferris, a tall, rangy boxer with a fair punch but, like McAlinden, not the possessor of a sturdy jaw, is not remembered as one of the outstanding occupants of the British heavyweight throne. He might have gone further in the game had he possessed the burning ambition to succeed that is so vital a part of a fighter's make-up. But his performances often revealed that he wished he was off doing something else. He lost the British title at the first defence to another veteran, Neville Meade, a Wales-based Jamaican, who crushed him in two and a half minutes of the opening round.

More British title-holders; and a couple of record breakers

Since the late 1960s, Northern Ireland has produced an impressive list of British champions and two of them etched their names in the record books for unique achievements. Des Rea became the first holder of the newly created junior welterweight title. He lost it in his first defence and lost again when he tried to regain it. They were the only three contests for that particular title before the British Board of Control abolished it. And Hugh Russell performed a strange 'double' by winning the British bantamweight championship, and then moving down a weight to pick up the flyweight crown. It was the first time these titles had been won in 'reverse' order.

Another odd aspect of Des Rea's championship campaign is that all his three title fights were against the same man, Vic Andreetti, a Londoner of Italian extraction. The BBBC had introduced the new ten stone junior welterweight division as an experiment to cater for boxers who were too heavy for the lightweights and too light for the welterweights. Rea, born in Belfast, raised in Liverpool and domiciled in Wales, had the new Lonsdale Belt put around his waist in February 1968 after outpointing Andreetti in London. In the return match, exactly a year later, the Londoner turned the tables on him with another close 15-round decision. The third meeting between the pair, in October 1969, ended more decisively. Rea was counted out in the fourth round.

Undaunted, Rea took up the chase for the British welterweight title and boosted his reputation by taking the all-Ireland title with an 11th round knockout of Dubliner Gus Farrell in Belfast. But he spoiled his chances of a shot at the British crown by dropping a points decision to veteran Johnny Cooke, a former title-holder, again in Belfast. Rea, a crowd-pleasing southpaw who always kept his boxing kit packed in case he was called upon at short notice, was a thorough professional. He cared little about where or who he fought as long as the money was right. His career took him to Australia, South Africa, Denmark, France, Switzerland and the United States. He ended his campaign in Norway in 1974, when he was stopped in two rounds by Kristian Hoydahl. Rea's overall career record of 28 wins, five draws and 36 defeats does not appear too impressive until one takes into account the quality of many of his opponents. After being halted in six rounds by future world champion Bruno Arcari in a European title bout in 1968, Des showed almost suicidal zeal in making a trip to California to tackle the brilliant Cuban Jose Napoles, another upcoming world champion, Rea, floored and in trouble in the first round, stuck it out gamely until the fifth, when the ringside doctor advised the referee to stop the one-sided bout as blood flosed from the Irishman's damaged nose. Another one-time world title-holder, John H. Stracey, stoped Ria in two rounds in London and other British champions who beat him were Brian Curvis, Des Morrison and Pat Thomas (three times).

Like Rea, fellow-Belfastman Paddy Maguire was not the most talented boxer of his era, but he was plentifully endowed with the fighting spirit that lifts some ringmen to greater heights than their skills promise. Maguire won the British bantamweight title at the third attempt when he beat Dave Needham at the World Sporting Club, London, in 1975. Paddy's constant body bombardment, supplemented with sharp hooks to the head, overcame the better boxing of the defending champion. Maguire was just ahead on points when a badly cut eye suffered by Needham caused the referee to stop the contest in the 14th round. *Boxing News* voted it 'Fight of the Year', just as another Maguire fight for the British title, his losing clash with Johnny Clark two years earlier, was considered the best bout of 1973 by the same journal. In between these two bouts, Maguire had been thwarted in his second try for the title when Needham outscored him for the crown vacated by Clark.

Born less than a mile from the birthplace of the legendary John Caldwell, Maguire had a distinguished amateur career, highlighted by his taking the Irish senior flyweight and bantamweight championships and a silver medal in the 1966 Commonwealth Games. He also holds the distinction of being the only boxer to stop the great, eight-times Irish amateur champion, Mick Dowling. Encouraged by Scot Walter McGowan, the former world flyweight champion, to turn professional, Maguire won his first eight fights for pay in Belfast, but found the street violence of the period a serious handicap to his road training. He opted to pursue his career in London under the manager and trainer team of Paddy Byrne and Frank Duffett, a combination that had been so successful with the McCormack brothers. Although his first London outing resulted in a loss to Bob Allotey from Ghana, the wisdom of his move was borne out when he won the next seven on the trot, including a stoppage of British flyweight champion John McCluskey in a non-title bout leading up to his first try for the British bantamweight title.

Paddy's ambitions embraced the Commonwealth crown too, but he lasted less than eight rounds against the Australian title-holder Paul Ferreri at Melbourne Festival Hall. In an attempt to take the European title at Cluses, France, Maguire was very unlucky to receive only a draw against Daniel Trioulaire. He floored the Frenchman in the eighth round with a left hook to the ribs, the bell coming to Trioulaire's rescue as he rose at eight. Maguire also forced the title-holder to take a standing count in the 13th round. Ray Clarke, secretary of the BBBC, who was at the ringside, said he had no doubt that Maguire should have got the verdict, while Mickey Duff, the Irishman's new manager, said the decision was 'a joke'. Maguire did gain a second crack at the European crown in 1977 at Sardinia. As always, the Irishman's effort was underlined with courage, but that was not enough against the crafty 37-year-old Italian Franco Zurlo. Maguire's face was badly swollen and he had a nasty gash on his eyebrow when his seconds announced his retirement at the end of the eighth round. There was only one more ring date for Paddy after that. Defending his British title against lanky Johnny Owen he tried his best to bring the Welshman down to his level by pounding away to his body. But Owen kept him on the end of his long, raking punches and was giving the Irishman a painful lesson when the referee ended the unequal contest in the 11th round. While Maguire went into contented retirement, the ill-fated Owen's career ended tragically when he failed to recover consciousness after being knocked out in a world title bout by Lupe Pintor and died after 64 days in a coma.

The historic city of Derry had its first ring hero since Billy 'Spider' Kelly when Charlie Nash took British and European title honours during the 1970s, but failed in his bid for the World Boxing Council lightweight title. A slick-moving southpaw from the troubled Creggan area (his brother was one of 13 civilians shot dead by British troops on the infamous 'Bloody Sunday' in January 1972), Nash had a noteworthy amateur career before taking the plunge into the paid ranks at the relatively late age of 24. He was Irish senior lightweight champion five times, represented his country in 29 internationals, and fought in two European championships and in the 1972 Olympic Games, where he lost in the quarter-final to the eventual gold medallist. His professional campaign got off to an historic start when he fought for the all-Ireland title in his very first contest. He beat his old amateur rival Ray Ross on points over ten rounds in Derry to earn the title and make the final score in the series: Nash 6, Ross 0.

Thirteen straight victories, including defeats of former British title-holders Jimmy Revie and Joey Singleton, shot him into the leading contender spot for Jim Watt's British lightweight title. But the Scottish holder was in no hurry to accommodate him. A cut eye, a problem that was to hound Charlie throughout his career, caused his first defeat against Adolfo Osses, but in a return meeting he scored a knockout in the third round. When Jim Watt refused to defend his British crown in Derry against Nash, even though the Irishman's home town had won the right to stage it, the BBBC took away the Scot's title. Nash got his desserts when he beat Londoner Johnny Claydon for the vacant title at the Templemore Sports Complex, Derry, in February 1978. Referee Roland Dakin stopped the contest in the 12th round as he had the Irishman ten points ahead. But Claydon's cornermen were not so happy with the referee's interpretation of the rules. They reasoned that, with three rounds still to go and with Nash bleeding from the right eyebrow, their man was still in with a chance. The referee, however, explained that he had no option but to interpret the rules strictly, which stated that a boxer whose points tally was ten points in front automatically became the winner at that juncture.

Now managed by an ailing Jack Solomons, who conducted his business by telephone as he was not fit enough to travel, Nash cast his sights towards the WBC title, which had just been won by Jim Watt. He realised he stood even less chance of enticing Watt to defend his world crown in Northern Ireland than of getting him over when he was British title-holder. But the Derryman was willing to go anywhere to contest the major honour. He consolidated his position in the world ratings by taking the European title, vacated by Watt, with a comprehensive points win over Frenchman Andre Holyk in Derry. Charlie fought mainly on the retreat, his southpaw jab being rarely out of Holyk's face, and always

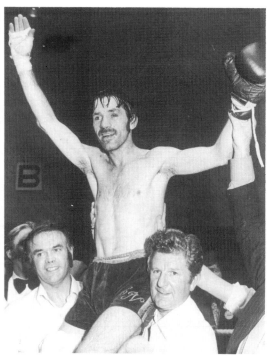

Charlie Nash after winning the European title

Hugh Russell after winning the British title

Sean Mannion (right) v Mike McCallum

slipping away beautifully from any threat of danger. Critics, however, noted that he had still to rid himself of his old amateur habits of dropping his hands, punching off balance and sticking his chin out invitingly.

Copenhagen was the odd setting for Nash's first defence of his European title, for his challenger was Scotsman Ken Buchanan, the former WBA lightweight champion. Nash kept his crown with a desperately close points decision. Charlie suffered a sad blow shortly afterwards when Jack Solomons died. Another prominent boxing figure, Mickey Duff, took over as his manager and secured for the Derryman his big chance at Jim Watt's WBC lightweight championship in March 1980. He had travel to Watt's home town of Glasgow for the opportunity but that didn't worry him as he had fought all over the world as an amateur and most of his professional bouts were away from home, due to the lack of promotions in riot-torn Northern Ireland. Nash made a bright start, using the ring well and poking Watt's head back with probing right leads. The Scot, taken aback at the challenger's smooth opening, had a bigger shock in store before the first three minutes were up. A perfectly placed left hook caught the world champion flush on the jaw and sent him to the floor. Up before a count could begin, he traded punches with a surprisingly agressive Irishman. There was a clash of heads and Nash backed off with blood seeping from the corner of his right eye. The injury did not worry Charlie unduly, but the Scot settled down to win the next two rounds with his more composed punching. Watt mounted a furious assault in the fourth round, driving the challenger across the ring. Nash, caught off balance, fell to the canvas and brought Watt down with him. The Derryman stayed on one knee until the referee, Sid Nathan, counted eight. Watt's controlled attack had Nash in dire trouble and a smashing right floored him for another count of eight. He rose on wobbly legs and the referee immediately stopped the fight. It was the end of Charlie's world title dreams.

He turned his sights back to the European title, now held by Francisco Leon of Spain. Dublin was the location for its first European championship contest since the riotous Billy 'Spider' Kelly v Ray Famechon affair at Donnybrook bus depot 25 years earlier. This time it was at the plush Burlington Hotel, with 500 patrons paying £50 a head for the dinner-boxing-cabaret show on 14 December 1980. For those who couldn't afford the admission charges Radio Telefis Eireann televised the bout live. The stay-at-home spectators were the lucky ones, for it was a drab 12-rounder with Nash proving too skilful for a champion of limited ability. Dublin was again the choice for Nash's defence of the European title five months later against Joey Gibilisco. The Italian, with only 19 wins in 27 outings, was considered a fair puncher but not a serious threat to the stylish Irishman. It didn't turn out that way. The chunky fighter never gave Nash a chance to get settled and forced him to a standing count in the second round from a series of hooks to the head. Blood flowed from Nash's right eye in the next round and he bled from the nose and mouth in the fourth, when he took another standing count. Battered to the canvas for seven in the sixth round, Nash was a sorry sight as he stood helpless, his eyes glazed and his face smeared with blood. The Italian smashed a left hook, followed by a tremendous right, to the champion's head. Nash fell straight back, out cold even before his neck bounced off the bottom rope. He lay there, badly dazed, for several minutes after the referee completed the formality of the count-out. Promoter Phil McLaughlin also lost out badly that night. Only 2,000 spectators braved the bitter cold of the outdoor Dalymount Park for the occasion.

Nash, whose 30th birthday was two days after the fight, should have realised that his best fighting days were behind him, but boxers are often the last to accept the harsh realities about themselves. He came back after a ten-month rest to win two contests in his home town, but took a trip to Birmingham to lose in three rounds to unbeaten prospect Tony Willis. Further humiliation hit the Derryman when, after signing contracts for a return match with Gibilisco for the European title and having it approved by the European Boxing Union, the match was vetoed by the British Board, who felt it was not in his best interests in view of his poor showing against Willis. Charlie had one last fling, travelling to Cologne in March 1983 to tackle the unbeaten German champion Rene Weller, who later won the European title. Nash put up a creditable performance, but he was cut under the left eye and on the forehead and was also bleeding from the nose when his seconds retired him as he sat in his corner after the fourth round.

In the same month that rarity of boxing occasions, a contest between two Irishmen for a British championship, drew a packed King's Hall on 2 March 1983, when Hugh Russell put his newly acquired bantamweight title on the line against Davy Larmour. Rivalry between the pair was intense, with Russell drawing his support from the Catholic New Lodge district of Belfast and Protestant Larmour enjoying the Loyalist backing of the Shankill population. To the credit of the boxers they made no attempt to exploit the religious difference between them. Nor did the crowd show any sign of the sectarian bitterness which marked so much of everyday life in the troubled Northern capital. Barney Eastwood was the promoter of this first boxing tournament at the King's Hall since that unforgettable bantamweight clash between Freddie Gilroy and John Caldwell 21 years earlier. Larmour, at 31 the older man by seven years, took his last chance at glory literally with both hands. Lacking the champion's greater skills, Davy simply 'walked through' Russell's punches and kept the pressure on so well that he stopped 'Little Red' from settling into his normal rhythm. Russell, dropped for eight in the fifth round and cut on his cheek, gamely stuck it to the finish, but referee Harry Gibbs had no hesitation in raising Larmour's hand at the end of the 12 rounds on a score of 118 points to 116 $\frac{1}{2}$.

It was Russell's honouring of a promise to make Larmour his first challenger that cost Hughie his title after holding it for only 36 days. Next to Frank Goddard's 23-day tenure as heavyweight title-holder in 1919, Russell's was the shortest reign of any British champion. Larmour, too, carved himself a slice of history that night. At 31, he was the oldest boxer ever to win the British bantamweight title. Russell had made a vow to defend his title against Larmour after narrowly outpointing him in their first meeting, a final eliminator for the British crown, in October 1982. He was true to his word at a heavy cost.

Both Russell and Larmour were stars of the amateur ring before fighting for pay. Hughie, with his distinctive head of ginger curly hair, was a dazzling southpaw who took home bronze medals from the Commonwealth Games in 1978 and the Olympics two years later. Larmour was already a veteran of 17 years' amateur campaigning, comprising some 400 contests, when he turned pro at the advanced age of 25. A bustling, aggressive battler, he was a gold medal winner at the 1974 Commonwealth Games and also took part in the world amateur championships, European championships and the 1976 Olympic Games, where he was beaten by American Leo Randolph the eventual gold medallist. Davy picked up a gold medal in an 18-nation tournament in Holland and West Germany in 1974. He turned pro in 1977, mainly for financial considerations, but lost three of his first five bouts, including stoppages by John Feeney and reigning British bantamweight champion Johnny Owen in a non-title bout. He did outscore his old amateur rival Neil McLaughlin to win the all-Ireland title at the Albert Foundry Social Club in Belfast. They had met no less than nine times as amateurs, with McLaughlin emerging on top in six if them.

Larmour managed five wins and a loss in his next six fights before dropping a decision to Dave Smith in a final eliminator for the British title. But thanks to Hugh Russell's generosity he got the opportunity to etch his name on the roll of British bantamweight champions. Larmour held the title for eight months before putting it on the line against former champion John Feeney. The Englishman was even more devastating than he had been in their first encounter. Larmour, after a bright opening, walked onto a left hook counter to the jaw and took a count of five. He was shipping heavy punishment against the ropes when the referee intervened in the third round. It was the end of the road for Davy Larmour, but he wasn't overly disappointed. Just winning the British title had been a bonus he hadn't dared to expect when he made his late entry to the professional ranks.

Hugh Russell's time spent as a paid fighter was even shorter than Larmour's. He was 26 when he called it quits after 19 contests (17 wins and two defeats) while still British flyweight champion in April 1985. Hughie was a highly popular performer during his four-year professional career, with his lively style, darting in and out behind a solid southpaw right jab and a nice variety of hooks from either hand. He would have been a standout boxer in any other era, but was unfortunate to be overshadowed by a bigger star in the same Barney Eastwood 'stable', Barry McGuigan. He was unbeaten in 11 contests when he challenged John Feeney for the British bantamweight title at the Ulster Hall in January 1983. It was the last British title fight to be scheduled for 15 rounds. The BBBC had decided to restrict title contests to 12 rounds but, as contracts had already been signed before the new rule was made, the bout went ahead over the old distance. As it ended in controversial circumstances in the 13th round, with Feeney being disqualified for 'persistent misuse of the head', it is interesting to speculate who might have won had it been restricted to 12 rounds. Opinions were sharply divided as to which boxer was ahead at the time of the stoppage. Referee Sid Nathan had Russell two rounds in front at the end of the 12th. Surprisingly, Barney Eastwood agreed with many ringside reporters who had Feeney ahead, although he was convinced his boy would have made up the deficit over the last three rounds.

After losing the bantamweight title to Davy Larmour, Russell caused considerable surprise by dropping down to the flyweight division. The experts who felt his decision was unwise appeared justified when he struggled to outpoint a couple of mediocre opponents. Not even his home-town fans were all that confident he could take the British flyweight title from Welshman Kelvin Smart, even at the King's Hall. But 'Little Red' gave one of the best performances of his career to outbox and outfight the defending champion. Smart complained that he was unable to see out of his badly swollen left eye and retired at the end of the seventh round. But any ambitions Russell harboured of chasing after the world title came a cropper when Mexican Jose Torres shocked him with a fifth round stoppage in Belfast. It brought home to him the stark fact that he lacked the ruggedness so vital for top-level professional boxing. He successfully defended his British flyweight title against Danny Flynn and Charlie Brown to win the Lonsdale Belt outright (the only other Irishman to do so was Freddie Gilroy) but had to come back from near defeat to halt Brown in the final round. By now, Hughie had secured a job as a photograper with the Belfast daily newspaper, *The Irish News*, and he wisely decided to concentrate fulltime on his new career. He is now a regular attender at Belfast big fight nights, but performs his job from the safe side of the ropes.

One Irishman who tried the American way to the top was Sean Mannion, who emigrated to Boston from Rosmuc, a small Connemara town nestling in the shadows of the picturesque Twelve Pins mountain range. A former Irish amateur junior champion while with the Oliver Plunket's Club in Girley, County Meath, he worked his way into a shot at the WBA light-middleweight title with an impressive points win over the previously undefeated Korean Inchul Baek. When the WBA stripped Roberto Duran of his world title for failing to meet top contender Mike McCallum, Mannion was chosen to contest the vacant crown with McCallum. The Galwayman, with his widowed mother and other members of his family at New York's Madison Square Garden on 19 October 1984 to cheer him on and Radio na Gaeltachta broadcasting the fight live for his Irish-speaking home fans, made a brave try for glory. The unbeaten Jamaican, however, proved vastly superior in all-round skills and punching power and was an overwhelming winner on points over 15 rounds. The 27-year-old Irishman showed boundless courage in lasting the limit, but it was once again emphasised that courage alone doesn't win world titles.

If anyone is handing out bravery awards at the end of the decade they should reserve an extra special one for Dave 'Boy' McAuley, a 25-year-old part-time chef from Larne, County Antrim, who went down fighting in a thrilling bid to relieve Columbia's Fidel Bassa of his WBA flyweight title at the King's Hall, Belfast, on 25 April 1987. Unlike Mannion, McAuley had the punching power to upset the odds. Unfortunately the proverbial 'luck of the Irish' deserted him when the world crown was within his grasp. After being floored and cut in the opening minute, McAuley battled back to drop Bassa in the third round. Fortunes swayed one way and then the other until the sensational ninth round when the Irishman, who had won the vacant British title by halting Scot Joe Kelly in nine rounds the previous October, overcame a shaky start to the round and smashed the world champion to the canvas for two counts of eight. One more knockdown and the fight would have automatically been stopped under the WBA's three knockdowns in one round rule. But McAuley just couldn't find the strength or the accuracy to land that one more big punch. By the 13th round the Irish challenger had nothing left and it was Bassa who delivered the knockout. McAuley vowed he would be back for another try at a world title, perhaps in the light-flyweight (7st 10lbs) division.

Barry McGuigan after winning the European title

Eight

Oh, Barry Boy!

IT HAD BEEN a long time coming - 35 years to be exact - but Irish fight fans had their first world champion since Rinty Monaghan to cheer when Barry McGuigan, the pride of Clones, County Monaghan, brilliantly outpunched Panama's Eusebio Pedroza to capture the World Boxing Association featherweight title at Queen's Park Rangers football ground, London, on 8 June 1985. 'The Clones Cyclone' not only beat one of the modern greats in Pedroza, who had foiled the best efforts of 19 prior challengers in a seven-year championship reign, but it was the way he did it that delighted everyone. His controlled aggression from the start paved the way for a sensational seventh round that saw him floor Pedroza with a perfect right to the jaw. The wily veteran title-holder managed to survive, however, and was still upright at the end of 15 memorable rounds. The referee and both judges gave their verdicts for McGuigan by wide margins. Some experts expressed the view that the Irishman had proved himself as good a boxer-fighter, pound for pound, as anyone else in the world, perhaps only marginally behind contemporaries Marvin Hagler and Don Curry.

Just as intriguing was the comparison made between McGuigan and past Irish greats. He might even be the best of all the Irish-born battlers, it was suggested with sound justification. But was he really better than Jimmy McLarnin, conqueror of 13 one-time world champions, Jack McAuliffe, never beaten in a career total of 53 contests, Tom Sharkey, who stood up to much-bigger James J. Jeffries for a combined 45 rounds in two brutal heavyweight battles, Nonpareil Jack Dempsey, first middleweight champion of the world and loser of only three of his 68 fights, Mike McTigue, winner of the world light-heavyweight title in Dublin in 1923 and an active professional for 21 years, or Rinty Monaghan, first 'homegrown' world champion and one of the most popular Irishmen ever to don a pair of boxing gloves? Without the benefit of hindsight, it is difficult to place McGuigan's ranking with the past greats. His shock loss of his WBA crown to Steve Cruz in the searing heat of the Nevada desert in June 1986 had some experts reassessing Barry's ability, but it was almost unanimously felt that the 110 degrees heat under the unrelenting Las Vegas sun had more to do with his downfall than the efforts of the Texan challenger. At the time of writing McGuigan was preparing for a comeback in the junior lightweight (or super featherweight) division and was setting his sights on one of the three versions of the world title at 9st 4lbs (130lbs).

On sheer all-round ability, McGuigan stands out in any company and in any era. His meteoric rise to world fame in the 1980s has given Irish fans a sense of pride they had not enjoyed since Rinty Monaghan's world title success in the late 1940s. Here, at last, was a boxer who could remind them of what real fistic talent was all about. Connoisseurs of the sport see in McGuigan the closest to the complete professional that can be found. His punching power is astonishing for a man of around nine stone (126lbs) and anyone who has been on the receiving end of those devastating left hooks, especially to the body, will testify to that account. His right hand is used more sparingly, but can still prove a potent weapon, as Eusebio Pedroza found out in losing his WBA title. For an almost exclusively attacking fighter, Barry is unusually adept at avoiding punches. He never presents a stationary target, twisting, turning and ducking while working his way in to find the chinks in his opponents' armour. Once inside, he unleashes those vicious hooks with power and accuracy. Thanks to a long reach, he also employs a good left jab, which is a useful points scorer was well as a 'softener up' for the heavier artillery. Critics have pointed out that he is not so impressive when forced to retreat, but few rivals have had the strength to make him go backwards for more than a few seconds. And even when he is caught with a hard punch, he has shown he can absorb the effect without too much discomfort. Allied to his natural talents is his complete dedication to the game. A fitness fanatic, the only real fear of his management team is the possibility that he might over-train. It's a problem many a boxer's handler would gladly suffer. Barry has the utmost confidence in his ability to overcome any obstacles set up by an opponent and to adapt his approach if the situation demands. A serious student of the sport, he goes into every strength and weakness of his prospective rivals before a fight, then concentrates on putting into practice his plan of campaign. If things don't work out, he's ready to try something else. And he is attentive to his cornermen's advice. In short, he is the true pro.

Not surprisingly, McGuigan is constantly 'claimed' by Britain, Northern Ireland and the Irish Republic. If he loses, say the cynics, the British will soon drop him. In fact, though born at Clones in County Monaghan, just south of the border, on 28 February 1961, he boxed for Northern Ireland in the Commonwealth Games, qualifying because his father was born at Killideas in County Fermanagh. And he took out

British naturalisation papers to fight for the British title and thus enhance his career prospects.   He now lives with his wife Sandra and three children, Blain, Denika and Jake, in a bungalow at Kilrooskey on the northern side of the border and just a short distance from his birthplace. His training is done in a makeshift gym attached to his parents' grocery store at The Diamond in Clones.

Barry, an adventurous youngster who frequently caused family consternation by getting up to mischievous stunts, was 13 when he transferred his energies into pounding the bag - and his sparmates - at the Wattlebridge amateur boxing club near Clones.   When the club disbanded he switched to the Smithboro club, where trainers Danny McEntee and Frank Mulligan honed the eager youth into such a capable fighter that he won the Irish senior bantamweight title in 1978. That same year, still only 17 years old, he struck gold at the Commonwealth Games in Toronto, despite a hand injury suffered in the quarter-final.   Many ringside observers thought he was lucky to get a split decision over Tumat Sogolik of Papua New Guinea in the final after taking two standing counts and incurring a public warning for holding. He went on to win two more gold medals in multi-nation tournaments in Holland and Rumania but the gold he wanted most, the Olympic Games prize, eluded him.   A hand injury suffered in beating rugged Dubliner Richie Foster in an Ulster *v* Dublin show again troubled him in the 1980 Irish championships and forced him to withdraw from the final.   To his relief the hand caused him no troubles in the European under-19 championships that year at Rimini, where he was the victim of a very bad decision in the final against the Soviet Union's Juri Gladychev, the world junior champion. Barry was so disgusted that he threatened to quit the amateur game, but decided to stay on and try for Olympic glory in Moscow. He got through his initial bout by stopping Issack Mabushi of Tanzania in three rounds, but fought well below his best form in the third series to lose on points to Zambia's Winfred Kabunda.

It was Barney Eastwood, a spectator at a McGuigan amateur bout at the Ulster Hall, who suggested to the youngster's father, Pat, that the three rounds of amateur boxing were too short for Barry to get into his stride.   Pat agreed.   When the time came to go professional, it was Eastwood that the McGuigans turned to.   It seemed to be a very wise decision. Barney Eastwood was different. He was not in boxing solely for the money. He was already a very wealthy man, having left school at 14 to work his way to the top of a bookmaking empire which now has 32 branches throughout Northern Ireland, with an estimated annual turnover of £15 million. A genuine fight fan, he enjoys his boxing involvement as a manager and promoter. It would be naive to suggest that Eastwood did not do well financially out of guiding McGuigan to the world championship, but his accumulated wealth proved of great benefit to the boxer in enabling him to import the best sparring partners and advisers. Sadly, what had seemed a mutually satisfying and profitable liaison ended in acrimony after McGuigan's loss of his world title to Steve Cruz. The boxer took his manager to the Northern Ireland High Court in a move to end the partnership. On the day the case was due to open, the pair reached a settlement. Eastwood would no longer act as McGuigan's manager and he handed over a sum of money, believed to be at least £250,000, as agreed 'compensation' for Barry's title defeat. It was also agreed that Eastwood would promote McGuigan's first comeback fights.

At the beginning of Barry's professional career Eastwood hired Eddie Shaw, a respected trainer whose own professional boxing career had been cut short by a nagging hand injury, to supervise McGuigan's gym work and help develop his natural abilities to their utmost. The thing that most impressed Shaw was Barry's willingness to accept advice and, indeed, to seek it. 'Far too many boxers think they know it all,' said Eddie, 'they just cannot or will not ask questions. A class boxer has to know the problems, try to find out what to do to counteract them and then be able to put into practice what he has learned through hours of sparring and training. Barry can do all that. He can out-think as well as out-fight his opponents.'

Dalymount Park, Dublin, was the setting for McGuigan's professional debut on 10 May 1981. Selvin Bell, a Manchester-based Jamaican, was no match for the eager 20-year-old Monaghan man and he was taking a severe pounding when the referee stopped the bout in the second round. McGuigan got the star treatment, with TV interviews in the ring and girl supporters dancing with delight around the ringside. 'You'd have thought he had just won the world title, instead of becoming the 43rd man to beat Selvin Bell,' was the wry comment of *Boxing News* editor Harry Mullan.

A fourth round win over Gary Lucas at Wembley Pool, London, preceded McGuigan's first setback in the professional ranks. Opposing local favourite Peter Eubanks at Brighton Corn Exchange, on a bill promoted by Dubliner Paddy Byrne, he lost a close points decision over eight rounds. 'McGuigan lets it slip away' was the headline in *Boxing News* and that about summed it up. After dominating the first round and flooring his rival in the second round, he was too casual the rest of the way. It was Eubanks' greater work-rate that earned him referee Roland Dakin's verdict by 78$\frac{1}{2}$ points to 78. There were many in the audience who felt McGuigan had done enough to win. But Barry learned his lesson well. Four months later, with the roars of the packed Ulster Hall behind him, he wiped out the blot on his record by stopping Eubanks in the eighth round. Five wins in six starts earned McGuigan the *Boxing News* accolade of 'Best Prospect of 1982'. The trade paper especially praised the way he had overcome the tough Belgian Jean Marc Renard, who dropped the Irishman momentarily and offered stiff resistance before losing on points.

The most distressing episode of McGuigan's career, the memory of which will haunt him for the rest of his life, was the tragic encounter with Nigerian Alimi Mustafa, who boxed as Young Ali, on 5 October 1982.

Ali, knocked out by a solid right to the jaw in the sixth round before an exclusive audience at the World Sporting Club in London's Mayfair, collapsed in his manager's arms on leaving the ring. For five months he lay in a coma. When he died, it had a numbing effect on McGuigan. He thought long and deeply about giving up boxing altogether, but concluded: 'Boxing is a risk business. It could have been me who was badly injured that night. Boxing is my whole life. It's the only livelihood I have, so I have to carry on and try to forget that tragic incident.'

He was back in the ring four months after the Ali fight to stop Jimmy Duncan in four rounds. He showed that he had put all thoughts of the tragedy behind him by pounding previously unbeaten Paul Huggins to a fifth round defeat in a final eliminator for the British featherweight championship. Title-holder Steve Sims relinquished his claim in order to contest the European crown, leaving McGuigan to meet Welshman Vernon Penprase for the vacant British title. Penprase had lost six times in 24 contests, but he had never been stopped. McGuigan spoiled that record in no uncertain manner. In a performance of chilling perfection he chopped down the taller Welshman with consummate ease, dropping him twice before the referee called a halt in the second round. Penprase, announcing his retirement from boxing, said: 'I've never been hit so hard in my career. His jab has the kick of a mule. It felt like he had a brick in his glove.' It was the shortest British featherweight title fight since 1917.

An American trip to pick up experience by sparring with top featherweights and lightweights cost manager Eastwood nearly £15,000, but it was partly paid for by Barry's appearance on a Chicago bill which saw him dispatch Loval McGowan inside a round. Next on the championship list was the European title, which had just been relinquished by Loris Stecca. Another Italian, Valerio Nati, was brought to Belfast to contest the vacant prize with McGuigan. Nati was counted out in the sixth round after taking two left hooks to the jaw. The honours continued to shower on the Irish hero's head as the British Boxing Writers Club voted him 'Young Boxer of 1983' and *Boxing News* also named him 'Fighter of the Year'.

Not that it was all plain sailing and easy wins. Rugged Charm Chiteule, from Zambia, gave McGuigan a very hard fight in a final eliminator for the Commonwealth title at the King's Hall. And Barry's careless body punching almost earned his disqualification after being warned several times about low blows. 'Once more and you're out,' referee Roland Dakin told him in his corner at the end of the ninth round. Barry later apologised to Chiteule, blaming his badly swollen right eye for hampering his vision. A barrage of punches as he trapped the Zambian in a corner forced the referee to call a halt in the tenth round. It has been Barry's toughest outing so far. There was no hint of his controversial body punching when he took on Jose Caba of the Dominican Republic in an eliminator for the WBC title, again at the King's Hall. This time it was McGuigan the master boxer, as he speared

Caba with a succession of accurate left jabs before stepping up the pace to force a seventh round stoppage. It was a brilliant performance by the Monaghan man, for Caba had gone 15 rounds with Eusebio Pedroza in a WBA title encounter

The world was getting to hear about this fighting Irishman and an estimated audience of 82 million watched his meeting with New Yorker Paul De Vorce. The fight was televised live in the United States from the King's Hall. After seeing McGuigan stop De Vorce in five rounds, Mort Sharnik, boxing consultant for the CBS network, enthused: 'Your boy has everything ... acceleration, intensity, personality and good looks. He's a real good fighter, the best I've seen in Europe for many a day.' The fight that proved McGuigan really was world class was his ten-rounder with Juan Laporte at the King's Hall in February 1985. The Puerto Rican had been WBC featherweight champion less than a year before and, although at 25 only a year older than McGuigan, was much more experienced among top-flight opposition. McGuigan came through his toughest test with flying colours. He didn't manage to stop Laporte, but referee Harry Gibbs gave him six rounds, with two to the visitor and two even. Barry was also called upon to demonstrate his resistance to a hard punch. In the fifth round, he was forced to take two good rights to the head. He staggered backwards and took another right. The normal 'Here we go' chant of the King's Hall faithful fell ominously silent as McGuigan grasped his opponent for a couple of seconds until the referee called 'break'. But he had come through the test. Before the bell rang to end the round, he was back on the attack. If there was any lingering doubts about his completeness as a fighter, they had now been dispelled.

It cost Barney Eastwood the best part of £1 million to lure WBA featherweight champion Eusebio Pedroza to London to defend his title against McGuigan at Queen's Park Rangers soccer stadium in Loftus Road on 8 June 1985. It was the best investment of the shrewd businessman's life. McGuigan was magnificent as he took the world title from the Panamanian on a unanimous points decision over 15 enthralling rounds. And he came very close to scoring a knockout in the seventh round that had the 25,000 paying customers and the millions of TV viewers in 12 countries leaping to their feet with excitement as he threw a right over the champion's lowered guard and caught him flush on the side of the jaw. A left hook connected as Pedroza sagged to the floor. On his feet again by four, the groggy but wily title-holder used his wits and his nifty footwork to steer clear of further big trouble until the bell. At the end of the ninth round, Pedroza was sent reeling before another McGuigan onslaught, but refused to go down. The din from the crowd was so loud that neither the boxers nor the referee heard the bell and McGuigan landed several heavy blows after the round had ended. Pedroza stayed in the fight with the fluid boxing skills that had carried him through 19 successful title defences, but no one needed the announcement at the close of the 15 rounds to know that Ireland had its first world champion in 35 years. Referee Stan Christodoulo of South Africa gave it to McGuigan by 148 points to 138, while judges Ove Oveson (Denmark) and Fernando Viso (Venezuela) marked it 149-139 and 147-140 respectively.

Fleet Street was rapturous in its acclaim of the new WBA champion's performance. 'If he took a backward step, I didn't notice it,' said Fred Bucombe in the *News of the World.* 'He attacked from the start and his pressure was relentless. For all of his 12 years in the ring, Pedroza can rarely have been confronted by such a mass of energy.' Hugh McIlvanney of the *Observer* said that 'no one now is entitled to oppose very strenuously the claims some of us have made that this young man is the most dramatic fighter to emerge from these islands in half a century.' Alan Hoby in the *Sunday Express* said it was the best performance he had seen in a British ring since Randolph Turpin beat Sugar Ray Robinson in 1951. 'The 24-year-old Irishman, fighting out of his American-style crouch, came through against a world champion second only to Marvin Hagler in malevolence and menace,' he stated. Patrick Collins in the *Mail on Sunday* wrote: 'McGuigan was massive, inspired by the prevailing passion and by the prospect of the prize to be won, he offered a performance which will add his name to the litany of Turpin, Conteh, Buchanan and the rest.'

A wildly cheering, flag-waving crowd of some 40,000 lined the main streets of Belfast to welcome the conquering hero, while the entire population of Clones turned out for his home town arrival. But Dublin was the biggest surprise of all. The police had expected around 25,000 for the lunchtime parade through the city centre to the Mansion House where Barry was welcomed by Lord Mayor Michael O'Halloran. In fact, over 100,000 jammed the route of the open-topped bus, bringing traffic to a standstill.

McGuigan repaid the fans for their loyalty and support by making his first two defences of his WBA title in Ireland, even though he could have made much more money fighting in the United States, or even in England. Belfast was first, with Barry accommodating the number one contender, Bernard Taylor from Tennessee. A brilliant boxer, Taylor was unbeaten in 34 contests, with only a draw in a title challenge to Eusebio Pedroza to mar an otherwise 100% record. For five rounds Taylor had the 6,000 King's Hall crowd choking on their 'Here we go ' and 'Barr-ee, Barr-ee' chants as he outboxed and outmanoeuvred the champion. But once McGuigan got his range and began to dig in those lethal body thumps, the American challenger lost all heart for the affair. He quit in his corner at the end of the eighth round, claiming heat exhaustion and dehydration.

Dublin was next, with the first world title fight since Mike McTigue took the light-heavyweight crown from Battling Siki 63 years earlier. Danilo Cabrera from the Dominican Republic, a late replacement for injured Argentinian Fernando Sosa, gave McGuigan plenty of trouble before the referee stopped the contest in the 14th round with the confused challenger trying to pick his gumshield off the canvas. Referee Ed Eckert of the United States had actually called a halt at the end of the eighth round as McGuigan pounded Cabrera in a corner, only to be told that the bell had rung before he made his decision. The champion's work lacked much of its usual precision and power, but he was able to step up the pace again in the 14th round to force the stoppage. Quite a lot of the cheers of the Royal Dublin Society's showgrounds were reserved for the game challenger, who had been written off by the pundits as a 'no hoper'. McGuigan was badly marked around both his eyes and had to have six stitches in the gash under his left eye. Compensation for the pain and the bruises came with the promise that, along with his ring earnings, he could gather juicy pickings from advertising and endorsement of various products. Marketing the 'commodity' that is Barry McGuigan could make him Ireland's first multi-millionaire boxer.

But it was the chase after the 'fast buck' that proved disastrous for McGuigan's immediate future plans when manager Eastwood unwisely agreed to a title defence at Las Vegas on 23 June 1986. It was a sad and upsetting experience for the 2,000 Irish fans who made the trip to see their hero perform and for those at home who stayed up for the mid-morning live telecast to watch a completely drained McGuigan wilt in the unbearable conditions and stagger through a nightmare last round to lose a unanimous points verdict to a willing, but unremarkable, opponent. Punches that would normally not have bothered the Irishman had him floundering around the ring in that 15th round as Cruz pressed home for a deserved victory. Barry, unable to finish off the tough Texan in the early rounds as he had hoped, used up every ounce of his energy in going after Cruz in the 13th and 14th rounds, with the result that he had nothing left when the American came back at him in the final round. Had McGuigan been able to sustain his attack over those last three minutes and had he not lost a point for a low blow in the 12th he would have just scraped home on points and his precious world title would have been intact. Such are the uncertainties of boxing, however, that McGuigan surrendered his title status and his potential for immediate lucrative earnings was drastically reduced.

The decision to fight in Las Vegas under a blinding June sun was, without question, a major blunder. It was a gamble that a man with Eastwood's experience as a bookmaker and astute businessman should have known better than to take. Of course it is easy to be wise after the event and there was not one boxing expert who predicted that McGuigan would lose, even under the extremely unfavourable conditions. But it was just too much to expect even a boxer of McGuigan's proven talents to overcome the oven-like temperature and fend off the grimly-determined challenger, who was rated ninth by the WBA. Cruz was brought in as a substitute for Fernando Sosa, who had to withdraw when he was found to have detached retinas in both eyes. It was a bitter blow for Sosa, who had previously had to forego a crack at McGuigan's title in Dublin four months earlier because of a broken finger. Barry was unhappy about having to face a new opponent in Cruz, as his training had been geared towards a fight with the Argentinian. But the promoters threatened to sue if he failed to go through with the fight, so McGuigan had no option but to comply.

Barry gambled on a quick finish before the heat forced him to slow down, but when Cruz refused to yield it was clear that the gamble had failed. McGuigan's punches carried little of their customary power and, strangely, it was he who seemed most affected by the blows of a man who was far from the strongest puncher he had ever met. Though he was comfortably ahead on points after the half-way stage, Barry was failing to have his challenger in any real trouble, whereas he looked in some distress when Cruz put together a few good combinations. The first proof of the gruelling pace and conditions on McGuigan came in the tenth round when a neat left hook sent him tumbling into a corner. He took a count of seven on one knee. With Cruz keeping up the pressure over the next couple of rounds, the Irishman realised his title was slipping away. Cut around both eyes, television viewers could plainly hear him pathetically pleading with his cornermen to 'Say a prayer for me' as the fight moved into its closing stages. Somehow he found the strength and raw courage to mount an offensive throughout the 13th and 14th round, but the effort proved totally exhausting and it was something of a miracle that he survived the last round. A left hook sent him to the canvas and he was down again from a right when a mere push would have floored him. He had not been knocked down by any other boxer since Jean Marc Renard of Belgium had him down briefly in 1981. As Cruz's seconds hoisted their man aloft in anticipation of the verdict, McGuigan slumped dejectedly on his stool as his cornermen attended to his cuts. Judge Angel Tovar, of Venezuela, scored it 143 to 142, with Cruz winning the last round by two points. Canadian Guy Jutres made it 142-141, with Cruz taking the final session by 10-7. The third offical, Melardo Villa Lobos, of Panama, had Cruz the winner by a wide margin, 143 to 139. So it was unanimous. Steve Cruz was the new WBA featherweight champion; and Barry McGuigan was left to lick his wounds and wonder why it all went wrong. He spent the night in hospital suffering from the effects of dehydration and having a brain scan, which showed there was no permanent damage.

Post-fight inquests largely pointed the finger of blame towards Eastwood for not foreseeing the dangers of boxing in an open-air arena in Las Vegas in the height of summer and at a time of the day when the sun was at its hottest. But it seems unfair to blame the debacle solely on the manager. McGuigan knew only too well that a boxing champion's career can be a short one and he must cash in while he is in the driving seat. He could have chosen to stay at home and confine his title defence to Belfast, Dublin or London. But the United States is the place where the big money is to be made. If Barry wanted financial security he knew he had to play it the American way. It is the major television companies which dictate where and when the big fights take place and McGuigan, despite being a hugely popular personality in Ireland and Britain, was not sufficiently well known in America to command large purses for his fights. That is why he was forced, against his wishes, to set aside his susceptibility to homesickness and the absence of his family and undertake a strenuous three-week tour of 12 American cities, giving television and press interviews, in order to project his image to audiences there. It was also on Barry's insistence, and not to Eastwood's approval, that he took his wife and family over to Las Vegas as he prepared to fight Cruz. It is a long-standing belief among boxing managers that keeping a fighter away from his family makes him meaner and more aggressive when he gets into the ring. The lessons of Las Vegas have been hard earned and only time will tell if Barry McGuigan can profit from the bitter experience. Perhaps under his new manager, Londoner Frank Warren, he can make a successful return on the hardest road of all: the comeback trail.

The next round

Thanks mainly to modern television networks boxing maintains a high popularity profile throughout the world. Whether it will survive the recurring demands for its abolition from various medical and humanitarian bodies remains to be seen, but the sport commands huge public interest whenever a big fight is screened. Barry McGuigan's loss of his WBA featherweight title to Steve Cruz at Las Vegas on 23 June 1986 was carried by over 40 television stations around the world, from Latin America to Japan, from South Africa to Thailand, from Indonesia to Britain and Ireland. In the United States, viewers on the East Coast packed theatres to enjoy the action on closed-circuits screens, while the rest of the country doled out $15 a head to a cable company to receive the fight on the pay-for-view television system. For his own exertions and part compensation for the loss of his title, McGuigan picked up nearly a million dollars. It was quite a step up from the £400 he had earned for stopping Selvin Bell on his professional debut at Dalymount Park, Dublin, five years earlier.

While today's mind-boggling financial dealings in big-time boxing would be the envy of the old-time promoters and managers, the backstage boys of long ago knew a thing or two about the power of the pound also. When Colonel O'Kelly slipped £100 to Bill Darts to forfeit his English bare-knuckle championship to Irishman Peter Corcoran in 1771 he hardly considered, and probably cared less, that he almost killed boxing off with his shameless act of skullduggery. One of the refreshing aspects of modern boxing is that the enormous sums earned by world champions and top contenders has all but eliminated the possibilities of 'fixed' contests. One still hears accusations of a 'frame-up' whenever there is an upset result in a big fight, but the charge cannot really stand up. No champion would sacrifice his crown, with its potential for further lucrative earnings, for a one-off bribe. It just wouldn't pay him to 'lie down' in the ring and almost certainly cut off his source of more big pay-days.

For Irish professional boxers, one thing has not changed since the bare-knuckle days. They still must travel abroad to cash in on their talents and to take up the championship chase. The likes of Barry McGuigan can continue to pull in huge crowds wherever he appears, but even a promoter of Barney Eastwood's considerable business acumen and organisational ability had his fingers burned when he staged shows at the Ulster Hall that did not have Barry McGuigan to top the bill. Local boys with winning potential like Dave 'Boy' McAuley and Roy Webb have their sizeable followings, but they don't have superstar appeal. In a perverse way McGuigan's success could be said to have been bad for Irish boxing, in that the fans have become 'spoiled' by his thrilling performances and are not prepared to settle for anyone else. If Barry weren't around, they would be patronising lesser heroes like McAuley and Webb.

But where McGuigan has been of enormous benefit to Irish boxing is in the inspiration he has provided for youngsters launching their first tentative jabs in amateur clubs all around the country. Ambitious kids are flocking to join clubs and the number of clubs and tournaments are on the increase. The national junior championships in December 1985 attracted the largest number of entries in over 20 years and there are similar success stories from juvenile tournaments. These boys have been fired by the success of McGuigan. If he could become champion of the world then so can they. Only a tiny minority, of course, will achieve major championship status but that is the same in any sport where a beginner hopes to emulate his idol. Trying is what counts. The most refreshing aspect of McGuigan's hero-worship is that the youngsters are inspired by what can be achieved by hard work, dedication, fitness and a readiness to listen to advice, if they have the natural basic ability to go with it. That can only mean good for the future of boxing in Ireland. We haven't heard the last of The Fighting Irish yet.

Nine

On The Record

Irish-Born Title-holders

Bare Knuckles

English heavyweight champions: Peter Corcoran, born Athy, Co. Kildare (birthdate unknown), died in London (date unknown). Championship reign 1771-76. Duggan (Jack) Fearns, birthplace and date unknown, place and date of death unknown. Championship reign 1779.

American heavyweight champions and title claimants: Yankee Sullivan, born James Ambrose, Bandon, Co. Cork, 1813, died in San Francisco, 31 May 1856. Claimed title 1849-53. John Morrissey, born Templemore, Co. Tipperary, 1831, died in Saratoga, Florida, 1 May 1878. Championship reign 1858. Joe Coburn, born Middletown, Co. Armagh, 20 July 1835, died in New York, 6 Dec. 1890. Claimed title 1863. Mike McCoole, born 12 Mar. 1837 (exact birthplace unknown), died in New Orleans, 17 Oct. 1886. Claimed title 1867-73. Jim Dunne, born Co. Kildare, 4 Oct. 1842, died at Elizabeth, New Jersey, 26 June 1906. Claimed title 1863. Jim Elliott, born Athlone, Co. Westmeath, 1838, died in Chicago, 1 Mar. 1883. Claimed title 1867-68. Ned O'Baldwin, born Lismore, Co. Waterford, 19 May 1840, died in New York, 25 Sept. 1875. Claimed title 1868. Paddy Ryan, born Thurles, Co. Tipperary, 15 Mar. 1853, died at Green Island, near Troy, New York, 1901. Championship reign 1880-82.

American middleweight champion: Tom Chandler, born Waterford, 6 Nov. 1842, place and date of death unknown. Championship reign 1867.

American lightweight champions: Owney Geohegan, born 1840 (exact birthplace unknown), place and date of death unknown. Championship reign 1861-63. Tommy Kelly, born 2 Jan. 1839 (exact birthplace unknown), died in Crescent Beach, Massachusetts, 6 Sept. 1887. Championship reign 1869 to late 1870s.

American featherweight champion: Tommy Kelly (see lightweight champions). Claimed title 1869.

Gloves

Light-heavyweight: George Gardner, born Lisdoonvarna, Co. Clare, 17 Mar. 1877, died in Chicago, Illinois, 8 July 1954. Championship reign 1903. Pro. career 1897-1908. Contests 65, won 41, drew 10, lost 11, no decision 2, no contest 1. Mike McTigue, born Ennis, Co. Clare, 26 Nov. 1892, died in Queens, New York, 12 Aug. 1966. Championship reign 1923-25. Pro. career 1909-30. Contests 146, won 81, drew 6, lost 23, no decision 36.
Middleweight: Nonpareil Jack Dempsey, born John Kelly, Clane, Co. Kildare, 15 Dec. 1862, died in Portland, Oregon, 2 Nov. 1895. Championship reign 1884-91. Pro. career 1883-95. Contests 68, won 50, drew 12, lost 3, no decision 3.
Welterweight: Jimmy Gardner, born Lisdoonvarna, Co. Clare, 25 Dec. 1885, place and date of death unknown. Claimed title 1908. Pro. career 1900-13. Contests 100, won 51, drew 22, lost 6, no decision 21. Tom McCormick, born Dundalk, Co. Louth, 8 Aug. 1890, died in France, 1916. Claimed title 1914. Pro. career 1911-15. Contests 46, won 35, drew 2, lost 9. Jimmy McLarnin, born Hillsborough, Co. Down, 19 Dec. 1907. Championship reign 1933 to May 1934, Sept. 1934-35. Pro. career 1923-36. Contests 77, won 63, drew 3, lost 11.
Lightweight: Jack McAuliffe, born Meelin, Co. Cork, 24 Mar. 1866, died Forest Hills, New York, 5 Nov. 1937. Claimed title 1886-94. Pro. career 1884-97. Contests 53, won 41, drew 9, lost 0, no decision 3.
Featherweight: Ike O'Neil Weir, born Lurgan, Co. Armagh, 5 Feb. 1867, died in USA, 12 Sept. 1908. Claimed title 1889-90. Pro. career 1885-94. Contests 41, won 29, drew 8, lost 3, no decision 1. Dave Sullivan, born Cork, 19 May 1877, place and date of death unknown. Championship reign 1898. Pro. career 1894-1905. Contests 58, won 28, drew 16, lost 12, no decision 2. Barry McGuigan, born Clones, Co. Monaghan, 28 Feb. 1961. Championship reign (WBA) 1985-86. Pro. career began 1981. Contests (to Sept. 1987) 31, won 29, lost 2.
Bantamweight: John Caldwell, born Belfast, 7 May 1938. Claimed title (European Boxing Union and British Boxing Board of Control version) 1961-62. Pro. career 1958-65. Contests 35, won 29, drew 1, lost 5.
Flyweight: Rinty Monaghan, born Belfast, 21 Aug. 1908, died Belfast, 3 Mar. 1984. Championship reign 1947-50. Pro. career 1934-50. Contests 66, won 51, drew 6, lost 9.

Lightweight: Charlie Nash, born Derry, 10 May 1951. Championship reign 1979 to Mar. 1980, Dec. 1980-81. Pro. career 1975-83. Contests

30, won 25, lost 5.

Featherweight: Barry McGuigan (see world champions). Championship reign 1983-85.

Bantamweight: John Kelly, born Belfast, 17 Jan. 1932. Championship reign 1953-54. Pro. career 1951-57. Contests 28, won 24, lost 4. Freddie Gilroy, born Belfast 7 Mar. 1936. Championship reign 1959-60. Pro. career 1957-62. Contests 31, won 28, lost 3.

Flyweight: Rinty Monaghan (see world champions). Championship reign 1949-50.

BRITISH EMPIRE OR COMMONWEALTH CHAMPIONS

Heavyweight: Petty Officer Matt 'Nutty' Curran, born Lisdeen, Ennis, Co. Clare, Nov. 1882, died in Sydney, Australia, 1938. Championship reign 1911. Pro. career 1908-20. Contests 86, won 45, drew 3, lost 33, no contest 5. Dan McAlinden, born Newry, Co. Down, 1 Jun. 1947. Championship reign 1972-75. Pro. career 1969-81. Contests 45, won 31, drew 2, lost 12.

Welterweight: Tom McCormick (see world champions). Championship reign 1914.

Featherweight: Jim 'Spider' Kelly, born Derry, 25 Feb. 1912. Championship reign 1938-39. Pro. career 1928-48. Contests 150, won 105, drew 12, lost 33. Billy 'Spider' Kelly, born Derry, 21 Apr. 1932. Championship reign 1954-55. Pro. career 1950-62. Contests 83, won 56, drew 4, lost 23.

Bantamweight: Freddie Gilroy (see European champions). Championship reign 1959-62. John Caldwell (see world champions). Championship reign 1964-65.

Flyweight: Rinty Monaghan (see world champions). Championship reign 1948-50.

BRITISH CHAMPIONS

Heavyweight: Dan McAlinden (see Empire/Commonwealth champions). Championship reign 1972-75. Gordon Ferris, born Enniskillen, Co. Fermanagh, 21 Nov. 1952. Championship reign 1981. Pro. career 1977-82. Contests 26, won 20, lost 6.

Light-heavyweight: Dennis Haugh, born Tipperary (date unknown). Place and date of death unknown. Claimed championship 1913-14. Pro. career 1909-16. Contests 45, won 21, drew 4, lost 17, no decision 2. 'Young' John McCormack, born Dublin, 11 Dec. 1944. Championship reign 1967-69. Pro. career 1963-70. Contests 42, won 33, drew 1, lost 8.

Middleweight: Mick Leahy, born Cork, 12 Mar. 1935. Championship reign 1963-64. Pro. career 1956-65. Contests 72, won 46, drew 7, lost 19.

Welterweight: Tom McCormick (see world champions). Championship reign 1914.

Junior-welterweight: Des Rea, born Belfast, 8 Jan 1944. Championship reign 1968-69. Pro. career 1964-74. Contests 69, won 28, drew 5, lost 36.

Light-welterweight: Pat McCormack, born Dublin, 28 Apr. 1946. Championship reign 1974. Pro. career 1968-75. Contests 49, won 30, drew 1, lost 18.

Lightweight: Charlie Nash (see European champions). Championship reign 1978-79.

Featherweight: Jim 'Spider' Kelly (see Empire / Commonwealth champions). Championship reign 1938-39. Billy 'Spider' Kelly (see Empire/Commonwealth champions). Championship reign 1955-56. Barry McGuigan (see world champions). Championship reign 1983-85.

Bantamweight: John Kelly (see European champions). Championship reign 1953-54. Freddie Gilroy (see European champions). Championship reign 1959-63. John Caldwell (see world champions). Championship reign 1964-65. Paddy Maguire, born Belfast, 26 Sept. 1948. Championship reign 1975-77. Pro. career 1969-77. Contests 35, won 26, drew 1, lost 8. Hugh Russell, born Belfast, 15 Dec. 1959. Championship reign 1983. Pro. career 1981-85. Contests 19, won 17, lost 2. Davy Larmour, born Belfast, 2 Apr. 1952. Championship reign 1983. Pro. career 1977-83. Contests 18, won 11, lost 7.

Flyweight: Rinty Monaghan (see world champions). Championship reign 1948-50. John Caldwell (see world champions). Championship reign 1960-61. Hugh Russell (see British bantamweight champions). Championship reign 1984-85. Dave McAuley, born Larne, Co. Antrim, 15 Jun. 1961. Championship reign 1986 to date. Pro. career 1983 to date. Contests (to Sept. 1987) 14, won 11, drew 2, lost 1.

Championship Bouts Involving Irish Boxers

Bare Knuckles

NOTE: Bare-knuckle contests were fought to a finish, when either man was knocked unconscious or was unable to continue. Rounds were of indeterminate length, ending only when a man fell to the ground. For this reason, the number of rounds fought, as well as the duration of the contest (where they are recorded) are given. Contests allegedly 'fixed' in advance are marked with an asterix.

ENGLISH HEAVYWEIGHT CHAMPIONSHIP (BROUGHTON'S RULES)
*18 May 1771 Peter Corcoran (Ire.) beat Bill Darts (Eng.), 1 round, at Epsom Race-course, Surrey.
*10 Oct. 1776 Harry Sellers (Eng.) beat Peter Corcoran (Ire.), 38 rounds (28 mins.), at Staines, Middlesex.
*25 Sept. 1779 Duggan Fearns (Ire.) beat Harry Sellers (Eng.), 1 min. 30 secs., at Slough, Buckinghamshire.
19 Dec. 1787 Tom Johnson (Eng.) beat Michael Ryan (Ire.), 30 mins., in Buckinghamshire.

11 Feb. 1789   Tom Johnson (Eng.) beat Michael Ryan (Ire.), 33 mins., near Rickmansworth, Hertfordshire.

22 Dec. 1800   Jem Belcher (Eng.) beat Andrew Gamble (Ire.), 5 rounds (7 mins.), at Wimbledon Common, Surrey.

7 Jan. 1824   Tom Spring (Eng.) beat Jack Langan (Ire.), 77 rounds (2 hrs. 20 mins.), at Worcester.

8 June 1824   Tom Spring (Eng.) beat Jack Langan (Ire.), 76 rounds (1 hr. 48 mins.), at Birdham Bridge, near Chichester, Sussex.

12 July 1831   Jem Ward (Eng.) beat Simon Byrne (Ire.), 33 rounds (1 hr. 17 mins.), at Willeycut.

30 May 1833   James 'Deaf' Burke (Eng.) beat Simon Byrne (Ire.), 99 rounds (3 hrs. 6 mins.), near St Albans, Hertfordshire.

AMERICAN HEAVYWEIGHT CHAMPIONSHIP (LONDON PRIZE RING RULES)
NOTE: Early bare-knuckle prize-fighting in America was disorganised and there were often several rival claimants to the title at the same time. The following contests were announced as championship fights.

7 Feb. 1849   Tom Hyer (USA) beat Yankee Sullivan (Ire.), 16 rounds (17 mins.), at Rock Point, Maryland.

12 Oct. 1853   John Morrissey (Ire.) beat Yankee Sullivan (Ire.), 37 rounds, at Boston Corners, New York.

20 Oct. 1858   John Morrissey (Ire.) beat John C. Heenan (USA), 11 rounds, at Long Point, Canada.

5 May 1863   Joe Coburn (Ire.) beat Mike McCoole (Ire.), 67 rounds (1 hr. 10 mins.), at Charlesworth, Maryland.

13 May 1863   Jim Dunne (Ire.) beat Jim Elliott (Ire.), 12 rounds, near Weehawken, New Jersey.   Elliott was disqualified for fouling.

10 May 1867   Jim Elliott (Ire.) beat Bill Davis (USA), 9 rounds (11 mins.), at Point Pelee Island, Lake Erie, Canada.

19 Sept. 1867   Mike McCoole (Ire.) beat Aaron Jones (Eng.), 34 rounds (26 mins.), at Busenbark Station, Ohio.

29 Oct. 1868   Ned O'Baldwin (Ire.) fought Joe Wormwald (Eng.) for 10 mins., then police intervened and bout was abandoned, at Lynnfield, Massachusetts.

12 Nov. 1868   Jim Elliott (Ire.) beat Charlie Gallagher (Canada), 23 rounds (1 hr. 17 mins.), at Peach Island, near Detroit, Michigan.

15 June 1869   Mike McCoole (Ire.) beat Tom Allen (Eng.), 9 rounds, at Foster's Island, Mississippi.

11 May 1871   Joe Coburn (Ire.) fought Jem Mace (Eng.) for 1 hr. 17 mins., no verdict was rendered, at Port Ryson, Canada.

30 Nov. 1871   Joe Coburn (Ire.) fought Jem Mace (Eng.) for 12 rounds (3 hrs. 48 mins.), contest drawn, at Bay St Louis, Missouri.

23 Sept. 1873   Tom Allen (Eng.) beat Mike McCoole (Ire.), 7 rounds (20 mins.), near St Louis, Missouri.

9 May 1879   Johnny Dwyer (Newfoundland) beat Jim Elliott (Ire.), 12 rounds (12 mins. 40 secs.), at Long Point, Canada.

30 May 1880 Paddy Ryan (Ire.) beat Joe Goss (Eng.), 87 rounds (1 hr. 24 mins.), at Collier's Station, West Virginia.

7 Feb. 1882 John L. Sullivan (USA) beat Paddy Ryan (Ire.), 9 rounds (10 mins. 30 secs.), at Mississippi City.

AMERICAN MIDDLEWEIGHT CHAMPIONSHIP

13 Apr. 1867 Tom Chandler (Ire.) beat Dooney Harris (USA), 23 rounds, at Port Isabel, California.

AMERICAN LIGHTWEIGHT CHAMPIONSHIP

18 Apr. 1861 Owney Geoghan (Ire.) beat Eddie Tuohey (USA), 45 rounds (1hr. 10 mins.), in New York.

10 May 1869 Tommy Kelly (Ire.) beat Ted Timmoney (USA), 10 rounds, at Campobello Island, Canada.

AMERICAN FEATHERWEIGHT CHAMPIONSHIP

20 May 1860 Nobby Clarke (Eng.) beat Jim Elliott (Ire.), 34 rounds (1 hr. 2 mins.), at Weehawken, New Jersey.

7 Oct. 1868 George Seddons (Eng.) beat Tommy Kelly (Ire.), 96 rounds (1 hr. 39 mins.), at Portsmouth, New Hampshire.

Gloves

WORLD CHAMPIONSHIP CONTESTS (MARQUIS OF QUEENSBERRY RULES)

KEY: w = won; ko = knockout; pts = points; rsf = referee stopped fight; rtd = retired; disq = disqualified.

Heavyweight

11 Nov. 1895 James J. Corbett (USA) announced retirement and 'presented' his world title to Peter Maher (Ire.) after Galwayman's 63-second knockout of Steve O'Donnell (New Zealand) at Long Island, New York. But Maher was not seriously recognised as champion and forfeited any claim when knocked out in 95 seconds by Bob Fitzsimmons (Eng.) at Langtry, Texas, on 21 Feb. 1896. Corbett then returned to reclaim the title and lost to Fitzsimmons on St Patrick's Day 1897.

3 Nov. 1899 James J. Jeffries (USA), champion, w pts 25 Tom Sharkey (Ire.), challenger, at Coney Island, New York.

17 Mar. 1908 Tommy Burns (Canada), champion, w ko 1 Jem Roche (Ire.), challenger, at Theatre Royal, Dublin.

Light-heavyweight

4 July 1903 George Gardner (Ire.), challenger, w ko 12 Jack Root (Austria), champion, at Fort Erie, New York.

25 Nov. 1903 Bob Fitzsimmons (Eng.), challenger, w pts 20 George Gardner (Ire.), champion, at San Francisco, California.

17 Mar. 1923 Mike McTigue (Ire.), challenger, w pts 20 Battling Siki (Senegal, French West Africa), champion, at La Scala Opera House,

Dublin.

31 May 1925 Paul Berlenbach (USA), challenger, w pts 15 Mike McTigue (Ire.), champion, at Yankee Stadium, New York.

7 Aug. 1927 McTigue reclaimed title after champion Jack Delaney, who had beaten Berlenbach, gave it up to compete as a heavyweight. McTigue was recognised by some authorities, but National Boxing Association of America (NBA) named Jim Slattery (USA) champion after he beat Maxie Rosenbloom (USA).

7 Oct. 1927 Tommy Loughran (USA) w pts 15 Mike McTigue (Ire.), for vacant title, as recognised by all but NBA, at Madison Square Garden, New York. Loughran then beat Slattery for undisputed title.

Middleweight

30 July 1884 Nonpareil Jack Dempsey (Ire.) w ko 22 George Fulljames (Canada) at Great Kills, New York. This is generally regarded as the first middleweight title fight.

3 Feb. 1886 Nonpareil Jack Dempsey (Ire.), champion, w ko 27 Jack Fogarty (USA), challenger, in New York.

4 Mar. 1886 Nonpareil Jack Dempsey (Ire.), champion, w ko 13 George La Blanche (Canada), challenger, at Larchmont, New York.

13 Dec. 1887 Nonpareil Jack Dempsey (Ire.), champion, w ko 45 Johnny Regan (USA), challenger, at Long Island, New York.

27 Aug. 1889 George La Blanche (Canada), challenger, w ko 32 Nonpareil Jack Dempsey (Ire.), champion, at San Francisco, California. La Blanche was not recognised as champion as he was overweight for the fight and also used an illegal 'pivot punch' to knock out Dempsey.

18 Feb. 1890 Nonpareil Jack Dempsey (Ire.), champion, w ko 28 Australian Bill McCarthy, challenger, at San Francisco, California.

14 Jan. 1891 Bob Fitzsimmons (Eng.), challenger, w ko 13 Nonpareil Jack Dempsey (Ire.), champion, at New Orleans.

Light-middleweight

19 Oct. 1984 Mike McCallum (Jamaica) w pts 15 Sean Mannion (Ire.) for vacant World Boxing Council (WBC) title at Madison Square Garden, New York.

Welterweight

23 Apr. 1908 Mike 'Twin' Sullivan (USA), champion, w pts 25 Jimmy Gardner (Ire.), challenger, at Los Angeles, California. Sullivan relinquished title late in 1908 and the championship fell into dispute. Among the many claimants to the title were Gardner and fellow Irishman Tom McCormick. There was no universally accepted champion until Ted 'Kid' Lewis (Eng.) beat Jack Britton (USA) in 1915. During that period, the following four contests were billed as world title fights:

7 Nov. 1908 Jimmy Gardner (Ire.) w pts 15 Jimmy Clabby (USA) at New Orleans.

26 Nov. 1908 Jimmy Gardner (Ire.) drew 20 Jimmy Clabby (USA) at New Orleans.

24 Jan. 1914 Tom McCormick (Ire.) w disq 6 (low blow) Waldemar

Holberg (Denmark) at Melbourne, Australia.

21 Mar. 1914 Matt Wells (Eng.) w pts 20 Tom McCormick (Ire.) at Sydney, Australia.

29 May 1933 Jimmy McLarnin (Ire.), challenger, w ko 1 Young Corbett III (Italy), champion, at Los Angeles, California.

28 May 1934 Barney Ross (USA), challenger, w pts 15 Jimmy McLarnin (Ire.), champion, at Long Island Bowl, New York.

17 Sept. 1934 Jimmy McLarnin (Ire.), challenger, w pts 15 Barney Ross (USA), champion, at Long Island Bowl, New York.

28 May 1935 Barney Ross (USA), challenger, w pts 15 Jimmy McLarnin (Ire.), champion, at Polo Grounds, New York.

Lightweight

1855 John Monaghan (Irl.) w ko 45 Little Jim Hart (USA) at Island Pond, Canada. He lost to Hart in ten rounds in a return match the following year. Monaghan's claim to the world title was not widely supported.

27 Feb. 1886 Jack McAuliffe (Ire.) w ko 17 Jack Hopper (USA), for vacant title, in New York.

29 Oct. 1886 Jack McAuliffe (Ire.), champion, w ko 21 Bill Frazier (USA), challenger, at Boston, Massachusetts.

14 Jan. 1887 Jack McAuliffe (Ire.), champion, w ko 28 Harry Gilmore (Eng.), challenger, at Lawrence, Massachusetts.

16 Nov. 1887 Jack McAuliffe (Ire.) drew 74 Jem Carney (Eng.) at Revere, Massachusetts, for undisputed world title.

10 Oct. 1888 Jack McAuliffe (Ire.), champion, w ko 11 Billy Dacey (USA), challenger, at Dover, New Jersey.

13 Feb. 1889 Jack McAuliffe (Ire.), champion, drew 64 Billy Myer (USA), challenger, at North Judson, Illinois.

5 Sept. 1892 Jack McAuliffe (Ire.), champion, w ko 15 Billy Myer (USA), challenger, at New Orleans.

21 May 1928 Sammy Mandell (USA), champion, w pts 15 Jimmy McLarnin (Ire.), challenger, at New York.

14 Mar. 1980 Jim Watt (Scot.), champion, w rsf 4 Charlie Nash (Ire.), challenger, at Glasgow, Scotland, for WBC title.

Featherweight

31 Mar. 1889 Ike O'Neil Weir (Ire.) drew 80 Frank Murphy (Eng.) at Kouts, Indiana (police stopped fight).

13 Jan. 1890 'Torpedo' Billy Murphy (New Zealand) w ko 14 Ike O'Neill Weir (Ire.) at San Francisco Athletic Club, California, for vacant title.

26 Sept. 1898 Dave Sullivan (Ire.), challenger, w rtd 5 Solly Smith (USA), champion, at Coney Island, New York. (Smith broke his arm.)

11 Nov. 1898 George Dixon (Canada), challenger, w disq 10 Dave Sullivan (Ire.), champion, at New York. Sullivan's seconds illegally entered the ring.

23 June 1983 Irving Mitchell (USA), champion, w pts 15 Richie Foster

(Ire.), challenger, at San Diego, California, for World Athletic Association title. The WAA, however, is not generally accepted as a major boxing authority and the Mitchell v Foster contest is not regarded as a legitimate world title fight.

8 June 1985   Barry McGuigan (Ire.), challenger, w pts 15 Eusebio Pedroza (Panama), champion, for WBA title, at Queen's Park Rangers football ground, London.

28 Sept. 1985   Barry McGuigan (Ire.), champion, w rtd 8 Bernard Taylor (USA.), challenger, for WBA title, at King's Hall, Belfast.

15 Feb. 1986   Barry McGuigan (Ire.), champion, w rsf 14 Danilo Cabrera (Dominican Republic), challenger, for WBA title, at RDS, Dublin.

23 June 1986   Steve Cruz (USA), challenger, w pts 15 Barry McGuigan (Ire.), champion, for WBA title, at Caesar's Palace, Las Vegas, Nevada.

Bantamweight

18 Oct. 1897   Pedlar Palmer (Eng.), champion, w pts 20 Dave Sullivan (Ire.), challenger, at London.

25 Oct. 1960   Alphonse Halimi (Algeria) w pts 15 Freddie Gilroy (Ire.) at Wembley Pool, London, for EBU and BBBC version of world title.

27 May 1961   Johnny Caldwell (Ire.), challenger, w pts 15 Alphonse Halimi (Algeria), champion, at Wembley Pool, London, for EBU and BBBC version of title.

31 Oct. 1961   Johnny Caldwell (Ire.), champion, w pts 15 Alphonse Halimi (Algeria), challenger, at Wembley Pool, London, for EBU and BBBC version of title.

18 Jan. 1962   Eder Jofre (Brazil), NBA champion, w rtd 10 Johnny Caldwell (Ire), EBU and BBBC champion, at Sao Paulo, Brazil, for undisputed title.

Flyweight

20 Oct. 1947   Rinty Monaghan (Ire.) w pts 15 Dado Marino (Hawaii) at Harringay Arena, London, for NBA of America and Irish Boxing Board of Control version of world title.

23 Mar. 1948   Rinty Monaghan (Ire.) w ko 7 Jackie Paterson (Scot.) at King's Hall, Belfast, for undisputed title.

5 Apr. 1949   Rinty Monaghan (Ire.), champion, w pts 15 Maurice Sandeyron (France), challenger, at King's Hall, Belfast.

30 Sept. 1949   Rinty Monaghan (Ire.), champion, drew 15 Terry Allen (Eng.), challenger, at King's Hall, Belfast. Monaghan thus retained title.

25 Apr. 1987   Fidel Bassa (Colombia), champion, w ko 13 Dave McAuley (Ire.), challenger, for WBA title, at King's Hall, Belfast.

EUROPEAN CHAMPIONSHIP CONTESTS
Middleweight
9 Oct. 1964   Laszlo Papp (Hungary), champion, w pts 15 Mick Leahy (Ire.), challenger, at Vienna, Austria.
Light-welterweight

21 Aug. 1968 Bruno Arcari (Italy), champion, w rsf 6 Des Rea (Ire.), challenger, at San Remo, Italy.

Lightweight

27 June 1979 Charlie Nash (Ire.) w pts 12 Andre Holyk (France) for title vacated by Jim Watt (Scot.), at Derry.

6 Dec. 1979 Charlie Nash (Ire.), champion, w pts 12 Ken Buchanan (Scot.), challenger, at Copenhagen, Denmark.

Feb. 1980 Charlie Nash relinquished European title, to concentrate on world title fight with Jim Watt.

14 Dec. 1980 Charlie Nash (Ire.), challenger, w pts 12 Francisco Leon (Spain), champion, at Burlington Hotel, Dublin. Nash thus regained title.

10 May 1981 Joey Gilbilisco (Italy), challenger, w ko 6 Charlie Nash (Ire.), champion, at Dalymount Park, Dublin.

Featherweight

27 May 1955 Ray Famechon (France), champion, w pts 15 Billy 'Spider' Kelly (Ire.), challenger, at Donnybrook bus garage, Dublin.

16 Nov. 1983 Barry McGuigan (Ire.) w ko 6 Valerio Nati (Italy), for title vacated by Loris Stecca (Italy), at King's Hall, Belfast.

30 June 1984 Barry McGuigan (Ire.), champion, w ko 3 Esteban Eguia (Spain), challenger, at Royal Albert Hall, London.

19 Dec. 1984 Barry McGuigan (Ire.), champion, w ko 4 Clyde Ruan (Eng.), challenger, at Ulster Hall, Belfast.

26 Mar. 1985 Barry McGuigan (Ire.), champion, w rtd 2 Farid Gallouze (France), challenger, at Wembley Pool, London. Barry McGuigan relinquished European title to concentrate on world title challenge.

Bantamweight

3 Oct. 1953 John Kelly (Ire.), challenger, w pts 15 Peter Keenan (Scot.), champion, at King's Hall, Belfast.

27 Feb. 1954 Robert Cohen (French Algeria), challenger, w ko 3 John Kelly (Ire.), champion, at King's Hall, Belfast.

3 Nov. 1959 Freddie Gilroy (Ire.), challenger, w pts 15 Piero Rollo (Italy), champion, at Empire Pool, Wembley, London.

19 Mar. 1960 Freddie Gilroy (Ire.), champion, w rsf 13 Billy Rafferty (Scot.), challenger, at King's Hall, Belfast.

25 Oct. 1960 Freddie Gilroy lost in a world title fight against Alphonse Halimi (France) and the EBU declared the European title vacant.

27 May 1961 Pierre Cossemyns (Belgium) w rtd 9 Freddie Gilroy (Ire.), for vacant title, at Brussels, Belgium.

16 Jan. 1976 Daniel Trioulaire (France), champion, drew 15 Paddy Maguire (Ire.), challenger, at Cluses, France. Trioulaire thus retained title.

28 Sept. 1977 Franco Zurlo (Italy), champion, w rtd 8 Paddy Maguire (Ire.), challenger, at Cagliari, Italy.

Flyweight

5 Apr. 1949 Rinty Monaghan (Ire.), challenger, w pts 15 Maurice Sandeyron (France), champion, at King's Hall, Belfast.

30 Sept. 1949 Rinty Monaghan (Ire.), champion, drew 15 Terry Allen

(Eng.), challenger, at King's Hall, Belfast. Monaghan thus retained title.

Prior to 1970 Commonwealth title-holders were classed as champions of the British Empire.

Heavyweight

18 Jan. 1911 Petty Officer Matt 'Nutty' Curran (Ire.) w disq 1 Bill Lang (Australia) at Olympia, London, for vacant title. (Lang struck opponent while down).

27 July 1972 Dan McAlinden (Ire.), challenger, w ko 2 Jack Bodell (Eng.), champion, at Birmingham.

13 Jan 1975 Bunny Johnson (Eng.), challenger, w ko 9 Dan McAlinden (Ire.), champion, at World Sporting Club, London.

4 Nov. 1975 Richard Dunn (Eng.), champion, w ko 2 Dan McAlinden (Ire.), challenger, at Wembley Pool, London.

Light-heavyweight

17 May 1923 Jack Bloomfield (Eng,), champion, w rtd 13 Dave Magill (Ire.), challenger, at Olympia, London.

31 Jan. 1927 Tom Berry (Eng.) w pts 20 Dave Magill (Ire.) at Manchester, for vacant title.

12 Feb. 1968 Bob Dunlop (Australia) w rsf 7 'Young' John McCormack (Ire.) at Sydney, Australia, for vacant title.

Middleweight

22 Oct. 1963 Gomeo Brennan (Bahamas) w pts 15 Mick Leahy (Ire.) for vacant title.

Welterweight

10 Jan. 1914 Tom McCormick (Ire.), challenger, w pts 20 Johnny Summers (Eng.), champion, at Sydney, Australia.

14 Feb. 1914 Tom McCormick (Ire.), champion, w ko 1 Johnny Summers (Eng), challenger, at Sydney, Australia.

21 Mar. 1914 Matt Wells (Eng.), challenger, w pts 20 Tom McCormick (Ire.), champion, at Sydney, Australia.

31 Oct. 1961 Brian Curvis (Wales), champion, w ko 8 Mick Leahy (Ire.), challenger, at Wembley Pool, London.

Featherweight

23 Nov. 1938 Jim 'Spider' Kelly (Ire.) w pts 15 Benny Caplan (Eng.) at King's Hall, Belfast, for vacant title.

28 June 1939 Johnny Cusick (Eng.), challenger, w rsf 12 Jim 'Spider' Kelly (Ire.), champion, at King's Hall, Belfast.

2 Oct. 1954 Billy 'Spider' Kelly (Ire.), challenger, w pts 15 Roy Ankrah (Ghana), champion, at King's Hall, Belfast.

22 Jan. 1955 Billy 'Spider' Kelly (Ire.), champion, w pts 15 Sammy McCarthy (Eng.), challenger, at King's Hall, Belfast.

19 Nov. 1955 Hogan 'Kid' Basey (Nigeria), challenger, w ko 8 Billy 'Spider' Kelly (Ire.), champion, at King's Hall, Belfast.

Bantamweight

10 Jan. 1959 Freddie Gilroy (Ire.), challenger, w rsf 11 Peter Keenan

(Scot.), champion, at King's Hall, Belfast.

5 Dec. 1959 Freddie Gilroy (Ire.), champion, w ko 5 Bernie Taylor (S. Africa), challenger, at King's Hall, Belfast.

19 Mar. 1960 Freddie Gilroy (Ire.), champion, w rsf 13 Billy Rafferty (Scot.), challenger, at King's Hall, Belfast.

3 Mar. 1962 Freddie Gilroy (Ire.), champion, w ko 12 Billy Rafferty (Scot.), challenger, at King's Hall, Belfast.

20 Oct. 1962 Freddie Gilroy (Ire.), champion, w rtd 9 Johnny Caldwell (Ire.), challenger, at King's Hall, Belfast.

5 Mar. 1964 Johnny Caldwell (Ire.), w rsf 7 George Bowes (Eng.) at ABC Cinema, Belfast, for title vacated by Freddie Gilroy.

22 Mar. 1965 Alan Rudkin (Eng.), challenger, w rsf 10 Johnny Caldwell (Ire.), champion, at Nottingham.

7 Mar. 1975 Paul Ferreri (Australia), champion, w rsf 8 Paddy Maguire (Ire.), challenger, at Melbourne, Australia.

Flyweight

23 Mar. 1948 Rinty Monaghan (Ire.), challenger, w ko 7 Jackie Paterson (Scot.), champion, at King's Hall, Belfast.

30 Sept. 1949 Rinty Monaghan (Ire.), champion, drew 15 Terry Allen (Eng.), challenger, at King's Hall, Belfast. Monaghan thus retained title.

8 Feb. 1980 Ray Amoo (Nigeria) w pts 15 Neil McLaughlin (Ire.) at Lagos, Nigeria, for vacant title.

BRITISH CHAMPIONSHIPS CONTESTS

Heavyweight

11 Feb. 1910 Petty Officer Matt 'Nutty' Curran (Ire.), challenger, w ko 15 William 'Iron' Hague (Eng.), champion, at Plymouth, but fight was not officially recognised as title bout because it did not take place at NSC, London, the self-proclaimed ruling body in Britain until the formation of the BBBC in 1929.

30 June 1913 Bombardier Billy Wells (Eng.), champion, w ko 13 Pakey Mahoney (Ire.), challenger, at NSC, London.

31 Mar. 1916 Bombardier Billy Wells (Eng.), champion, w ko 5 Petty Officer 'Nutty' Curran (Ire.), challenger, at Plymouth. Not recognised as title bout by NSC.

18 Dec. 1916 Bombardier Billy Wells (Eng.), champion, w rsf 2 Private Dan Voyles (Ire.), challenger, at NSC, London.

12 July 1933 Jack Petersen (Wales), champion, w disq 2 (low punch) Jack Doyle (Ire.), challenger, at White City, London.

27 June 1972 Dan McAlinden (Ire.), challenger, w ko 2 Jack Bodell (Eng.), champion, at Birmingham.

13 Jan. 1975 Bunny Johnson (Eng.), challenger, w ko 9 Dan McAlinden (Ire.), champion, at World Sporting Club, London.

3 Nov. 1975 Richard Dunn (Eng.), champion, w ko 2 Dan McAlinden (Ire.), challenger, at Wembley Pool, London.

3 Mar. 1981 Gordon Ferris (Ire.) w pts 15 Billy Aird (Eng.) at Birmingham, for title vacated by John L. Gardner (Eng).

12 Oct. 1981 Neville Meade (Wales - born Jamaica), challenger, w ko 1 Gordon Ferris (Ire.), champion, at Birmingham.

Light-heavyweight
9 June 1913 Dennis Haugh (Ire.) w ko 1 Sid Ellis (Eng.) at NSC, London, for vacant title.
10 Nov. 1913 Dennis Haugh (Ire.), champion, w rsf 8 Private Dan Voyles (Ire.), challenger, at NSC, London.
19 Jan. 1914 Dennis Haugh (Ire.), champion, w pts 15 Dick Smith (Eng.), challenger, at NSC, London.
9 Mar. 1914 Dick Smith (Eng.), challenger, w pts 20 Dennis Haugh (Ire.), champion, at NSC, London.
19 June 1967 'Young' John McCormack (Ire.) w rsf 7 Eddie Avoth (Wales), at NSC, London, for vacant title.
22 Nov. 1967 'Young' John McCormack (Ire.), champion, w ko 7 Derek Richards (Wales), challenger, at Solihull, Warwickshire.
13 Jan. 1967 Eddie Avoth (Wales), challenger, w rtd 11 'Young' John McCormack (Ire.), champion, at World Sporting Club, London.
6 Apr. 1970 Eddie Avoth (Wales), champion, w disq 8 (alleged butting) 'Young' John McCormack (Ire.), challenger, at Nottingham.

Middleweight
28 May 1963 Mick Leahy (Ire.), challenger, w rsf 1 George Aldridge (Eng.), champion, at Nottingham.
14 Dec. 1964 Wally Swift (Eng.), challenger, w pts 15 Mick Leahy (Ire.), champion, at Nottingham.

Welterweight
10 Jan. 1914 Tom McCormick (Ire.), challenger, w pts 20 Johnny Summers (Eng.), champion, at Sydney. Australia.
14 Feb. 1914 Tom McCormick (Ire.), champion, w ko 1 Johnny Summers (Eng.), challenger, at Sydney, Australia.
21 Mar. 1914 Matt Wells (Eng.), challenger, w pts 20 Tom McCormick (Ire.), champion, at Sydney, Australia.
10 May 1915 Johnny Basham (Wales), champion, w rsf 13 Tom McCormick (Ire.), challenger, at NSC, London.
31 Oct. 1961 Brian Curvis (Wales), champion, w ko 8 Mick Leahy (Ire.), challenger, at Wembley Pool, London.
15 Dec. 1975 Pat Thomas (Wales - born West Indies) w ko 13 Pat McCormack (Ire.) at Walworth, London, for title vacated by John H. Stracey.

Junior-welterweight
27 Feb. 1968 Des Rea (Ire.), w pts 15 Vic Andreetti (Eng.), at Bethnal Green, London, for vacant title.
17 Feb. 1969 Vic Andreetti (Eng.), challenger, w pts 15 Des Rea (Ire.), champion, at Nottingham.
13 Oct. 1969 Vic Andreetti (Eng.), champion, w ko 4 Des Rea (Ire.), challenger, at Nottingham.
These were the only three contests staged for the British junior-welterweight (10st) title, which was then abolished. In 1973 the BBBC

introduced a new championship at 10st, called light-welterweight.

Light-welterweight

26 Mar. 1974 Pat McCormack (Ire.), challenger, w ko 11 Des Morrison (Eng. - born Jamaica), champion, at Royal Albert Hall, London.

21 Nov. 1974 Joey Singleton (Eng.), challenger, w pts 15 Pat McCormack (Ire.), champion, at Liverpool.

11 Oct. 1978 Clinton McKenzie (Eng.) w rsf 10 Jim Montague (Ire.) at Maysfield Leisure Centre, Belfast, for title vacated by Colin Power (Eng.).

Lightweight

28 Feb. 1978 Charlie Nash (Ire.) w rsf 12 Johnny Claydon (Eng.) at Templemore Sports Complex, Derry, for title taken from Jim Watt (Scot.) for refusing to defend it against Nash in Northern Ireland.

Feb 1980 Nash relinquished title to concentrate on world title fight with Jim Watt.

Featherweight

23 Nov. 1938 Jim 'Spider' Kelly (Ire.) w pts 15 Benny Caplan (Eng.) at King's Hall, Belfast, for vacant title.

28 June 1939 Johnny Cusick (Eng.), challenger, w rsf 12 Jim 'Spider' Kelly (Ire.), champion, at King's Hall, Belfast.

22 Jan. 1955 Billy 'Spider' Kelly (Ire.), challenger, w pts 15 Sammy McCarthy (Eng.), champion, at King's Hall, Belfast.

4 Feb. 1956 Charlie Hill (Scot.), challenger, w pts 15 Billy 'Spider' Kelly (Ire.), champion, at King's Hall, Belfast.

7 Oct. 1957 Charlie Hill (Scot.), champion, w ko 10 Jimmy Brown (Ire.), challenger, at Nottingham.

10 Apr. 1962 Howard Winstone (Wales), champion, w rsf 14 Derry Treanor (Ire.), challenger, at Wembley Pool, London.

12 Apr. 1983 Barry McGuigan (Ire.) w rsf 2 Vernon Penprase (Eng.), at Ulster Hall, Belfast, for vacant title.

19 Dec. 1984 Barry McGuigan (Ire.), champion, w ko 4 Clyde Ruan (Eng.), challenger, at Ulster Hall, Belfast. Barry McGuigan relinquished British title on becoming world title-holder.

Bantamweight

3 Oct. 1953 John Kelly (Ire.), challenger, w pts 15 Peter Keenan (Scot.), champion, at King's Hall, Belfast.

21 Sept. 1954 Peter Keenan (Scot.), challenger, w ko 6 John Kelly (Ire.), champion, at Paisley, Scotland.

11 Dec. 1954 Peter Keenan (Scot.), champion, w pts 15 George O'Neill (Ire.), challenger, at King's Hall, Belfast.

10 Jan. 1959 Freddie Gilroy (Ire.), champion, w rsf 11 Peter Keenan (Scot.), champion, at King's Hall, Belfast.

19 Mar. 1960 Freddie Gilroy (Ire.), champion, w rsf 13 Billy Rafferty (Scot.), challenger, at King's Hall, Belfast.

3 Mar. 1962 Freddie Gilroy (Ire.), champion, w ko 12 Billy Rafferty (Scot.), challenger, at King's Hall, Belfast. Gilroy thus won Lonsdale Belt outright.

20 Oct. 1962 Freddie Gilroy (Ire.), champion, w rtd 9 Johnny Caldwell (Ire.), challenger, at King's Hall , Belfast.

5 Mar. 1964 Johnny Caldwell (Ire.) w rsf 7 George Bowes (Eng.), at ABC Cinema, Belfast, for title vacated by Freddie Gilroy.

22 Mar. 1965 Alan Rudkin (Eng.), challenger, w rsf 10 Johnny Caldwell (Ire.), champion, at Nottingham.

20 Mar. 1973 Johnny Clark (Eng.) w pts 15 Paddy Maguire (Ire.) at Royal Albert Hall, London, for title vacated on Alan Rudkin's retirement.

10 Dec. 1974 Dave Needham (Eng.) w pts 15 Paddy Maguire (Ire.) at Nottingham, for title vacated on Johnny Clark's retirement.

20 Oct. 1975 Paddy Maguire (Ire.), challenger, w rsf 14 Dave Needham (Eng), champion, at World Sporting Club, London.

29 Nov. 1977 Johnny Owen (Wales), challenger, w rsf 11 Paddy Maguire (Ire.), champion, at National Sporting Club, London.

25 Jan. 1983 Hugh Russell (Ire.), challenger, w disq 13 (persistent misuse of head) John Feeney (Eng.), champion, at Ulster Hall, Belfast.

2 Mar. 1983 Davy Larmour (Ire.), challenger, w pts 12 Hugh Russell (Ire.), champion, at King's Hall, Belfast.

16 Nov. 1983 John Feeney (Eng.), challenger, w rsf 3 Davy Larmour (Ire.), champion, at King's Hall, Belfast.

Flyweight

23 Mar. 1948 Rinty Monaghan (Ire.), challenger, w ko 7 Jackie Paterson (Scot.), champion, at King's Hall, Belfast.

30 Sept. 1949 Rinty Monaghan (Ire.), champion, drew 15 Terry Allen (Eng.), challenger at King's Hall, Belfast. Monaghan thus retained title.

30 Mar. 1950 Rinty Monaghan retired as undefeated world, European, British Empire and British flyweight champion.

8 Oct. 1960 Johnny Caldwell (Ire.), challenger, w ko 3 Frankie Jones (Scot.), champion, at King's Hall, Belfast.

May 1961 Johnny Caldwell relinquished British flyweight title on winning EBU and BBBC recognition as world bantamweight champion by beating Alphonse Halimi.

25 Jan. 1984 Hugh Russell (Ire.), challenger, w rtd 7 Kelvin Smart (Eng.), champion, at King's Hall, Belfast.

13 Nov. 1984 Hugh Russell (Ire.), champion, w rsf 8 Danny Flynn (Scot.), challenger, at Ulster Hall, Belfast.

23 Feb. 1985 Hugh Russell (Ire.) w rsf 12 Charlie Brown (Scot.), challenger, at King's Hall, Belfast. Russell thus won Lonsdale Belt outright.

20 Oct. 1986 Dave McAuley (Ire.) w ko 9 Joe Kelly (Scot.) at St Andrew's Sporting Club, Glasgow, for title vacated by Duke McKenzie (Scot.).

Irish championships

Contests for all-Ireland professional championships are a rarity, primarily due to the lack of regular promotions in the Irish Republic and the absence of any real prestige attaching to the winning of such titles. Although there have been occasional bouts billed for Irish championships, no known complete record of them exists.

NORTHERN IRELAND CHAMPIONSHIP CONTESTS
All fights staged in Belfast, unless otherwise stated.
Heavyweight
10 Aug. 1946 Alex Woods w rtd 3 Pat Duffy.
25 Dec. 1948 Paddy Slavin w rsf 2 Alex Woods. Paddy Slavin retired.
22 Nov. 1966 Barney Wilson w rsf 5 Jim Monaghan. Barney Wilson retired.
21 May 1975 Sean McKenna w ko 3 Des Reynolds.
26 July 1977 Dan McAlinden w rsf 2 Sean McKenna, in Derry. McAlinden relinquished title.
Light-heavyweight
5 Feb. 1944 Alex Woods w ko 14 Frank Hayes.
22 Oct. 1947 Alex Woods w ko 8 Matt Locke. Alex Woods retired.
11 Oct. 1952 Tom Meli w pts 12 Garnett Denny. Tom Meli relinquished title.
1 Apr. 1969 Terry McTigue w ko 5 Gerry Hassett. McTigue retired.
4 Mar. 1976 Ian Glenn w ko 2 Roy Baillie.
28 Oct. 1976 Tony Monaghan w rtd 2 Ian Glenn, in Ballymena. Tony Monaghan retired.
22 Sept. 1980 Trevor Kerr w rsf 7 Mick Fellingham.
17 Feb. 1981 Liam Coleman w pts 10 Trevor Kerr, in Leeds.
30 Nov. 1981 Liam Coleman w rtd 6 Trevor Kerr, in Enniskillen.
Middleweight
11 Mar. 1938 Jack McKnight w pts 15 Pat Cowley. Jack McKnight relinquished title.
28 Oct. 1947 Jackie Wilson w pts 15 Frank Boylan.
19 Aug. 1949 Freddie Webb w pts 12 Jackie Wilson.
27 Jan. 1951 Jackie Wilson w pts 12 Freddie Webb.
1 Dec. 1951 Tom Meli w rtd 4 Jackie Wilson.
22 Jan. 1955 George Lavery w pts 12 Tom Meli.
21 Apr. 1956 George Lavery w pts 12 Sammy Hamilton. George Lavery retired.
12 Oct. 1965 Al (Peter) Sharpe w rsf 9 Henry Turkington.
21 Feb. 1967 Al (Peter) Sharpe w pts 12 Terry McTigue. Al (Peter) Sharpe retired.
Welterweight
22 Mar. 1938 Jack Walsh w pts 15 Ginger Lecky.
22 Mar. 1939 Tommy Armour w rsf 3 Jack Walsh.
29 Jan. 1944 Patsy Quinn w pts 15 Tommy Armour. Patsy Quinn relinquished title.
30 Nov. 1949 Tommy Armour w pts 12 Jackie King.
28 Apr. 1951 Tommy Armour w rtd 10 Billy O'Neill. Tommy Armour forfeited title.

11 Oct. 1952 Bunty Adamson w pts 12 Mickey O'Neill. Bunty Adamson relinquished title.

25 Dec. 1954 Roy Baird w rtd 5 Mickey O'Neill.

30 June 1956 Roy Baird w rtd 9 Gerry Smyth. Roy Baird retired.

18 Apr. 1959 Al (Peter) Sharpe w pts 12 Paddy Graham.

3 Mar. 1962 Paddy Graham w pts 10 Al (Peter) Sharpe. Paddy Graham retired.

29 Sept. 1965 Des Rea w pts 10 Bob Sempey, in London. Des Rea relinquished title.

Light-welterweight

26 Apr. 1977 Jim Montague w pts 10 Ray Ross, in Derry. Jim Montague relinquished title.

25 Feb. 1980 Davy Campbell w rtd 7 Ray Heaney. Davy Campbell retired.

3 Dec. 1985 Gary 'Peppi' Muir w ko 1 Vinnie Vahey.

Lightweight

21 July 1938 Al Lyttle w pts 15 Patsy Ouinn.

21 Feb. 1940 Al Lyttle w rsf 14 Dave Warnock.

18 Nov. 1940 Al Lyttle w pts 15 Jim Keery. Al Lyttle relinquished title.

11 Mar. 1944 Mick Magee w pts 15 Jim McCann. Mick Magee relinquished title.

30 Nov. 1949 Mickey O'Neill w rtd 9 Gerry Smyth.

16 June 1950 Mickey O'Neill w rtd 12 Jim Keery.

23 Feb. 1952 Gerry Symth w pts 12 Mickey O'Neill.

27 June 1953 Ricky McCulloch w pts 12 Gerry Smyth.

25 Sept. 1953 Gerry Smyth w pts 12 Ricky McCulloch.

26 Mar. 1955 Gerry Smyth w pts 12 Paddy Graham. Gerry Smyth retired.

23 Nov. 1957 Al (Peter) Sharpe w rtd 8 John McNally.

2 Aug. 1958 Jimmy Brown w ko 6 Al (Peter) Sharpe.

4 Oct. 1958 Jim 'Spike' McCormack w pts 12 Jimmy Brown. Jim 'Spike' McCormack relinquished title.

2 Oct. 1975 Charlie Nash w pts 10 Ray Ross, in Derry. Charlie Nash relinquished title.

Junior-lightweight

10 Feb. 1970 Sammy Lockhart w disq 4 Sean McCafferty. Weight division abolished.

Featherweight

2 Sept. 1935 Jim 'Spider' Kelly w rsf 14 Frank McAloran.

25 Feb. 1938 Jim 'Spider' Kelly w ko 3 Dan McAllister. Kelly relinquished title.

3 Oct. 1942 Jim McCann w pts 15 Charlie Brown. Jim McCann relinquished title.

18 Mar. 1944 Harry McAuley w rtd 12 Billy Donnelly.

26 Dec. 1949 Jim McCann w pts 15 Harry McAuley.

28 Dec. 1949 Jim McCann w pts 15 Dave Watson.

22 Feb. 1950 Jim McCann w pts 15 Eddie Magee. Jim McCann retired.

13 June 1953 John Griffen w rsf 4 Pat Kelly.

29 July 1953 Billy 'Spider' Kelly w pts 12 John Griffen, in Derry. Billy 'Spider' Kelly relinquished title.

18 Dec. 1954 Joe Quinn w rtd 7 Billy Smith.

26 Mar. 1955 Joe Quinn w pts 12 John McNally. Joe Quinn retired.

23 Feb. 1965 Peter Lavery w pts 10 Brian Smyth. Peter Lavery retired.

4 Mar. 1969 Jim McAuley w pts 10 Jim Henry.

26 Apr. 1977 Damien McDermott w rtd 4 Jim McAuley, in Derry. Damien McDermott retired.

Bantamweight

11 June 1938 Jack Mussen w rsf 8 Jack Bunting.

4 Mar. 1940 Jim McCann w rtd 12 Jack Mussen. Jim McCann relinquished title.

28 Apr. 1945 Tommy Madine w pts 15 Joe Meikle.

24 Mar. 1947 Tommy Madine w pts 15 Max Brady.

5 May 1947 Eddie 'Bunty' Doran w ko 4 Tommy Madine.

26 Dec. 1951 Eddie 'Bunty' Doran w pts 15 Jackie Briers.

27 June 1953 John Kelly w rtd 11 Eddie 'Bunty' Doran. John Kelly relinquished title.

4 Oct. 1958 Billy Skelly w pts 12 George O'Neill. Billy Skelly retired.

12 Oct. 1965 Jim McCann w rsf 9 Alex O'Neill.

13 Dec. 1966 Jim McCann w pts 12 Sean McCafferty. Jim McCann retired.

26 July 1977 Neil McLaughlin w rsf 5 Terry Hanna, in Derry.

27 Oct. 1978 Davy Larmour w pts 10 Neil McLaughlin.

5 Oct. 1982 Hugh Russell w pts 12 Davy Larmour.

2 Mar. 1983 Davy Larmour w pts 12 Hugh Russell. Davy Larmour retired.

Flyweight

23 Nov. 1938 Tommy Stewart w rsf 10 Jim McStravick. Tommy Stewart relinquished title.

14 Nov. 1942 Eddie 'Bunty' Doran w ko 6 Harry Rodgers.

19 Feb. 1944 Eddie 'Bunty' Doran w ko 3 Ike Weir.

6 Nov. 1945 Rinty Monaghan w ko 4 Eddie 'Bunty' Doran. Rinty Monaghan relinquished title.

26 Nov. 1948 Jackie Briers w rtd 6 Frank McCoy. Jackie Briers forfeited title.

6 Oct. 1951 Frank McCoy w rsf 2 Mickey McLaughlin. Frank McCoy forfeited title.

2 Feb. 1957 Dave Moore w pts 12 Jim Loughrey. Dave Moore relinquished title.

Amateur honours

OLYMPIC GAMES MEDAL WINNERS
Silver: John McNally, bantamweight, Helsinki 1952; Fred Tiedt, welterweight, Melbourne 1956. *Bronze:* Tony 'Socks' Byrne,

lightweight, Melbourne 1956; Freddie Gilroy, bantamweight, Melbourne 1956; John Caldwell, flyweight, Melbourne 1956; Jim McCourt, lightweight, Tokyo,1964; Hugh Russell, flyweight, Moscow 1980.

WORLD CHAMPIONSHIPS MEDAL WINNER
Bronze: Tommy Corr, light-middleweight, Munich 1982.

EUROPEAN CHAMPIONS
Paddy Dowdall, *featherweight*, Dublin 1939; Jimmy Ingle, *flyweight*, Dublin 1939; Gerry O'Colmain, *heavyweight*, Dublin 1947; Maxie McCullagh, *lightweight*, Oslo 1949.

BRITISH COMMONWEALTH CHAMPIONS
Terry Milligan, *middleweight*, Wales 1958; Jim McCourt, *light-welterweight*, Jamaica 1966; Davy Larmour, *flyweight*, New Zealand 1974; Gerry Hamill, *lightweight*, Canada 1978; Barry McGuigan, *bantamweight*, Canada 1978.

World champions of Irish descent

Heavyweight: John L. Sullivan (father from Tralee, County Kerry; mother from Athlone, County Westmeath), James J. Corbett (father from Shrule, near Tuam, County Galway; mother from Dublin), Bob Fitzsimmons (father from Omagh, County Tyrone; mother English), Jack Dempsey (of Irish, Jewish and Cherokee Indian descent), Gene Tunney (father from Killeaden, near Kiltimagh, County Mayo; mother from Gortgoriff, also near Kiltimagh), James J. Braddock (both parents Irish who spent some time in Mottram in Lancashire before settling in USA). Muhammad Ali's grandfather, on his mother's side, was an O'Grady from County Clare. *Light-heavyweight:* Philadelphia Jack O'Brien, Jack Dillon, Tommy Loughran, Jimmy Slattery, Billy Conn. *Middleweight:* Mike O'Dowd, William Brian Downey, Harry Greb, Mickey Walker (also welterweight champion), Freddie Steele, Ken Overlin, Paul Pender. *Welterweight:* Paddy Duffy, Mysterious Billy Smith, Matty Matthews, Billy 'Honey' Mellody, Mike 'Twin' Sullivan, Jimmy Clabby, Mike Glover, Jack Britton, Tommy Freeman, Freddie 'Red' Cochrane. *Lightweight:* Jimmy Goodrich, Lew Jenkins, Sean O'Grady. *Featherweight:* Terry McGovern, Johnny Kilbane, Joey Archibald. *Bantamweight:* Tommy 'Spider' Kelly, Jimmy Barry, Harry Forbes, Frankie Neil, Jimmy Walsh, Johnny Coulon, Joe Lynch. *Flyweight:* Benny Lynch.

Famous non-champions of Irish extraction include Patsy Brannigan, Frankie Burns, George 'K.O.' Chaney, Gerry Cooney, Henry Cooper, Tommy Farr, Dick 'Honeyboy' Finnegan, Mike and Tom Gibbons, Joe Goddard, Ace Hudkins, Jake Kilrain, Willie Lewis, George 'Elbows' McFadden, Packey McFarland, Kid McPartland, Tommy Milligan, Ritchie Mitchell, Frank Moran, Carl Morris, Harlem Tommy Murphy, Shawn O'Sullivan, Jerry Quarry, Frank 'Paddy' Slavin, Midget Smith, Jack 'Twin' Sullivan and Joe Thomas.

Bibliography

Andrews, Eamonn (editor), *Boxing Review*, Dublin 1945

Andrews, Eamonn, (editor), *Amateur Boxing Spotlight*, Dublin 1946

Anonymous, *The Fancy, or True Sportman's Guide*, London 1826

Batchelor, Denzil (editor), *Best Boxing Stories*, London

Batchelor, Denzil, *Big Fight, the story of world championship boxing*, London 1954

Batchelor, Denzil, *British Boxing*, London

Batchelor, Denzil, *Jack Johnson and His Times*, Sportman's Book Club edition, London 1957

Batchelor, Denzil (editor), *The Boxing Companion*, London 1964

Bowes, Leo, *Irishmen in the Olympic Games*, Dublin (nd)

Bowes, Leo, *The Sporting Irish*, Dublin (nd)

Buchanan-Taylor, W, (with James Butler), *What Do You Know About Boxing?* London 1947.

Butler, James and Frank, *The Fight Game*, Sportsman's Book Club edition, London 1956.

Caprani, Vincent, *Rowdy Rhymes and 'Rec-im-itations'*, Dublin 1982

Carpenter, Harry, *Boxing: A Pictorial History*, Glasgow and London 1975

Cooper, Henry, *The Great Heavyweights*, Middlesex 1978

Corbett, James J, *The Roar of the Crowd*, New York and London 1925

Corry, Eoghan, *McGuigan: the unauthorised biography*, Dublin 1985

Crosbie, Paddy, *Your Dinner's Poured Out*, Dublin 1982

Edmundson, Joseph, *Great Moments in Boxing*, London 1974

Egan, Pierce, *Boxiana, sketches of ancient and modern pugilism* (vols 1-4), London 1812-28

Farr, Finis, *Black Champion, the life and times of Jack Johnson*, London 1964

Fitz-Barnard, Capt L, *Fighting Sports*, first published 1921, new edition Hampshire 1975

Fleischer, Nat, (with Sam Andre), *A Pictorial History of Boxing*, London 1959

Fleischer, Nat, *Fifty Years at the Ringside*, London 1960

Fleischer, Nat, *Jack McAuliffe, the Napoleon of the Prize Ring*, New York 1944

Fleischer, Nat, *Ring Record Book and Boxing Encyclopedia*, New York 1962 and 1980

Fleischer, Nat, *The Heavyweight Championship*, Sportsman's Book Club edition, London 1954

Ford, John, *Prizefighting, the age of Regency boximania*, Devon 1971

Ford, John, *This Sporting Land*, London 1977

Furniss, Harry, *The By-ways and Queer-ways of Boxing*, London (nd)

Gains, Larry, *The Impossible Dream*, London (nd)

Golding, Louis, *The Bare Knuckle Breed*, London 1952

Golesworthy, Maurice, *The Encyclopedia of Boxing*, London 1971

Green, Benny, *Shaw's Champions, GBS and Prizefighting from Cashel Byron to Gene Tunney*, London 1978

Grombach, John V, *The Saga of the Fist*, New Jersey and London 1977

Gutteridge, Reg, *The Big Punchers*, London 1983

Haldane, R A, *Champions and Challengers*, London 1967

Heller, Pete, *In This Corner*, New York 1973

Henderson, Eugene, *Box On*, Sportsman's Book Club edition, London 1959

Henning, F W J, *Fights for the Championship*, 2 vols, published by Licensed Victualler's Gazette 1902

Hugman, Barry J, *British Boxing Yearbook*, Middlesex 1984 and 1985

Ingle, Jimmy, *The Jimmy Ingle Story*, Dingle 1984

Johnson, Jack, *In the Ring and Out*, first published USA 1927, new edition (edited by Gilbert Odd) London 1977

Langley, Tom, *The Life of John L Sullivan*, Leicester 1973

Leigh-Lye, Terry, *From the Ringside*, London 1958

Leigh-Lye, Terry, *In This Corner*, London 1963

Liebling, A J, *The Sweet Science*, New York 1956

Lloyd, *Alan, The Great Prize Fight*, London 1977

Lynch, Bohun, *The Prize Ring*, London 1925

McInnes, Peter, *Clouting for Cash*, London 1962

McInnes, Peter, *Ten and Out*, Bournemouth 1961

Mendoza, Daniel, *The Memoirs of Daniel Mendoza*, first published 1816, new edition (edited by Paul Magriel) London 1951

Miles, Henry Downs, *Pugilistica, the History of British Boxing* (vols 1-3), Edinburgh 1906

Myler, Patrick, *Regency Rogue: Dan Donnelly, his life and legends*, Dublin 1976

Myler, Thomas, *Irish Ringside Yearbook*, Dublin 1975

Nolan, Liam, *The Savage Square*, Dublin 1982

Odd, Gilbert, *Boxing: the Great Champions*, Middlesex 1974

Odd, Gilbert, *Boxing: the Inside Story*, London 1978

Odd, Gilbert, *Encyclopedia of Boxing*, London 1983

Odd, Gilbert, *Great Moments in Sport: Heavyweight Boxing*, London 1973

Odd, Gilbert, *The Fighting Blacksmith, the story of Bob Fitzsimmons*, London 1976

O'Donnell, Patrick, *The Irish Faction Fighters of the 19th Century*, Dublin 1975

O'Reilly, John Boyle, *Ethics of Boxing and Manly Sport*, Boston 1888

Prestidge, Dennis, *Tom Cribb at Thistleton Gap*, Leicestershire 1971

Reid, J C, *Bucks and Bruisers: Pierce Egan and Regency England*, London 1971

Shepherd, T B (editor), *The Noble Art, an anthology*, London 1950

Sheridan, Jim, *Leave the Fighting to McGuigan: the offical biography of Barry McGuigan*, London 1985

Solomons, Jack, *Jack Solomons Tells All*, London 1951

Strong, L A G, *Shake Hands and Come Out Fighting*, London 1938

Sullivan, John L, *I Can Lick any Sonofabitch in the House*, first published 1892, new edition (edited by Gilbert Odd) Nevada and London 1979

Watters, E, and Murtagh M, *Infinite Variety: Dan Lowrey's Music Hall 1879-97*, Dublin 1975

Whiting, George, *Great Fights of the Sixties*, London 1967

Wignall, Trevor C, *Prides of the Fancy*, London 1928

Wilson, Peter, *Old Holborn Book of Boxing*, London 1969

Wilson, Peter, *Ringside Seat*, London 1948

Wilson, Peter, *More Ringside Seats*, London 1959

Newspapers and Periodicals

Belfast Telegraph

Blackwood's Magazine

Boxing and Wrestling

Boxing Illustrated

Boxing International

Boxing News (incorporating *Boxing*)

Boxing News Annuals (1949 to date)

Boxing Pictorial

Boxing World

Combat

Evening Herald (Dublin)

Evening News (London)

Evening Press (Dublin)

Evening Standard (London)

Gentleman's and London Magazine (Feb 1792)

Ireland's Own

Irish Independent

Irish News

Irish Press

The Irish Times

Jack Solomons' International Boxing Annuals (1949-52)

Newsletter (Belfast)

Ringsider

Sport (Irish weekly newspaper 1910-16)

Sport (Irish monthly magazine 1946-48)

Sunday Independent

Sunday News (Belfast)

Sunday Press

Sunday Tribune

The Bell (vol VII, No 1, Oct 1943; vol XV, No 4, Jan 1948)

The Ring

Tuam Herald